THE JOY OF
HOME
WINEMAKING

THE JOY OF HOME WINEMAKING

TERRY GAREY

AVON BOOKS NEW YORK

AVON BOOKS
A division of
The Hearst Corporation
1350 Avenue of the Americas
New York, New York 10019

Copyright © 1996 by Terry A. Garey
Cover art by Tom Nikosey
Interior photographs © 1995 by David Dyer-Bennet
Published by arrangement with the author
Library of Congress Catalog Card Number: 95-44219
ISBN: 0-380-78227-8

Library of Congress Cataloging in Publication Data:

Garey, Terry A.
   The joy of home winemaking / Terry Garey.
       p.   cm.
Includes bibliographical references and index.
1. Wine and winemaking—Amateurs' manuals.   I. Title.
TP548.2.G37   1996   95-44219
641.8'72—dc20   CIP

First Avon Books Trade Printing: June 1996

AVON TRADEMARK REG. U.S. PAT. OFF. AND IN OTHER COUNTRIES, MARCA REGISTRADA, HECHO EN U.S.A.

Printed in the U.S.A.

OPM   10 9 8 7 6 5 4 3 2

This book is for

Dennis Lien
for the usual, the unusual,
and most of the good jokes

and for
Joel Rosenberg
with much gratitude

ACKNOWLEDGMENTS

Thanks to Erik Biever for yeast and advice, and to Karen Schaffer and Mog Decarnin for patience and inspiration. Special thanks to Jeanne Gomoll for heaps of patience. Thank-you David Dyer-Bennet for the photos, and Lydia Nickerson, photographer's assistant and model. Many thanks to Shawna McCarthy for taking a chance.

Many thanks also to Tim Furst for that first taste of raspberry wine, to my mother for liking it when I made it, to Phil and Irene Garey for computer and printer support, to Jerry Kaufman and Suzle Tompkins for making me write nonfiction, to Myrna Logan for bravery, to Janet Belwether for the first recipe, to St. Paul Campus Library Technical Services for jokes, work, research, and time, and to the Minnesota Science Fiction Society for being there.

Thank you, Charlotte Abbott, for helping me make sense.

Thanks, finally, to The Flying Karamazov Brothers—Randall Nelson and Steve Jobs—for the gone but never forgotten Kaypro. "Look, a computer from out of the crowd!"

Do the best you can and don't worry!

—My grandmother Garey *during an earthquake*

Contents

List of Illustrations
and Photographs

Introduction

If you can follow a simple recipe, you can make wine. You can make it in the tiniest kitchen apartment. You don't need much specialized equipment. You don't have to be Italian or French or a chemist. You have to be an adult over eighteen or twenty-one (depending on where you live) with a sense of adventure, curiosity, and patience.

Home winemaking is easy, as I'll show you. Do yourself a favor, though, and read through at least the first three chapters of this book before you start. Nothing wastes more time than undue haste.

Here's how I got started.

Many years ago I spotted some Danish strawberry wine in a shop. I was young, but I had had good wine and knew what it should taste like. My father bought the pretty bottle for me, since I wasn't yet twenty-one, but he cautioned me that I wouldn't like it.

Opening and tasting the strawberry wine was a disappointment. I won't call it a bitter disappointment, because it was so sweet that it made my teeth curl. My father laughed. So did I. As I remember, my grandmother used it over vanilla ice cream so it wouldn't go to waste. It lasted a long time!

Many years after that a friend came to dinner, bearing with him a bottle of homemade raspberry wine. Friends of his in the Santa Cruz mountains had made it.

I trusted his judgment. We opened the wine.

When I read about wine as a child, I imagined it tasting a particular way. The little sips my parents gave me of what they were drinking were nice, but not what I had imagined.

The raspberry wine from Santa Cruz was the wine of my dreams. It smelled softly of ripe raspberries and was dry, clean; flavorful, yet subtle. I instantly felt that this was the way I had always dreamed wine could be.

Please understand that I love grape wines. I honor and respect the winemaking traditions of the world. It is true however that I tend to drink American wines over French and German due to habit, chauvinism, and economy. It is also true that I have no illusions about my chances of duplicating Bordeaux in my basement. But that's okay. I don't want to. The Bordeaux region does what it does just fine.

Fruit wines are my first love.

A year after I moved to the Midwest from California I made my first gallon of apple wine with a recipe a friend had given me. It featured frozen apple juice and lemonade. It wasn't bad, but it wasn't good.

Another friend sipped some of it. The next time I saw him he handed me a packet of champagne wine yeast and said, "Try this on the next batch." He was a beer brewer and knew that yeast was important, you see. I had been using bread yeast.

So I tried it. He was right; it was much better. He suggested I learn to bottle. I did. He was right; the wine was better yet.

More than a year after my first excursions, I decided to try to make wine out of real fruit.

It wasn't easy. I didn't know anyone who did it, and couldn't find any current information about making wine. My partner found some old British books dating from the 1960s and 1970s in used bookstores. Painstakingly, I cobbled together a method, crossed it with what I had already learned on my own, and there it was, my first batch of strawberry wine: dry, a bit thin, but quite nice, thank-you very much. And a year after that, the first of the raspberry was born. I had done it! I had made raspberry wine!

I've made apple wine, grape, cranberry, raspberry, mint, potato, carrot, raisin, dandelion, blueberry, pineapple sage, and all sorts of other wines from fruits, flowers, herbs, and combinations of fruits. I've made mead, melomel, cyser, and metheglin. The most popular ones among me and my friends are raspberry, apple, strawberry, carrot, and blueberry, made from the whole fruit, on the dry side. And the fruit melomels.

You may gag at the idea of carrot wine (it's OK, I'm used to it), but I assure you, it's wonderful. It doesn't taste like carrots, oddly enough, but vaguely like a dry Rhine.

What wine goes with what? Almost any homemade wine will go with Chinese food, light pastas, salads, sandwiches, chicken, salmon, and vegetable dishes. Almost any homemade wine will go with anything, although you meat eaters may find you still need a rich red grape wine for beef, which is difficult to achieve with non-vinifying fruits unless you use grape concentrate or a grape wine kit.

You can also cook with homemade wine.

For Chinese cooking, instead of sherry I'm still using a batch of raisin wine I made five years ago. The older it gets, the better it is.

A dash of raspberry or apricot wine in the sauté pan at the right moment does wondrous things to pork, turkey, chicken, fish, and vegetables.

I've used my homemade wines in desserts, mustards, sauces, and salad dressings.

And, last but not least, I give it to people who I know will appreciate it.

Do I sell it? Absolutely not. Which brings us to the next section.

IS THIS LEGAL?

It sure is. By federal law you are allowed to make 100 gallons of wine a year for your own consumption, and 200 gallons a year if you are a household of two or more adult people. You don't have to fill out a form or anything. You can just do it.

Be aware, however, that there are some states and counties where the regulations are different. Check with the local authorities to be absolutely sure winemaking is legal where you live.

Under no circumstances should you sell or distill wine.

If you eventually find that your enthusiasm knows no bounds, you can get a commercial license for a winery, of course.

DEFINE YOUR TERMS

Wine, technically, is fermented grape juice with an alcohol content of 8–14 percent. The grape is the only fruit that is sweet enough to provide enough sugar and acid on its own (and in the olden days, its own yeast) to make that much alcohol.

Wine yeasts will tolerate only 14 percent alcohol content before they are killed off. Fortified wines, such as sherry and port, are made with yeasts that can survive up to about 18 percent: then the wine is "fortified" with brandy to bring the alcohol content up to 20–25 percent to make it more stable.

In this book most of what we will be discussing we will call fruit wines, made of fruit and sugar.

True grape wines are made using nothing but grapes and yeast with no added sugar. It takes a lot of grapes, around eighteen pounds per gallon. Go to the store and start loading up a scale with table grapes and then imagine that in your kitchen. The cost is also prohibitive unless you grow your own wine grapes.

Fruit wines are made with smaller amounts of fruits and added sugar. They are less expensive and less trouble to make. Some people scorn fruit wines and call them false wines, claiming only grape wine can be called wine. I disagree and refuse to quibble. I make wine.

Fruit and vegetable wines are not easily bought commercially. That's one of the reasons I decided to learn to make them, and it's where most of my experience lies. In this book I'll give you a basic recipe for making true grape wines, but it is not the true focus of this book.

If we make wine with honey and nothing else, it's mead; if we make fruit wine with honey, it's melomel; if we make herbal wine using honey, it's metheglin.

In most of my wines, I tend to use a bit of honey in addition to sugar. Though I'm not sure what most people would call it, I call it wine.

There is a sort of murky area between ciders and beers and ales and wines in the 6–8 percent alcohol area, but what we want here is something that will keep for several years, and you need a higher alcohol content for long-term storage.

STYLES OF WINES

Most people in the United States are familiar with three basic commercial wine styles: red, white, and sparkling. Everyone has heard of French wines, Italian wines, and California wines. Maybe they've explored some of the German wines, and Hungarian.

Grape wines have a tremendous range. Go to a liquor store that specializes in wines, and take a tour. You'll find everything from the lightest white to the heaviest red. There are wines meant to be drunk with food, aperitif wines (wines to spark the appetite), ports, sherries, Tokays, dessert wines, and celebratory sparkling wines.

You won't find many fruit wines. Most of the ones you do find will be "pop" wines made for people who just want a bit of a buzz, and heavy sweet fruit wines, which are an acquired taste.

Once in a while you'll find a nice surprise—a dry apple wine, or cranberry, or maybe pineapple.

However, if you look around your area no matter where it is or you ask at the local wine supply store, or you look through a list of agricultural businesses, you will likely hear of a small, regional fruit winery that uses local fruits to produce a range of wines and meads. Look also for wine competitions at state and county fairs, and see what you can find.

Washington, Oregon, and California produce many wonderful fruit wines. Massachusetts also has several, and so do New York, Minnesota, Wisconsin, Illinois, Iowa, Hawaii, and Missouri. I've had peach wine from Georgia, dandelion from Ohio, and many others I simply can't remember. There's a good chance that nearly every state in the Union produces fruit wines of some sort.

Just as there are many styles in grape wines, there are many in fruit wines. "Blueberry" describes the fruit, but it doesn't describe the style. It can be a table wine, a dessert wine, or a social wine like port or sherry. It's fun to explore the varieties.

One thing no one can tell you is what kind of wine you should like. Tastes are individual. It's true that for most people a red grape wine goes better with meat and heavy sauces than most white grape wines, but if you like white wine with roasts and red wine with fish, whose business is it but yours? If the people at the next table shudder and look faint, well, they can look the other way.

The same theory follows with fruit wines, and this area is less fraught with traditions and experts. The idea of blueberry wine with ravioli might seem startling at first, but you might like it— you never know. How about dry peach wine with chicken chow mein, or raspberry with grilled vegetables? Elderberry with meat loaf or strawberry-pineapple with jack cheese tamales? You'll never know until you try.

WHY MAKE YOUR OWN?

Making your own wine allows you to make wine to your exact tastes, inexpensively, though it's best to keep in mind that if your tastes run to Chateau La Salle, you have to buy a certain wineyard in France.

You can make grape wines from concentrates and kits available from your local wine supply store, or by mail. You can even make wine from real grapes, if you grow your own, or pick them. One of our local wine supply stores orders California wine grapes and gets them shipped out here to the Midwest every year. There are also winemaking clubs that share the use of wine and cider presses.

But fruit wine, and mead—now, that's something not everyone can have, except those who make their own.

On top of everything, it's fun to serve something you've made yourself. When you make your own wine, your creativity, experience, and judgment go into it. What comes out of the bottle is different from what anyone else makes. It's not mass-produced. It's homemade by someone who cares about the product, and who better than you?

You can use fewer chemicals than the commercial wineries do. You can use finer ingredients. You can age your wines longer and with more care.

You can do your own blending and experimenting. You can

make 200 gallons of rhubarb champagne, if that's your bag, or you can make 15 to 20 gallons of various fruit wines. It's up to you.

Then there's money. The most any of my wines has ever cost was $6.00 a gallon one year when raspberries were hard to get hold of. That's $1.50 a bottle. Usually, a gallon of homemade wine runs from $1.00 to $3.00 a gallon to produce. That's four to five bottles. I mostly make wine in five-gallon batches these days, and buy or gather fruit in bulk to save time and money.

If you are like me, you won't stop buying wine at the wine shop. There's nothing like a good Cabernet or zinfandel. But there's nothing in the wine store like my raspberry, either. If there were, it would cost five times what it costs me to make it.

IT TAKES SO LONG!

Yeah. So? Time will fly. You'll be busy doing other things. You aren't going to sit there and watch the jug for six months! Before you know it, a few months or a year has gone by, and you get to taste and try something new.

Time is on your side as a winemaker. You have to have patience. It takes a couple of years to get up to speed. There are no "instant" wines. You can have a drinkable product in as little as three months with the beginners' recipe, if you make it in the summer. Quite frankly though, it's not really worth it to make something just drinkable. You want it to be GOOD. So take your time. After a few batches, your tongue and brain will know what to expect and you won't mind so much about the time it takes.

WILL THIS STUFF KILL ME OR MAKE ME GO BLIND?

No. Don't worry. Unless you do something really silly like use contaminated equipment and ingredients, or unless you drink too much, winemaking is very safe. If it goes bad, you'll know, and you won't drink it.

There are a lot of horror stories left over from Prohibition days about bathtub gin and homemade beer and wine. Some of them are probably true. People made alcohol out of nearly anything, and some of it was poisonous. The distilled stuff was the worst.

You aren't making wine just for a cheap high, you're making it with good equipment and good ingredients; barring accidents, like mistaking deadly nightshade for blackberries, everything should be just fine. Later on I'll give you a list of poisonous plants and tell you how to care for your equipment.

HOW DO I DUPLICATE A CHABLIS?

You don't, unless, as I said before, you own a vineyard or use a commercial wine kit. Lots of people ask me questions like this.

Some home winemakers are really into duplicating grape wines using other fruits. They caution against using raspberry as a table wine because it "tastes too much of the fruit." My philosophy is: so what? I like fruit.

If you want a Chablis or a Burgundy, buy some! I just love reading descriptions of grape wines that say they have "overtones of blackberry," or a "slight strawberry flavor." Grapes are a marvelously complex fruit. Over the centuries they have been nurtured and bred and fermented and blended into a huge variety of wines.

But if blackberry is what you want or what you have, make it! My blackberry has overtones of blackberry, that's for sure! It has many of the characteristics of a red wine, and if I added some elderberries and messed around with it, I could probably come up with something that tasted close to an inexpensive red Burgundy. But unless I lived in a very out-of-the-way area with no wine stores, I can't see the point. If I wanted Burgundy, I would make it with grapes, not blackberries.

You can make wines from this book that don't taste particularly of any specific fruit. Many of the blends in the advanced section are like that. Sometimes a "generic" red, rosé, or white is what is needed. They might remind you of some of the classic wines ("Ah, a slight overtone of Gewürztraminer"), but they aren't going to be exact duplicates. And that's OK by me. Don't worry if the apricot comes out tasting of apricot. Don't expect it to be a Clairette de Die, either. If it happens to remind you of that wine, well, mazel tov!

MODERATION IN ALL THINGS

Alcoholism is no joke. It's a very real thing. Respect alcohol and the effect it can have on you and others. Never force or trick someone into drinking alcohol. Don't ask why if someone says no thanks. Just accept the no with good grace.

If you give a gift of wine, be sure it will be an acceptable present. Be sensitive to other peoples' feelings.

As for yourself—use good sense. You can get just as drunk on wine and beer as you can on hard spirits. It takes more to do it, of course, but alcohol is alcohol. Be moderate in what you imbibe, and keep it a pleasure, not a destructive compulsion. Don't drink and drive. Don't drink if you are pregnant, underage, or caring for vulnerable people. Don't make me sorry I wrote this book.

HOW TO USE THIS BOOK

Read at least the first three or four chapters before you start anything. Then try the first simple recipe, going through the steps carefully and waiting a month or two to see if you like the results. You can start two or three variations of the first recipe at the same time if you like.

It might be fun and instructive if you and a friend start your first batches at the same time; that way you can compare notes and results. Once your other friends hear that you've tried this and indicate interest, show them how to make their own so they won't try to wheedle you out of your favorites!

Then read the rest of the book. Study what I have to say about equipment and ingredients, and start some of the intermediate wines made with whole fruit. Fermentation alone is a fascinating subject. Get to know what to expect, and refine your methods.

After that, have fun doing what interests you in the other sections of the book. Buy other books on home winemaking and get to know other people who make wine. If you have a computer and modem, check out the various winemaking discussion groups on-line. Join a club or enter some of your wines in competitions.

Most home winemakers are interesting, generous people. They give advice freely and are interested in hearing what someone else is doing. Occasionally you find someone who is convinced that their way is the only way of doing something, but not very often. And remember, there will *always* be someone who knows more about winemaking than you do.

JOI DE VIVRE

Have fun! Don't get bound up in the details and forget to enjoy yourself when you use this book. As long as you are happy with what you are doing, and getting pleasure from it, you're doing it the right way! Almost anyone can make wine. Almost anyone can make GOOD wine. You are probably one of them. Like my grandmother said: Do the best you can and don't worry.

PART ONE

Beginning
Winemaking

CHAPTER ONE

A Brief History of Winemaking

NOTE: If you want to start making wine right away, you can skip on ahead to chapter 2 and read this later. However, I thought it would be nice to know a little of the history you're about to be part of.

Winemaking is an art that is thousands of years old. It isn't clear how many thousands of years, though wine residue has been found in clay jugs that were dug up in the ruins of an old Middle Eastern fort from 1000 B.C. Generally, archaeologists think it dates from over three thousand years before the Romans, probably in what is now Turkey. There is evidence that wine of some sort was being made at that time in China, as well, from plums, apricots, and rice. The poet Li Po had much to say about drinking wine in China, but not, alas, much about methods used to make it.

13

The skins of wild grapes carry wild yeasts, which were probably responsible for that first bowl or container of grape juice's accidentally fermenting into wine. We'll never know how it first got started. Maybe a woman crushed grapes to feed her baby the juice. Maybe some whole grapes in a tightly woven basket got a bit squashed and developed a winey odor instead of a spoiled smell.

Grapes were an important food source in the Mediterranean area. No one wanted to waste food; preservation was vital, even among nomadic people.

It's certain that people quickly noticed that the "funny" grape juice kept longer after fermentation, and that it gave a warm, happy feeling to those who drank it.

It's possible that even before the advent of the clay jar, wine was made by storing grapes or grape juice in sewn animal skins (with the fur on the outside) and hoping for the best. The clay jar had to be an improvement. Probably, at that point, the first wine snob evolved: "Oh, the old wine-in-a-skin? Never touch the stuff."

Wineskins still exist. One can still buy the staple container of yesteryear's free concerts and hiking trips.

The Egyptians made wine as well as beer. The Greeks picked it up from the Egyptians and the Persians. It was made not only from grapes (as the sugar source) but also from dates and honey.

Wine was viewed as both a food and a medicine, and it had great trade value. Imagine the value of a substance that was both food and drink. On top of everything, it stored easily, would keep for a decent amount of time, and was portable. The world's first convenience food?

Many ancient shipwrecks in the Mediterranean are full of wine jars and the oddly shaped amphorae.

Wine was an important part of many religions, as both a sacrament and a sacrifice. People even paid their taxes with wine. I don't think the IRS would go for that today.

It's thought that wine was drunk young for the most part, usually within the first year. Experts feel that it was probably thin and sweet, turning to vinegar within a few months or a year, depending on how it was stored. Jars were not cheap, nor were they airtight. Bottles had been invented, but they were tiny, valuable objects used to store expensive perfumes and salves. No one would have put wine into a bottle. Too extravagant!

The Greeks preserved some of their wines by adding acids to them, and coating and sealing the jars with pitch, resins, or even plaster. They added seawater and various other flavorings and preservatives. Retsina is probably left over from those days.

The ancient Greeks were responsible for spreading the art of winemaking around the Mediterranean region. They felt that any group of people who couldn't make wine were ignorant barbarians. Beer was a drink fit only for foreigners. Many of the beautifully illustrated vases from that period depict satyrs and even the gods themselves making and drinking wine.

There was a god of wine, whose name was Dionysus. He was not one of the "all-gods," but he was important enough for Euripides, the Greek playwright, to use as a major character in his drama *The Bacchae*.

The wild cult of Bacchus, worshipers of ecstasy, mysticism, wine, and dance, is looked upon today with amusement. At the time it was a disturbing, disruptive force in the lives of the ancient Greeks.

The Romans picked up wine and winemaking from the Greeks, as they did many other things, such as literature and science. Most wine was drunk diluted with water. The stuff was probably pretty sweet with unfermented sugars. Also, a good Roman was supposed to be a sober Roman, for a drunken Roman made a lousy soldier. They had learned that lesson from the Greeks, as well.

A banquet was not a banquet without wine. Nobles all had country estates and vied with each other to produce the perfect vintage. The sunny Mediterranean climate and gentle hills produced abundant crops and predictable results.

Those Romans got around—conquering, pillaging, spreading their culture, and the vine and wine. The Romans even planted vineyards in Great Britain. Such optimists.

In what is now France, the Celts became famous for their barrel-making, a more durable alternative to the fragile amphorae. Viticulture spread through the area via river traffic.

Gradually, grapevines and winemaking spread throughout Northern Africa and Europe. In the far northern parts of Europe, shaggy barbarians were making mead, or honey wine.

By the Middle Ages, wine was everywhere. Wooden barrels had been perfected, ships became bigger, trade routes were more stable, and populations grew. Wine was plentiful and cheap. There were many regulations about who could grow what kinds of vines, who could make wine and beer, and even who could drink it. Wine and beer were safer to drink than water in most towns. Diluted wine was drunk with meals. People even drank weak beer for breakfast.

The Christian Church had become the major religion in Europe. The church and the state were closely interconnected. No monarch ruled without sanction of the church, which declared the divine right of kings and princes. The church became rich from tithing and pardons. In those days wealth meant land and what you could produce on it. The monasteries owned vast vineyards, from which they made wines that began to take on distinguishing characteristics: rich and red here, heavy and sweet and white there, depending on the grapes of the region and the skill of the winemaker.

Most learning and most skills were centered in the monasteries. Few people could read; even kings were mostly illiterate. Anyone with an inclination to scholarship headed for the stability and peace of the monasteries.

Kings, nobles, and military leaders probably got the best of the wines. They used wine for tribute, bribes, gifts, and general trade. Vineyards were prized possessions, fought over in wars.

People in the Middle Ages and the Renaissance drank their wine young. As valuable as wine was, one can find references to the uneven quality, sediment, and sourness of wine at that time.

It was served in open jugs on the table. Servers flavored and sweetened it with honey, herbs, spices, and fruit juices, as well as various ingredients that were regarded as medicinal or magical. Grated "unicorn" horn was added to wine, pearls were dissolved into it, flecks of silver and gold were mixed into it. Amethysts were added with the belief that they kept one from getting drunk. Jewelers must have been very happy.

People too sick to eat were fed warmed sweetened wine to keep them going and ease their pain. Wine with poppy juice (that is, opium) was about the best painkiller there was.

France, with its temperate climate and limestone soil, became the European center for growing grapes and making wine. The British, especially after the loss of Bordeaux, became the most important importers and traders of wine. And the British, like the Romans, got around.

TECHNOLOGY CHANGES EVERYTHING, HURRAY

In Europe, up until about 1780, wine came from a barrel that was simply tapped until it went bad or got used up. Jugs and earthenware bottles were used to store smaller amounts of wine. It was possible to store wine in a barrel for a long time, but some would evaporate. It tended to age far too quickly unless it was carefully stored in a cool cellar.

The weather in Europe is very changeable, and vintners realized that they could blend an indifferent year's wine with another, good year's wine to come up with something that would taste and sell better.

People started getting the idea that many wines tasted MUCH better if they were allowed to hang around for more than a year. Blending of wines produced a much more balanced and more dependably tasty beverage.

The trade in wine from Europe was spreading around the world via ships. A wine from France could appear on the other side of the world in as little as six months from the time the bung was banged home in the barrel.

If you were moderately well off and liked wine, you could have a barrel or two of ordinary wine in the cellar and jugs of more expensive, rare wines for special occasions.

Then in France, someone got the idea of storing wine in glass bottles. Paired with bits of cork from Portugal, a revolution occurred. Barrels were still important, of course, but the glass bottle changed everything, from drinking to shipping. Glass was light and strong compared to pottery. If it was packed well, it could be shipped with relative ease. You could see the wine in the bottle.

In England in the mid–eighteenth century, it was discovered that the superior heat from coal made glass stronger than wood fires did. Someone invented the corkscrew, which meant that a cork could be driven all the way into the bottleneck and the new, stronger bottle could be stored on its side, keeping the cork wet. This avoided shrinkage, and meant the wine would keep even longer.

The monk Dom Perignon invented the champagne method, and champagne as we know it came about. Wines could be bottled on the estate where they were grown, or sold by the barrel and bottled by the wine merchant on the other end. Wine merchants could store especially good vintages for many years and sell them at a higher profit.

The first bottle of Chateau Lafite was laid down in 1781. It was wonderful. It was the fruit of technology.

In the mid–nineteenth century another innovation came along: a nasty little louse by the name of Phylloxera. Originally from North America, this creature attacked the vineyards of Europe. Almost 6.2 million acres were destroyed. It looked like the end of the glory of European wines. However, it was discovered that North American native grapes had developed a resistance to the disease spread by Phylloxera. Eventually, the disease was controlled by using North American native grapes as rootstock, even in the great vineyards of Bordeaux.

BUT WHAT ABOUT FRUIT WINES?

Ah. Well. During Roman, medieval, and Renaissance times there were wines made of things other than grapes. There are records of grape wines being "adulterated" with other fruits.

Granulated sugar as we know it didn't really exist. Sugarcane existed only in exotic climes. Sugar beets had not been bred. Sweetening was accomplished with honey, sweet fruits, and barley malt. Most fruit wines had to be made using honey, malt, or dates to supply the food for the yeast.

Bees were very important in those days, as you can imagine. A beekeeper was sometimes thought of as holy. Or crazy.

Fruit wines were really fruit meads. There aren't a lot of details about what plain folks ate, drank, or even did in those days, but I suspect that, along with the beer, cider, and perry, a certain amount of honey fruit wines were made and enjoyed while the wealthier swilled grape wine.

With the advent of colonialism, sugar became more widely available, though it was very expensive. Sugarcane must be grown in a warm climate. It takes a lot of work to grow the cane, harvest it, and refine the juice into sugar. With the help of slaves, sorry to say, this was done on a large scale.

Then Napoleon needed cheap food for his troops. In the early nineteenth century, the sugar beet was bred. And for the Western world many changes came about, including a gradual end to slavery. The sugar made from sugar beets was cheap enough so nearly anyone could afford it instead of the expensive cane sugar. It was cheap enough to be used to make wine.

Meanwhile, industrialism was getting a foothold. People lived in the towns and cities.

All along, fruit wines were being made. Not just by unregenerate peasants, either. *Mrs. Beeton's Book of Household Management,* first published in installments from 1859 to 1861, contained several recipes for fruit and flower wines made with sugar and lemons and what was probably bread yeast. They were clearly intended for household use. The method described was a trifle brief, but cleanliness was urged in the making of the wine. The wine was not aged very long, probably because it wouldn't keep very long.

Here's one from my files:

✺BLACKBERRY WINE✺

Bruise the berries well with the hands. To one gallon of fruit, add one-half gallon of water and let stand overnight. Strain and measure, and to each gallon of juice add two and one-half pounds of sugar. Put in cask and let ferment. Tack thin muslin over top, and when fermentation stops, pour into kegs or jugs.

And another:

✺SMALL WHITE MEAD✺

Take three gallons of spring water, make it hot, and dissolve in it three quarts of honey, and one pound loaf sugar. Let it boil about one-half hour, and skim it as long as any scum arises. Then pour it out into a tub, and squeeze in the juice of four lemons, put in the rinds but of two. Add twenty cloves, two races of ginger, one top of sweet briar, and one top of rosemary. Let it stand in a tub till it is but blood-warm; then make a brown toast, and spread it with two or three spoonfuls of ale yeast. Put it into a vessel fit for it, let it stand four or five days, then bottle it out.

And stand back, I should think. Sounds dangerous.

Many old cookbooks, going back even to medieval times, had

recipes for fruit wines using honey. In those days it was assumed that the reader would know the basics. Description of method was hazy. The important thing was the list of ingredients. One that I read included the body of a male chicken. No reason was given. I guess you were just supposed to take it on faith that the recipe's inventor was cocksure.

BACK IN THE U.S.A.

In the New World, Native Americans made mild alcoholic beverages. Pulque, tequila, and other drinks were made mostly in southern regions, including Central and South America. These beverages were not a major part of the culture. When the Spaniards and the Portuguese brought their vines with them, their wines quickly supplanted the native beverages.

In North America, the northern European colonialists brought with them collections of recipes that were very precious to them, handed down from generation to generation. They were mostly fruit and vegetable wines, or country wines, as they were sometimes called.

Even Martha Washington made wine. Unless their religion forbade it, most people made their own, since imported grape wines were terribly expensive.

Vineyards were established, both privately and for the manufacturing of wine to be sold. By the time of the Revolution the United States was chugging along pretty much in the same groove as Western Europe, with established wineries, breweries, and distilleries.

The country was mostly rural. Farm wives and husbands had their own methods of making beer and wine and even the harder stuff. Sugar wasn't too expensive, and there was always honey. Many a fine cordial or elderberry wine was made.

Then came Prohibition. It was a mess. Many producers and vineyards went out of business, never to return. Organized crime cheerfully poisoned and cheated millions of people. Bootleggers made the most horrible stuff and sold it as liquor and wine.

Prohibition lasted fourteen years. It took the American wine industry a long time to recover. First, there was the Great Depression of the '30s, when it was difficult to start a new enterprise of any kind. The money needed to establish a vineyard that wouldn't produce wine for several years was not easily found. Then there was the little matter of World War Two. Who had time to mess with wine when the fate of the world was at stake?

Gradually American wine came back into its own. By the '60s it was no longer considered embarrassing to admit you drank American wine. In the '70s, and '80s, some truly great grape wines were being made. Vineyards were popping up all over the country, but especially on the West Coast.

Homemade fruit wines were beginning to flourish, as well. The idea that only a desperate booze hound would make homemade wine was fading with the memory of Prohibition. In the '60s people experimented with alternative lifestyles in many different ways. Self-sufficiency was not a new concept, but it was being more widely explored. People were making bread with their own hands after years of eating only bakery bread. People began making their own beer and wine. For a while there, you could buy a winemaking kit from the Sears Roebuck catalog!

I drank some, once. Once was enough.

In the mid-seventies, the fad died back a little, but not out. Little by little, clubs and societies dedicated to home winemaking were born. A few winemaking supply houses hung on and did acceptable business. Gradually, more and more people began to experiment.

I think organizations such as the Society for Creative Anachronism and the various Renaissance festivals have had a lot to do with keeping winemaking going. Mead in particular has been explored in those circles, as well as ale and beer. That person who crunches out the code in the cubicle next to you could very well be known as Lady Montegreen on the weekends, specializing in peach melomel and juggling on the side.

More and more people have chosen a quieter life these last few decades, trading the corporate ladder for the apple tree ladder. The secretary might have a Ph.D. The janitor might be a science fiction writer. The guy who comes in as a consultant to figure out what went wrong in the assembly line might have a thriving herb farm. You never know.

The '80s weren't the age of conspicuous consumption for everyone. The standardization of consumer goods made a lot of folks decide they might want to get into planting stock instead of buying and selling it.

Many people are finding that making their own wine is an intriguing, satisfying hobby that takes them outside the bounds of crass commercialism after a hard day on the eighty-eighth floor.

Things are quietly booming in home winemaking. There are more people you can talk to, more supply houses, more books on the subject than ever before.

Think of what you can do! With a little time and effort you can have a respectable wine cellar (well, maybe wine closet?) with a different style of wine and flavor of wine for every week of the year. Chateau la Smith can swap recipes over the fence (or down the stairwell) with Chateau la Morgenstern.

It only takes a little time here and there. Skip the boob tube on Saturday morning and go to a local farmers' market, or out to a pick-your-own place. Six months later look with pride at the lovely row of strawberry melomel you've just put down for a long winter's nap. By next holiday season you'll have a wonderful wine to go with the turkey, ham, or cashew loaf. And that mint you bottled last winter? It will be a hit as a wine cooler at the Memorial Day picnic you're planning.

Spotted some berry bushes on a fishing trip up at the cabin? Take a half hour to gather some the night before you leave for home. In the next year or two you can serve guests your own elderberry sherry, your own woodruff aperitif, or after-dinner port-style blueberry. And maybe your guests will bring you a bottle of their specialty wine to enliven your next birthday or anniversary.

CHAPTER TWO

The First Gallon

(or, A Simple Apple Wine, I Think
You'll Admire Its Presumption)

Well, my friend, here's how to make your first gallon. Note the lack of glamorous, expensive equipment and ingredients. Do not be alarmed. You can spend more money later. Note the need for patience. You can use more of that later, too.

Think of winemaking as breadmaking, except that it takes six months to rise, and six months to bake. A lot of people shy away from making bread because they say it takes too long. Nonsense. It takes a mere half hour to make the stuff, assuming you do it by hand. You don't watch it rise, and you don't watch it bake. You set the timer, and do intensely important stuff like watching CNN or cleaning the garage in the meantime.

Same deal with wine. Of course, while waiting for the wine, you could be making several batches of homebrewed beer. Just a thought.

Pick a nice quiet time when you aren't likely to be interrupted by a call from the president or Hollywood, and put on some nice music. The first time always takes a while because it just does.

First, figure out a place you can put your wine to ferment. The first couple of days you'll want to watch it, but that will get old very quickly, and wine does best in subdued light or in darkness. In fact, strong light will fade the color (not a big deal in apple wine, but it's best to start good habits early).

The wine will also, ahem, have an odor as it ferments. Not a terrible odor, but some. All those little yeastie beasties are passing gas, you know. Bothers some people but not others.

You also want to keep it warm, but not too warm (60–80°F), and you don't want to move it around. You don't want it near vinegar, solvents, cleaning supplies, or your pile of dirty socks.

Panic-stricken already?

Look, it's OK. Do the best you can and don't worry. A corner of the kitchen or the back of a closet that isn't airtight is just fine. A cupboard is fine. A basement is OK for later, but it's not the best place right now. The attic is right out. Look around. You'll find a place. If the ideal place gets too much light, put a big cardboard box over your batch.

Equipment:

1 one-gallon glass jug—an ex-apple juice, cranberry juice, or wine jug that hasn't been used to store kerosene, vinegar, or nuclear waste
1 rubber band
1 4×4 in. square of heavy kitchen plastic wrap
1 medium-sized food grade funnel, plastic or metal
a long stick or rod for stirring (you can whittle down a wood spoon, but a long chopstick works just fine, too)
later: another gallon jug, 4 or 5 clean wine bottles, corks, a corker, and a 3–4 ft. length of clear plastic tubing from an aquarium shop or winemaking supply shop. For the latter, see complete description on page 54.

Ingredients:

1 12 oz. can frozen apple juice (any brand)
1 6 oz. can frozen lemonade or the juice of two lemons, strained (don't use bottled lemon juice, ugh)
1 lb. of sugar (two cups) or 1½ lb. mild honey

1 gallon of water, boiled and cooled while covered
1 packet of wine yeast (champagne or Montrachet)
$1/2$ teaspoon pectic enzyme (optional but recommended)
5 Campden tablets (optional but recommended)

NOTES

Later on in your winemaking career I will encourage you to use a proper rubber bung and air lock instead of the rubber band and plastic (to keep the air out and let the gas out of the bottle), but this is your first gallon, and this method should be OK.

The wine yeast, pectic enzyme, and Campden tablets can be purchased at your local wine supply or brewing supply store (or from any of the many mail order places listed in the back of this book). So can the rubber bung and air lock and any number of other interesting gadgets.

Wine yeast costs about fifty cents a packet. Don't use bread yeast or beer yeast. They don't come out just right, although they will work in a pinch. Wine yeast is best because it doesn't make "off" flavors, and it tolerates higher alcohol content. One packet makes one to five gallons of wine.

The pectin naturally present in fruit is nice for making jelly but not for making wine. It can create a harmless, but less than aesthetic, haze. Pectic enzyme eats the pectin, helping the wine to clear as it ferments. If the idea of the pectic enzyme is too complicated or weird to you, leave it out for right now, but really, this is not a big deal.

The Campden tablets are for sterilizing the jug. They are sodium metabisulphite. If you are sensitive to sulphites, don't use these. Many winemakers use them to sterilize the juices in the wine as well, but we don't need to worry about that so much in this case. If you can't or don't want to use Campden tablets (some people are very sensitive to this chemical, though it's perfectly safe for most), I'll give you an alternative method as we go along.

Many jugs these days are actually 4 liters, somewhat less than a U.S. gallon. Try to find a gallon jug, but don't worry if you can't. It won't make any real difference in this recipe.

FINALLY: Ignore everything else in the wine supply store until you know what you are doing and have finished this book. If you *must* look, don't buy. Yet. Later on, you can buy as much as you want. Talk to the clerks, who are usually the owners, and often possess a wealth of knowledge, which they will cheerfully pass on to you.

PROCEDURE

Boil most of the water in a stainless steel or enamel pot and let it cool, covered. In most areas, this isn't really necessary, but it certainly doesn't hurt.

Boil the sugar or honey with one quart of the water, and let it cool, stirring a little to make sure the sugar dissolves. Add an extra half cup of sugar if you are using lemons instead of lemonade. Take the cans of juice out of the freezer to let them defrost.

Sanitize the 1 gallon jug by boiling it in a large pot (such as a canning kettle or stockpot) of water for 1 to 15 minutes, or wash and clean it with a bottle brush, rinse, then swoosh it out with the Campden solution. To make the Campden solution, with the back of a spoon crush the tablets as finely as possible, and dissolve the powder in one cup of cool water, which you have placed in a jar with a tight-fitting lid. Shake up the jar like mad to facilitate the dissolving. You will never get all the lumps out, but do the best you can and don't worry.

Pour this solution into the clean jug (a funnel makes it easy) and swoosh it around the inside, making sure you cover the entire surface, then pour it back out into the jar. You can reuse this solution as long as it still smells like sulfur.

Another method is simply to soak the jug in a solution of unscented bleach and water for 20 minutes. An ounce or two of bleach to 5 gallons of water will sanitize the jug just fine. Rinse it out with really hot water to get rid of as much of the chlorine smell as possible. I worry that the chlorine will affect the taste of the wine, so I use the Campden method, but I have used bleach in emergencies.

Cleanliness in winemaking is not quite as essential as it is in beermaking, but it is still very important.

When the sugar water is still a bit warm, pour it into the jug, using a funnel that has either been rinsed in the Campden solution or boiled. Add the thawed apple juice and the strained lemonade or lemon juice. Then add the plain, cool water up to where the neck of the jug starts to slant upward. Add the pectic enzyme if you are using it. Stir with a long wooden or metal stick, over which you have poured boiling water. A long chopstick also works fine. Put the piece of plastic over the top and secure it with the rubber band. Store it someplace out of the light and out of the way. Twenty-four hours later, take off the rubber band and tap the packet of wine yeast into the jug. Replace the plastic with a new piece, and put the rubber band back on snugly.

Put the whole thing in a warm (75°F), preferably dark, place for one month to ferment. The temperature should be in the range of about 60–80°F. After the first day, you should see a bit of froth at the top of the liquid (or *must,* as it is called). This means the yeast is happily eating the sugar and making alcohol. It will be fairly active for the first couple of weeks, then it will settle down.

After a few weeks, you will notice a sediment at the bottom of the jug, and nearly clear wine above. You need to *rack* the wine, or separate the good stuff from the dead yeast and sediment. To do this, sanitize another jug and the tubing. I *strongly* recommend that you use the sulphite solution for the tubing, rather than boil it.

Then boil another cup or so of water.

Place the jug of wine on a table, moving it carefully so as not to disturb the sediment. Put the empty jug directly below on the floor. Remove the plastic again, and carefully insert one end of the tubing down into the wine until it rests a few inches above the sediment and hold it there with one hand, or have a friend hold it. Squat down above the empty jug and suck gently on the end of the tube. Be sure to rinse your mouth out before you do this. (Some people swish out with vodka!)

The wine should start flowing up out of the high jug into the tube, heading for the lower point of gravity, which just happens to be the end of the tube, which is between your lips. Quickly remove it from your lips, insert it into the empty jug, and let the wine flow into the jug. Try to avoid vigorous splashing. If you have to stop for a second, just pinch the tube firmly. Be sure to keep the bottom of the upper part of the tube in the liquid, or, of course, the flow will stop. Continue to siphon until just before the sediment begins to enter the tube. Then remove the tube from both jugs.

Top up the wine by adding the boiled water to it until the

Racking from the primary fermenter to the five-gallon carboy using a racking tube. Notice the casual, but alert stance of the model, and the open-mouthed admiration of the rubber lizard. Wearing loose, older clothes is a good practice when racking or bottling.

mixture reaches the bottom of the bottle neck, replace the old plastic with new. Add the rubber band. Don't fill the jar all the way up to the top. You need room for the gases. If you taste the wine it will probably taste pretty raw, but don't worry. Time is on your side.

At the end of about two months (or sooner if the weather is warm), you should check the wine again. You can tell if the wine has finished fermenting (has eaten all the available sugar) by gently tapping the jug to see if any little bubbles rise to the top. If they do, it's still fermenting. Be patient. There will be more sediment on the bottom of the jug, but not a whole lot. Later on you will acquire a hydrometer, and you can be a lot more scientific about the fermentation process.

When at last the wine is finished fermenting, and fairly clear (one to three months), you can do several things. You can rack the wine again and drink it. It won't be too bad. You can rack it and leave it in the jug for another six months and then drink it. It will be lots better.

Apple wine tastes best chilled, though it's awkward to store a whole gallon in the fridge. After you take some out of the gallon jug, the chances of the rest going bad rise quickly.

You see where I am gently leading you by the hand, don't you? Yes, the solution is to bottle it.

BOTTLING

Use old clean wine bottles, washed and sanitized. These days, they are mostly 750 ml, not the old fifths. You may have acquired some already. You can also get them from friends, caterers, some recycling centers, or, if all else fails, you can buy them rather expensively at the wine supply shop.

There is no point in using a bottle with any dubious matter in it, nor is there any point in using a bottle that has been used to store Uncle Joe's Karburetor Kleener, vinegar, frogs, lead paint chips, or anything else of that ilk. The world is full of wine bottles. Get ones that have held only wine.

They must be the kind that came with a genuine cork. You want four or five. If they have mold on the bottom, or any specks of weird stuff, soak them in the mild solution of water and chlorine bleach we spoke of earlier, overnight, submerging them. Rinse out with hot water until you get all the stuff out. Use a bottle brush if necessary. Or you can use the old trick of putting in a handful of dry beans and swishing them around inside with a little water to dislodge any crud. You can avoid all of this mess by rinsing out wine bottles after you use them, and storing them upside down in a wine carton to avoid the entrapment of curious centipedes and spiders.

After getting them very clean, it's best to sanitize them again, just before you want to bottle. Use the Campden tablet solution or the bleach treatment, if you must.

Now you need a corker and new corks from the wine supply store. The corker costs about fifteen dollars. A package of corks costs about three dollars for twenty-five. NEVER use old corks. False economy. Corks are porous and should be used for wine only once. After that, they are cat toys and hat decorations.

Buy the best-quality corks you can. You might have to buy a whole bag of twenty-five. Bring in your bottle and ask the clerk to help you figure out the right size. Sometimes you can get coated corks that do not need soaking, but they are not always easy to find.

Buy a lever action corker while you are at it. There is a simpler, cheaper plunge corker, which I have never used because it takes a lot of work and time. Then there's the old method of banging the cork in with a rubber mallet, left over from the days of smaller corks and dangerous living best left to history.

There are also nice bench corkers available in some areas and by mail, running from $70 to $100. They are an investment that you should consider if you make more than twenty gallons of wine a year.

If you want to justify the cost of the corks and corker, remember that you can now buy bulk wine in jugs and bottle it yourself. On the other hand, you can borrow a corker if you know anyone else who makes wine, or possibly rent one from a wine supply place.

Heat up five or six corks in some boiling water, simmer them very gently for a few minutes, turn off the heat, and submerge the corks with a saucer that is a little smaller than the pan. Soak the corks for four hours, or overnight.

Why soak extra corks? (They aren't cheap!) Well, things happen. You may drop them. They aren't as firm looking once they are soaked, so you may mis-cork and have to recork a bottle. Who knows? You don't want to be caught with full bottles and not enough corks.

OK. Got the wine, got the time, got the bottles nice and clean, got the corks, got the racking tube . . . we're off!

Rack the wine into the wine bottles. Put down some newspaper on the floor to catch any spills. Carefully bend or squeeze the tube so the wine doesn't overflow. Fill the bottles up to about two to three inches below the top. You have to leave room for the cork!

Overfilled? Don't panic. Just tip some out. Do the best you can and don't worry.

There will be some sediment (dead yeast) at the bottom of the jug. Better to throw out the last inch or two than have a bottle of cloudy-looking wine. It also might develop an off taste.

What usually happens, depending on the size of the jug and the size of the bottles, is that you end up with three or four full bottles and a half bottle. Ignore the half bottle for right now.

Take one of the soaked corks out of the soaking water, fit it into the corker and squeeze the handles to compress the cork. Depending on the model, you'll see how the cork fits in.

Place one end of the corker on top of the filled wine bottle,

Corker, ready for action. Note the cork is in position under the plunger, waiting for the two side handles to squeeze together and compress it so it can be pushed into the bottle.

Corking: My sturdy hands have compressed the cork and are about to plunge the cork into the bottle, which is being firmly steadied by the delicate hand of Lydia, the Human Light Stand. Normally, I wouldn't be wearing anything as silly as a fringy scarf when bottling, but it seemed like a good idea at the time.

having a friend hold the bottle steady on a flat surface (if you are fresh out of friends, you can kneel and put the bottle firmly between your knees, but the friend is easier and friendlier). Keeping the cork compressed in the corker with your strongest hand, plunge the lever down until you think the cork is seated.

There is usually a lot of resistance, and then it gives up and goes in.

Corking gets easier with practice, honest. It helps if you have two good strong arms and/or two people, in which case you'll have four good strong arms. Sometimes you need to put a little vegetable oil on the metal part of the plunger. Sometimes the cork doesn't go all the way in. Sometimes you can quickly push it the rest of the way in with your thumb, other times you will want to remove the cork and try again. I advocate practicing with some bottles of water a few times till you get the hang of it. So what if you waste a few corks? Better that than a bottle of your wonderful wine.

When all is said and done, it isn't that difficult.

Rinse off the bottles of newly corked wine to get rid of any spills that might make mold. Let the bottles dry, then label them clearly. I use gummed labels when I can get them, and stick on name tags or computer labels when I can't. My wine labels frequently look like this:

HELLO MY NAME IS
        High Pitched Wines
        FREEZER ROSÉ
        12%

Made Aug 93   Bottled Feb 94

Now that I have a laser printer, I think I'll try to make them look better. Many people use labels they buy in the wine supply store, or they make their own, sometimes using rubber stamps for elegant or silly effects. If you have access to a computer with a drawing program or graphics, you're in business.

On the label you want the name, the date bottled, and later, when you know it, the percent of alcohol. I have also come up with a code for the cork end, because these bottles will be joining others on their sides and reading the labels is not always easy. I use a ballpoint pen and ink to write, for example, A1 94, which stands for Apple—batch #1, 1994. It isn't foolproof because you run out of letters, but it saves quite a bit of trouble and shifting of bottles, anyway. (I keep thinking AP 93 is apple, but it's the apple peach I made—nothing's perfect.)

Lay your wine in a dark, cool place for a few months, and let your friend time do its work.

Chill the leftover wine and drink it with lunch or supper. If you are bottling two or more gallons, you can bottle the leftover stuff together and thus do your first blending. Sometimes these can be quite good. I remember that one bottle of Potato-Mint . . . well, I'll tell you about that later.

It's amazing how much better the wine is after even just a month in a bottle (six months is preferred). It is also amazing (though not preferred) to come down to the cellar and find a cork blown out and the floor sticky with wine.

With my first batch, you see, it hadn't quite finished fermenting when I bottled, and we had a warm spell. I should have waited longer, or stopped the fermentation with some stabilizer from the wine supply place. Or bottled it as champagne with the proper bottles and plastic champagne caps. But I didn't know any of this. *You, however, can benefit from my experience.*

Later on you will learn how to use more or less sugar, and to use a hydrometer for accuracy, and real fruit, and all that.

After a month, get the bottle and put it in the fridge to chill. Remove the cork, decant, if necessary, and get out some nice glasses. Carefully pour, trying to avoid disturbing any sediment at the bottom. There usually isn't much.

So, what does it taste like when you are done? Sort of like a strong apple cider: dry and crisp. *Nothing* like Annie Green Springs, thank-you very much. With this recipe you get 7–9 percent alcohol, which will keep a year or two. It's best drunk young.

All of this exposition for such a simple procedure! After you have done this once or twice, you can explore the process a bit more. You don't have to wait till the first batch is done. You can use grape juice or other frozen juices and move on up to real fruit, acid blend, yeast energizer, and tannin, all of which I will explain later. You'll also be using the proper equipment. You can use the many wine concentrates available in the wine supply stores. Most of them are quite acceptable, although you'll have to use five one-gallon jugs or a five-gallon carboy to make them. (The five-gallon carboy works better.)

TIME

This first, simple wine can take as little as two months to ferment out, or as long as six. But remember, time is on your side. Don't try to rush it.

SERVING

Serve your wine in nice wine glasses. Your wine deserves a chance to look its best. Inexpensive, clear wine glasses are easy to obtain. Only use colored glasses when the color of the wine isn't quite what you'd hoped, or when the relative who gave them to you is visiting.

French-style bistro glasses are also nice for casual sipping or social wines.

Try to avoid mason jars unless you're having some kind of

theme party. Don't use plastic with wine. It gives the wine an off taste.

MORE IDEAS

Here are some other ideas for making some simple, but very nice, wines in the beginner's mode.

Get a few more gallon jugs. Follow the apple recipe, but substitute ordinary frozen grape juice (purple or white, or both), orange juice, pineapple, cranraspberry, or whatever for the apple juice and lemonade. Easy, huh? Some you will like better than others, but having four or five nice light wines around isn't such a bad idea and you need to use up those corks.

Another idea: once you have the first batch of apple wine going, try making another batch with two, count them two, 12 oz. cans of juice, plus only the one 6 oz. can of lemonade, and sugar and see what you get.

After that, make up the frozen apple juice recipe with only the one 12 oz. can of juice, but with two lbs. of sugar instead of one lb.

These last two might take longer to ferment out, since they will have more alcohol, but when they are done and you compare the three it will be a good way for you to learn the different ways you can change flavors and strengths.

While you are at it, I suppose you could also try 12 oz. of lemonade by itself, though all lemonade might be a bit acidic, as might limeade.

You never know . . . there was this batch of mead I made once, which was mostly limeade and came out really fine. (I did it on a bet, OK?) You'll find the recipe further on. Look under ReinCo-nation Citrus Melomel.

Be aware that a lot of the frozen juices these days are not 100 percent juice. Many are merely flavored corn syrup, and aren't going to be very flavorful. Check the ingredients list to make sure you are getting as close to 100 percent fruit juice as you can. Reading labels is a good habit to get into.

I've tried a few of the "tropicals" with mixed results. If you look closely at the ingredients you'll notice that "white grape juice" is a key ingredient. This is tropical? Nothing wrong with it except that it's bland, and so is the bit of pineapple, guava or banana that is mixed in with it. I can't see any sense in making bland wine.

CANNED JUICES

Using canned juices is a bit more tricky, because a lot of them either have been cooked to death or have preservatives in them. The preservatives might inhibit your wine yeast. Some of the aseptically packaged concentrates have promise, though. I've used them a few times to pick up a five-gallon tutti-frutti that lacked zest.

If you want to try to use canned juice, buy some and drink it first to make sure you like it. If you think it tastes flat and metallic now, it's going to taste really flat and metallic later on. Silk purses and sow's ears and so forth.

A lot of the old British winemaking books from the '40s, '50s, and '60s have exuberant recipes for canned juices, but I think much of the enthusiasm was due to the cheapness of the resultant wine. Wine and hard liquor are heavily taxed in Britain, and were thus expensive. Beer was cheap, and there was no tax on home-made wine. Also, frozen fruit juice was not widely available at the time.

If you think the juice has any preservative in it, heat it up gently on the stove for a few minutes (do not boil) and let it cool down again. Heating up is NOT a foolproof way of getting rid of the preservatives, but it ought to improve your fighting chances.

☜CANNY APPLE WINE☞

48 oz. canned or bottled apple juice (any brand)
1 6 oz. can frozen lemonade or the juice of two lemons, strained (remember, don't use bottled lemon juice)
1 lb. of sugar (two cups) or 1½ lbs. mild honey
1 gallon of water, boiled and cooled while covered
1 packet of wine yeast (champagne or Montrachet)
1 teaspoon pectic enzyme (optional but recommended)
water
5 Campden tablets (optional but recommended)

Proceed as you did for the frozen apple juice on page 26, merely adding less water to the mixture, since you already have it in the apple juice. It should ferment out just as fast as the frozen variety.

If you want to try using other canned or bottled juices, go ahead, but I think the frozen ones are better. I don't recommend canned orange or grapefruit juice at all, but if you insist on trying, use only twenty-four ounces or less. Sometimes you can find apricot nectar, or pear nectar, or even more rarely, canned cherry juice. Follow the basic apple juice recipe using anywhere from twenty-four to forty-eight ounces of juice, and see what you get. You can never tell.

INSTANT WINE KITS

These are becoming available through gift catalogs that sell things other than winemaking supplies. You pour water into a mylar pouch, add yeast, and get grape wine a month or so later. They cost a lot, considering how much wine you get, and you don't learn much by using them. They are also available for beer.

For the same amount of money you could set up your basic home winemaking equipment, or buy a couple of bottles of *really* nice commercial wine.

NON-INSTANT WINE KITS

In Europe, many non-instant wine kits are available, especially for varietal grape wines. Some of them make excellent wines. They are now catching on here, too.

A good wine supply store will sell you the kit, which usually includes the grape concentrate, the proper yeast, instructions, etc. for forty to sixty dollars. Many places also sell a kit that includes the basic equipment you need plus the ingredients for making wine for under one hundred dollars. They want you to succeed so you will come back!

ONWARD

You can continue to use this simple method for making wine, or you can go a step further and use real fruit and more sugar in a two-stage fermentation process. I'll give you directions in the next chapter. It really isn't that much more difficult, and it is a heck of a lot more rewarding. I still make simple juice wines upon occasion, strengthening the alcohol content by using more juice and more sugar. I also combine the two techniques quite often, as

I will discuss later, in the section called The BIG TIME, where I will explain how to combine fruits, grains, vegetables, and methods.

The lists of equipment, terms, and ingredients in the next section may seem a little intimidating, but look them over while you are making a few wines from this first section, and familiarize yourself with them before you go on to making whole fruit wines. You'll quickly realize there isn't anything truly complicated; it just takes some time to describe some simple techniques. You'll be in the swing of it very quickly.

Welcome to home winemaking!

Part Two

Intermediate Winemaking

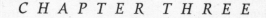

CHAPTER THREE

Equipment

(The Whole Fruit and Nothing but the
Fruit Except for Everything Else
That Goes In)

This section brings you up to using whole fruits and vegetables in your recipes. It's not that much more trouble, but you have to go through two stages of fermentation, and you need more equipment. I think you will like the results.

When you made the fruit juice wines in the previous chapters, that first, frothy stage of fermentation was where the yeast did most of its work. The second, quieter stage took longer but was necessary for the yeast to consume the last bits of sugar and die off.

When working with whole fruits and vegetables, we break the stages in two more completely, using the first, fast fermentation to extract sugars, flavors, and color from the fruits and vegetables. This is called *fermenting on the fruit.*

In the second stage of fermentation, the used-up material is discarded in order to let the fermentation proceed without the danger of producing off flavors from any solids.

The first stage is done in a large, sanitized food-grade plastic bin with a lid and a fermentation lock. It takes two weeks or less. The second stage happens in a glass container, again using a fermentation lock to guard against spoilage. It can take from two to six months for the fermentation to complete. After that, the racking and bottling procedures are no different from what you have already learned.

Please be sure to read over the descriptions of equipment, ingredients, and procedures before moving on to the actual recipes. To ensure consistent results, you need to understand more about what you are doing, what is happening, and what it is happening with. An hour or two of your time now will pay off in good results later.

These recipes are fairly simple; most require only one kind of fruit so that you will become familiar with the basic process of fermenting on the fruit. Besides, you need to learn the characteristics of each of the fruits and vegetables when they are translated into wine.

For example, strawberry wine sounds very romantic. It's the stuff of old folk songs and legends: lips like strawberry wine, etc. In your mind you probably have an imaginary taste for it already.

Believe me, your fantasy is going to differ from the actual wine, which will be drier, lusher, more acidic, or aromatic than you thought. This is not bad. In fact, it's quite good. But it isn't what you would think. It doesn't even look the way people think it should, usually being more straw color than berry.

Take carrot wine, for instance. I had no idea what to expect the first time I made it. I did it because it was winter, carrots were cheap, and I wanted to experiment. So I combed through the old recipes, and made some. Six months later, when I bottled the stuff, I was not pleased. It didn't taste like much. Certainly not like carrots. Six months later, same results.

My brother, the Ph.D., was visiting and insisted on taking a bottle back home with him. Over a year later, I was visiting him. He remembered the carrot wine and brought it up from the basement. "What's up, Doc?" I cried, "I've tried it, and it's not very good. Just throw it out."

We tried it anyway; it was wonderful. That's how I learned that vegetable wines take longer to age. But once again, it tasted nothing like carrots!

Before you get into both blending and the more advanced recipes, you must learn the basic flavor notes of the single fruit and vegetable and herb wines. This takes a few years, but so what? Time is on your side. So is experimentation. You can skip back and forth between this section and the next if you like, but it's best to make several wines from the middle section first.

Over the years I've come up with some wonderful surprises and some dismal failures. Watermelon was a wonderful surprise. Tangerine and brown sugar was a dismal failure.

Tastes differ. Someone else might have thought the tangerine juice wine was great.

I love the taste of sherry. My partner hates it. Anytime I end up with a sherrylike wine, I know he won't really like it, but I will. We both love the lushness of raspberry and blueberry, but I dislike what I think of as stringy, insipid whites, and he thinks they are great.

Neither of us liked the first five-gallon batch of what we termed Pink Plonk. It was too sweet. It was too thin. It was too pink. Luckily, we had some friends who adored it. David, it turns out, likes cold duck. To him, Pink Plonk was cold duck without the bubbles. To me, the bubbles are what make cold duck marginally bearable. I still respect David as a human being, but I'll never understand his taste in wine.

I suggest you make mostly one-gallon batches of a lot of different wines for the next couple of years, trying different fruits, vegetables, and herbs. The recipes given here are merely guidelines. Except for how you deal with the acid, most fruit wines are made the same way. Most vegetable and herb wines are made the same way. After you get the hang of it, you can range far and wide.

It's common for home winemakers to make only one or two kinds of wine, get used to the taste, and in the process have their taste go down the drain.

"Oh yes, there goes Chauncy, the one who makes battery acid out of all those luscious yum yum berries every year. Sad case."

You need to keep your taste buds awake and moving. OK, make LOTS of the raspberry, or apple, or rhubarb, but make other wines as well.

Taste commercial wines; you can learn a lot from the commercial wineries. I would have never tried pineapple wine if I hadn't found some from Maui in a wine store. Zinfandel is always in the back of my mind when I make blackberry or blueberry. I'm not trying to duplicate it, I'm just keeping a few of the flavor notes in mind.

Try to start a different wine each month. Make a heavy wine one month, and a lighter, drier wine the next. Keep track of your recipes. Your cellar will be much more interesting, and so will your tastes. Don't toss "mistakes." Keep them awhile to see if anything interesting happens.

When you bottle, try to bottle several gallons at once. For one thing, it's more efficient. For another thing, you learn what the wines taste like in comparison with each other as you bottle them. Write down your impressions. Just a few words in your wine log. "Stunk like old rotting leather," "Made me dream of a balmy summer night," "Didn't die, but wanted to," are more useful than "Pretty good," "OK," and "Could be worse," but any notes are better than nothing.

Invariably, there will be not quite enough for the rest of the bottle, and you will make your first steps in blending when you fill it up with the leftover Ring Tailed Wotsit. Don't label it something cute like Mystery Wine, either. For all you know, dandelion-raspberry-mint might be pretty good. You might want to know later what it was, unlikely as it seems now.

I bottled my first batch of potato and my first batch of mint at the same time. There wasn't quite enough potato for the fifth bottle, but there was leftover mint. With great hilarity, I topped up the fifth bottle with mint. We laughed gaily at the madness of the moment. We also labeled it.

Six months later an old friend was visiting. Proudly, I showed her my cellar. What would you like to try? I asked magnanimously.

To my chagrin she wanted to try the potato-mint. It was quite nice. You could have knocked me over with a mint sprig.

Common Causes of Failure (And Guidelines for Success):

- Using the wrong yeast. Use only fresh wine yeasts. Never use bread or beer yeast.

- Sloppy cleanliness and sanitation. Keep it clean, and keep it sanitary. It's easy.

- Old methods and recipes. It's OK to get ideas from old recipes, but don't copy the methods, or even the proportions! People were doing the best they could back then, but things have changed for the better in home winemaking. Don't use Great Uncle Jake's Elderberry Whoopee recipe with the beer yeast and the molasses scrapings set out in the sun in an open crock for umpteen days and expect it will come out OK.

- Use only the best fruits and vegetables. A moldy berry isn't going to taste any better in the bottle than it did before.

- Keep the secondary fermenter topped up. More on this later, but space for oxygen is space for oxidation.

- Keep the wine off the sediment. Rack at least once or twice during secondary fermentation—more, if you need to.

- Keep records! You'll be glad later!

- Give the wine a chance. Time is our friend, remember? Don't dump a batch unless it really has turned to vinegar, or you are now certain you hate it. Be patient!

Good news and bad news: The level of water in the airlock is just fine, but the rubber gecko looks in dismay at the level of the wine in this jug. Lack of topping off, and leaving the wine on the huge sediment—visible at the bottom of the jug—is a good way to get an oxidized, off-tasting wine. You'll be happy to know I put the jug out of its misery the next day by racking and topping off.

FOLLOWING RECIPES

Follow the recipe through for at least the first time you use it.

Read the recipe all the way through before you try it. Mostly, the instructions are pretty much the same, but on some, there are variations. You don't want any surprises halfway through. Make sure you understand what the recipe says.

Assemble all the ingredients and equipment before you start.

Make sure everything is clean and sanitized.

Follow measurements. Don't guess.

Do the best you can, and don't worry. This is supposed to be fun, remember?

EQUIPMENT AND ITS CARE

Primary Fermenter

You need a large container to hold both the liquid and the solids and all the froth the fermentation kicks up. You need to be able

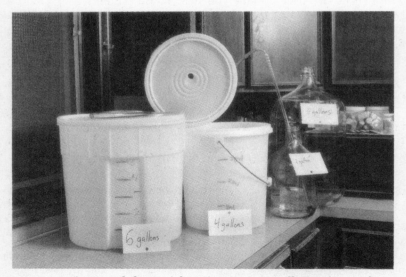

Large equipment, left to right: Six to seven-gallon primary fermenter and lid, four-gallon primary fermenter showing hole for air lock in lid, one-gallon jug, five-gallon carboy, and a racking tube carefully draped over all.

to stir the *must,* which is the water, sugar, and fruit before fermentation has set in, and to make additions to it. You also need to be able to keep it away from the open air.

People used to use stoneware crocks as primary fermenters. Sometimes they even put a piece of cheesecloth across the top to keep the flies out. The wine turned out well often enough to make it worthwhile doing again.

These days home winemakers mostly use six- or seven-gallon food-grade plastic bins as primary fermenters. They are easy to keep clean. They don't weigh much. They come with lids with a handy hole the size of a small rubber bung (a bung is like a plug) so you can fit them with an air lock. You can use them for the primary fermentation of one to five gallons of wine. The wine will always be fine as long as you practice good sanitation.

An alternative that's good for smaller batches of wine and that doesn't take up so much room is a smaller food-grade polyethylene bin or a glass jar. You need more room than one gallon, even for one-gallon batches, because the fruit takes up more room, and some wines make a lot of foam. So an ice cream tub won't work. You might have a friend in food service who can provide you with a small bin with a tight-fitting lid in which you can cut a hole for the bung and air lock. Bakeries and delis also have these bins and like to get rid of them.

Always make sure it's food-grade plastic and didn't contain vinegar or pickles. Don't use plastic bins from construction sites, or plastic wastebaskets.

Metal is out. In one of my favorite old out-of-print winemaking books, *How to Make Wine in Your Own Kitchen* (McFadden Books, New York; (1963), Mettja C. Roate advocated using unchipped galvanized canners as the primary fermenter. *Don't.* Food-grade plastic wasn't as easy to find in those days, and she was doing the best she could. Don't use anything but glass or food-grade plastic, or maybe a new crock.

I'm lucky to have some two-gallon clear glass jars that a friend gave me. She works in a lab, where they were unused surplus. Great for small batches of wine. I believe they were going to be used for pickling pathologic specimens!

If you happen to have a nice new stoneware crock (one that has never stored vinegar, and that is free of cracks or chips) that you know has a lead-free glaze, use it if you want to. Keeping it

A NOTE ON CLEANING: To sanitize the primary fermenter, proceed as you would for bottling or the gallon jug, although chemical means must be used. You can't boil anything this big. Rinsing it out with boiling water alone IS NOT GOOD ENOUGH. You might get away with it once or twice, but eventually, time and Mother Nature will punish you. Either soak it in the mild bleach solution for twenty minutes (including the lid), or swish it out carefully with Campden solution. You can use sulphite crystals if you like, but you must measure them accurately; for a sanitizing solution, mix 50–60 grams per 4 liters or a gallon of water. Like the Campden tablets, this solution can be used again and again as long as it smells like sulfur.

If you use bleach, rinse the fermenter with very hot water to remove the chemical smell. Don't forget the lid. Lids have crevices and little secret spots that mold and dirt love to settle into. You don't have to rinse if you use a sulphite solution. If you use any other commercial formula, follow the directions.

Do all of this just before you want to start a batch of wine. It isn't necessary or even desirable to dry the vessel out.

After the primary fermentation is finished, sanitize the fermenter right away all over again. Store it out of the way after it has dried out, with the lid on to keep out dust and arachnids. The reason for cleaning it up immediately is mold, which can grow almost anywhere. If you leave it, the least bit of food on it will grow. Yes, even on plastic. Plastic is soft. It scratches, making nice little valleys for mold spores to settle in. This goes for stoneware and glass, too: it should have no cracks and no chips.

Mother Nature loves us. But she loves mold and bacteria just as much. It's all the same to her!

ALWAYS clean up as soon as you can, and before you use your equipment again, sanitize it once more. Be picky. It pays off. I've never (she said, knocking on wood) had a batch go sour on me.

airtight will be a bit more difficult, since crocks don't come with airtight lids. You could use a sheet of food-grade plastic tied down with a giant rubber band (try making one out of a cross section of an old inner tube) as the lid. You will still have to sanitize the thing, don't forget. And it's heavy!

SECONDARY FERMENTERS

After two or three weeks of fermenting on the fruit, you will need to rack the wine into a secondary fermenter, which is either one or more one-gallon glass jugs or a five-gallon carboy. Use the five-gallon carboy only if you are going to fill it with five gallons of wine. During secondary fermentation, you want to avoid as much contact with air as you can.

If you planned to make three gallons of wine and have miscalculated and made, say, two and a half gallons of wine, use two gallon jugs and a half-gallon wine bottle. Or if you like, you can use a third gallon jug and top it up with some frozen juice and sugar and water, keeping in mind the acid content of what you are working with. If it is a low-acid juice (there will be a discussion of this later, don't worry), you will need to add some acid or lemon juice. The third gallon will throw a heavier deposit and it will need to be racked earlier.

Over the years I have found that it is better to keep five gallons of the same wine in a five-gallon carboy than in five one-gallon jugs. I'm not sure why this is, but the wine comes out better. It could also be that a large container is less susceptible to temperature fluctuations. Except for the weight, this approach is less fussy to rack and bottle, and less wine is wasted during racking.

I don't recommend keeping wine in the primary fermenter for more than a couple of weeks. I've done it, but I still don't think it's a good idea—too much risk of oxidation with all that exposed surface.

I've never used a plastic secondary fermenter, though I know collapsible plastic jugs are sold. In my humble opinion there is too much risk of strange flavors from the plastic, and contamination from an unseen scratch or imperfection.

Everything I have read has advised against using plastic as a secondary fermenter.

You are going to want to invest in a few five-gallon glass carboys almost immediately. Wine shops carry them new and used. Used, they run about twelve to fifteen dollars; new, they can cost up to twenty dollars. Sometimes you can luck out and find a used one at a thrift shop, or buy one from someone who is moving. Always clean a new or used carboy before you use it. Check for nicks around the top, and check the bottom for chips. Don't buy a carboy that has chips, nicks, or cracks. It isn't worth it.

Occasionally you will find a three-gallon, or even a two-gallon, carboy. Buy it. These are nice for smaller batches. The more sizes you have, the better off you are. Some shops sell special handles for carboys, to make it easier to haul them around when they are full.

A full carboy weighs a LOT! Fifty pounds or more of dead weight! Always handle them with care and respect. My partner and I were lifting one to empty out the sanitizing water one day and forgot to pad the edge of the laundry tub. The vessel shattered. Luckily we were not hurt, but the shards of glass were everywhere.

Many carboys fit snugly into some common sizes of plastic milk crates. These make handling the heavy carboys easier and safer. You can buy them in department stores and stores that specialize in closets and storage. Make sure that you buy sturdy ones, not the flimsy kind one finds at dollar stores. They have to hold more than fifty pounds of dead weight without the bottom falling out.

CARBOY AND BOTTLE BRUSHES

The carboy brush is curved and has a long handle. Get one, they're cheap. Ditto for bottle brushes.

AIR LOCKS

Air locks are inexpensive little gadgets with a stem that fits into a hole in the rubber bung, with which you will be sealing your primary and secondary fermenters. You fill the air locks about halfway with metabisulphate and water or some other sterile solution, drop the little cap over the hollow central stem, and put a little pill bottle cap over that. The pill bottle cap has a tiny hole that lets out the carbon dioxide that filters up from the fermenting yeast through the water in the lock but prevents the water in the lock from evaporating too quickly. As long as they have water in them, air locks will also keep out air, flies, and dust. Very simple; very effective. Long after the really active fermentation the wine needs to be protected until the final racking and bottling.

Some people fill the air lock with vodka, though I should think this would evaporate at a much higher rate than water. I use a metabisulfite/water solution. Sometimes plain water will develop mold, and you don't want that! You can keep a jug safe from harm for well over a year if you use an air lock and keep the solution at the proper level.

Get lots of air locks. I prefer the plastic multipart kind, which are easier to keep clean and harder to break. Get bungs to go with them to fit your various gallon jugs and your carboys, including a few small ones to go on your primary fermenter top and the occasional single bottle of "topping up" wine left over from a bigger batch.

When you finish bottling a batch of wine, check your air locks for mold and cracks. Sanitize the air locks by soaking them in our standard solution of water and bleach. Don't boil them; they melt. Leave them on a towel to dry, and sanitize them again before you use them.

It is false economy to use damaged air locks. In a pinch you can use the old plastic wrap and rubber band method, but I wouldn't for the long run, unless you are going away from your winery for an extended period and can't find someone to check your air locks for water once a month.

Replace your air locks when damaged, or every two or three years on general principle. There isn't that much plastic to them. Children who are old enough not to put them in their mouths like to play with them, using them for everything from rockets to doll cups.

Bungs

Bungs are cylindrical rubber plugs that fit snuggly into the openings of jugs, carboys, and barrels. They come in many sizes, from barely half an inch across which fits the average hole in the lid of a primary fermenter to huge ones for barrels. Most come with a hole drilled through the middle to accommodate the stem of an air lock, though you can obtain solid ones. Bungs are an inexpensive but important partner to the air lock.

When you are fitting a bung to a jug, remember that putting the stem of the air lock in it will firm up the bung a bit. I have a lot of jugs that fit the 7.5 and the 8 bung size; can I tell by eye which is which? Surely you jest. Some carboys have smaller openings than one-gallon jugs. Keep a variety of sizes around, as well as the tiny size for primary fermenters and individual wine bottles.

Assorted small equipment, back row, left to right excluding bottles: wine thief, corker, sulphite bottle marked with Mr. Ick, scale with air lock and bung on top, hydrometer and hydrometer tube, acid test kit, sanitizer, more bungs, assorted chemicals like tannin, acid blend, yeast nutrient and a nylon straining bag tastefully draped behind them. Front row, left to right: pectic enzyme, corks, assorted dry granular yeasts, measuring spoons, marking pen, labels, Champagne corks.

You might want to get some bungs without holes to fit gallon jugs. This way you can store a finished wine that you will be using in large quantities (for parties, etc.) without having to bottle so much. Wines can keep for two or more years this way.

Check the rubber bungs periodically. Keep them clean. Bleach isn't good for rubber, and metabisulphite isn't either, so don't soak them, though you can rinse them off in hot, hot water (not boiling!) and dunk them in and out of a sanitizing solution. Then let them dry and keep them in a plastic bag until you need them again.

Just before you are going to use your bungs, rinse them off in hot water, and then in sanitizer again, and keep them there for a few minutes until you fit them with an air lock and the whole thing goes into the neck or opening of the fermenter. Don't absentmindedly set them down on a dirty counter, on the edge of the washer, or on the garbage pail lid.

Remember, when the bung goes into the neck of the jug, its

bare little bottom will be hovering above your precious wine; if you slop the wine while carrying it, or the wine froths up in an excess of enthusiasm (which happens during primary fermentation, mostly), nasty things could get into your wine and ruin it. So keep the bungs clean!

When a rubber bung starts looking tatty, or loses its elasticity, get rid of it. They are very cheap, and they biodegrade. They make a fine hockey puck if you know some kids who could use a few.

NYLON STRAINING BAGS

In the old days, fruit was cut up or crushed and tossed into the primary fermenter and had to be strained out later, which was a very messy process. Today most home winemakers use a nylon straining bag to contain the fruit during the primary fermentation. They look like the laundry bags you can buy for washing delicate items in a washing machine, but with a much finer mesh.

Nylon straining bags come in small and large sizes. They are strong, inexpensive, easy to sanitize, and they last a long time. You can buy them at your wine supply store or by mail order. If you have a sewing machine or serger, you can make your own. Be sure you use fine, flexible nylon cloth if you make your own. Do not use stiff nylon netting or polyester.

Not only do nylon straining bags make removing the fruit or vegetables easier, but they also prevent clogs later on when racking. There's nothing like a stuck cherry pit or apple chunk to ruin a racking tube.

To sanitize, either boil or soak in sulphite or bleach solution.

To use, tie the bags closed with kitchen string that has been boiled along with the bag or soaked in sulphite solution. After the fruit has fermented in the primary container, merely lift the bag out of the fermenting wine and let it drip a bit, then get it to the sink without dripping everything all over the floor. I use a big pot lid or tray to accomplish this.

Fermented fruit is not a pretty sight when emerging from the bag, nor does it have a pleasant smell. Carefully cut the string (be sure you don't nick the bag) and dump the fruit dregs into the compost bucket or into a strong discardable plastic bag. As soon as you can, rinse the nylon bag out with hot water, get rid of all the fruit bits, and turn it inside out and back again to get rid of the crud. Wash in hot soapy water, and bleach to whiten it. Rinse the bag in hot water and hang it up to dry to be ready for the next time you need it.

Siphon and Racking Tube

A siphon is merely a long tube made of transparent flexible plastic. A racking tube is a piece of rigid transparent plastic that attaches to the siphoning tube. One kind of racking tube is open on one end and closed on the other, with a couple of holes drilled through about an inch above the closure. Another kind has a small foot of plastic, which fits over the bottom end to let the wine be drawn in when you rack but keeps the tube out of the sediment.

The racking tube is usually two to three feet long, for either one-gallon jugs or five-gallon carboys.

When you gently introduce the racking tube into the wine you want to rack, keeping the bottom of the rigid tube on the bottom of the jug, it sucks in the mostly clear wine through the little holes above the *lees,* or sediment at the bottom, leaving the gunk at the bottom of the vessel.

Of course, if you stick it in there and swish it around, the lees get stirred up and you've lost the advantage and will have to wait for the wine to settle down again. Toward the end, you can gently tip the jug to keep getting clear wine, before the sediment slips down all the way and starts to cloud.

Having two tubes around is a good idea, in case one cracks. You can get them in different sizes, as well.

Keeping the tubes clean can be tricky, but if you are consistent about it, you'll be OK. Always rinse your siphoning tube right after using it, letting LOTS of fresh hot water flow through every part of it. Then carefully let some sanitizing solution run through it, let that run out, and hang it up to dry.

Store your tube in a clean plastic bag to keep it from getting dusty or from having flies play in it like a hamster habitat.

Before using it to rack, soak·it in a dishpan of sanitizing solution, making sure that no air is in it and that it soaks in the solution on every surface INSIDE and OUT. Take the tube out and rinse it briefly with fresh hot water just before you use it. Never let it touch a dirty surface while you are using it. This can

seem complicated and it can get tricky, but with practice it is
easily done.

If I am bottling several batches, I carefully insert both ends of
the tube into the jug I've just siphoned off while I get the next
jug ready, because I know the inside of the bottle is pretty clean,
except for leftover wine and lees. It isn't necessary to clean the
siphon tube between wines as long as the wines themselves are
sound and you are moving quickly. Nothing awful is likely to
happen in those five or ten minutes.

I smell the next batch of wine very carefully with my nose to
make sure it's OK before I rack, and I also set out all of the new
bottles to be filled so I don't have to wave the tube around and
get it dirty by banging it on a wall, the counter, or the cat whilst
rounding up bottles.

BOTTLES

Always have plenty of bottles around, and keep them clean.
The 750 mm and 1.5 liter sizes that can lay on their sides are
best. The bigger the bottles, the fewer you have to cork! However,
big bottles take longer to age and are not always as convenient
as the smaller bottles.

There are many different styles of wine bottles, depending on
what kind of grape wine they were originally intended to hold. I
try to keep my reds and rosés in dark green glass, and whites in
white or brown. I try to use old sherry and port bottles for my
sherries and ports.

Champagne bottles should be used when you are making sparkling wines. Never use regular wine bottles for sparkling wines—
the bottles aren't strong enough (more on this in the sparkling
wine section).

When I am about to do some bottling, I choose the wines I am
going to bottle, and figure out the total number of bottles I will
need for the entire session. Table wines usually get more of the
big bottles than, say, a sherry-type or dessert wine. Always sanitize
a few extra.

Sometimes you can find those little half-size bottles. Grab them
and cherish them. They are a nice size for gifts and for very
special fortified or dessert wines.

For more tips, see the section in the previous chapter on bottles (page 29).

BOTTLE WASHER

This is a little brass gadget that fits on the end of most sink spouts and helps to rinse out the bottles, saving water and time. They are very useful, and don't cost much. By all means get one!

WINE THIEF, CORK SNATCHER, ETC.

A wine thief is a slightly more sophisticated turkey baster. It is used when you need a small amount of wine to test the fermentation process with a hydrometer (which will be discussed a little later on). You dip the sanitized tube into the must or wine, putting your thumb over the top, and gravity keeps the wine in the tube till you uncover the top. It works on the same principle as a drinking straw (remember when you were a little kid and played with your milk or pop). I used a turkey baster for years, but only for taking out wine, never for anything else. The wine thief is easier, cleaner, and costs only a few dollars.

The cork snatcher is pretty simple, as well. Every now and then you will lose a cork into a bottle. Put the curved wire ends of the cork snatcher in the bottle and fish around; with a little judicious jigging, you can ease the cork back out. Easier to use when the bottle is empty!

MORE ON CORKS

Corks come in different circumferences as well as lengths. Use the longer ones for wines you plan to keep more than a few years. Always get the best quality you can find.

CAPSULES AND CORK FOILS

These dress up your finished wines and give them a professional look. They come in different materials, from lead to plastics. You can buy them in a wine supply store or by mail order. Capsules and foils are not too expensive, but they do add to the cost of each bottle.

There are some drawbacks for those who store their wine in

areas that are subject to changes in temperature and humidity. For example, my basement is very humid in the summer and dry in the winter. If I get some leakage or mold, I want to know about it right away. Fancy foils tend to obscure such problems and might even add to the adverse conditions.

LABELS

You can make these or buy them, but remember, they must have room for the info you need, and you have to be able to get them off again! Wine supply stores and mail order sources have some lovely labels. However, cost quickly becomes a serious factor.

You can make your own by simply drawing them and having them reproduced at a copy center on pressure-sensitive labels. If you have a computer and printer, you can design and reproduce labels at home.

Try to use waterproof ink on your labels (computer printer ink varies in permanency), or, failing that, put clear tape over the important parts of the label.

To remove labels, try soaking the bottles in warm water and scraping off the wet paper and glue. There are many glues used today on labels. If soap and water don't work, try a household solvent like Citrasolv. Always be sure to rinse the bottles carefully.

DRYING RACK

I keep hoping Santa Claus will bring me one for Christmas. These can be very expensive. They look like upside-down Xmas trees or chandeliers and are used to prop up bottles that are drying upside down. Our best local wine store has some old wrought iron ones they use as decoration, and I covet them!

Usually I just put my bottles upside down in a cardboard liquor box to drain and dry before storing them because I'm going to be sanitizing and bottling with them wet, anyhow (but it would still be nice to have one).

WHAT'S A *HYDROMETER?*

A hydrometer tells you how tall your camel is.
No, sorry.

A hydrometer takes much of the guesswork out of winemaking. Hydrometers and air locks are the best things that happened to home winemaking since sugar was invented and glass bottles became cheap.

It looks like a big thermometer—a hollow glass tube bigger on one end than the other and weighted in the big end. Inside or on the instrument are several different scales.

With your wine thief or turkey baster, you put some of the must or wine you want to test into a glass or wide plastic test tube, but not one that is so wide that you waste a lot of wine. You can buy these at a wine supply store.

Gently drop the hydrometer into the liquid, giving the hydrometer a quick spin as it enters the liquid to get rid of air bubbles.

It will float in the liquid.

Now, if the liquid is plain water, the hydrometer will float at a specific height on the scale, which would be 1000 specific gravity, or 0 percent potential alcohol. If there is sugar in the water, the water will be thicker, and the hydrometer will tell you how much is in there. This is called measuring the Specific Gravity, or SG, in the must or wine.

Allowing for temperature fluctuations (the ideal temperature of the liquid would be 60°F or 15°C) and tiny specks of fruit suspended in the juice (you sort of have to wing it, there) you can learn how much sugar is present in the liquid, and therefore how much potential alcohol there is.

This is really useful, because you can add either more water or more sugar to your must, depending on the need. This way you avoid a wine too weak in alcohol to keep well (under 10 percent or so) and avoid having too much sugar in the wine, since the yeast can handle only 14 percent potential alcohol at best. If the reading says you've got 18 percent potential alcohol in there, you are going to have a very, very sweet wine if you don't thin it out.

If you take a reading before you add the yeast, and REMEMBER TO WRITE IT DOWN, and measure the wine at the end of fermentation, you will know how much alcohol is in the wine. Nifty, huh?

If you didn't take a reading at the beginning of the process, the hydrometer cannot tell you how much alcohol is in a wine. It's sad, but true. To do that you have to have a fancy, expensive gadget, which only the pros or serious (or rich) amateurs bother with.

The hydrometer also helps you keep track of the fermentation and offers a better way to know when it is done. When a recipe says, "Rack into a secondary fermenter until fermented out," you'll know, with the help of the hydrometer, when the sugar has fermented out and you have a dry wine.

It's best to buy a hydrometer at the wine supply store. If you make beer, you might already have one, but it might not have the range you need for winemaking. Take a look. You want one that measures the specific gravity from .990 to at least 1.160 and that also has a scale for potential alcohol from "blank" to 21 percent or 22 percent. Some also come with the added attraction of the Balling scale, which used to be standard in American home winemaking but is no longer. There's nothing wrong with it, I just don't feel the need for three different readings! If you are comfortable with the Balling scale, use it.

Why do you need to see readings of .990 and blank, if water is 1.000 or 0 percent? Temperature fluctuation and specks of fruit, that's why. All is not crisp and clean in science.

Place the tube on an even surface. (You can test this with a marble or ball bearing. If it rolls, the surface isn't even.) Put in the hydrometer and spin it a little to get rid of the air bubbles. Squat down and get your eyes even with the *level* of liquid, and see where the *level* is. Water tension makes the liquid bunch up a bit right up against the sides of the hydrometer, so the correct *level* is away from the edge, but not at the sides of the hydrometer.

Here's a sample of readings from a hydrometer:

SPECIFIC GRAVITY	POTENTIAL ALCOHOL
0.990	blank
1.000	0
1.005	
1.010	0.9
1.015	1.6
1.020	2.3
1.025	3.0
1.030	3.7
1.035	4.4
1.040	5.1
1.045	5.8
1.050	6.5

Specific Gravity	Potential Alcohol
1.055	7.2
1.060	7.8
1.065	8.6
1.070	9.2
1.075	10.4
1.080	11.2
1.085	11.9
1.090	12.6
1.095	13.4
1.100	14.0
1.105	14.9
1.110	15
1.115	16.4

Fear not if you feel lost. All will become clear if you look at the hydrometer and play with it in some fruit juice and water. (It's *your* toy; you can play with it.)

In reality, there are more increments on the hydrometer. On my hydrometer, the specific gravity scale runs right beside the potential alcohol, and the PA scale is done in whole numbers: 1, 2, 3, 4, etc. It is easy for me to compare them when I want to.

You'll notice that the SG scale gives you more accurate reading, but the PA is a lot easier to understand. In beermaking, using the actual SG is a lot more important because of beer's finicky nature. In this book, however, I will refer mostly to PA because I think it is easier for the beginner to understand. If you end up with a hydrometer without a PA scale on it, you can check the chart above. Most hydrometers from wine supply houses these days have them, though.

If the must is considerably warmer than 59°F or 15°C, you will need to adjust your calculations. The only way I know is to adjust by the SG.

Celsius	Fahrenheit	Correction to SG Reading
10	50	subtract .6
15	59	perfect
20	68	add .9
25	77	add 3.4
35	95	add 5

So, if your must is a little warm, your reading will be a little low, and if it is too cool, it will read high. Check the SG and compare it to the PA on your hydrometer. For the most part, as long as the must isn't over 70°F, don't worry. It's accurate enough for what you are doing.

When reading recipes from some books, especially older ones, you may notice that they sometimes leave off the first digit or two when they tell you what the SG should be. Instead of 1.050 they casually say 50.

Sometimes it's important to know EXACTLY what you are doing. Say, for example, you've obtained several gallons of lovely fresh apple cider that you want to turn into wine. You measure the PA. The lovely cider reads 6 percent PA. You know some of that is suspended fruit and the rest is sugar. So, say it has 5 percent PA in it. This is nice for hard cider, but it's not enough for the wine you want to make. The question becomes how much sugar or honey do you need to add to bring it up to 10 percent PA?

Relax. Be calm. You will need to add about 1 pound of sugar or honey per gallon to get 10 percent potential alcohol in the finished apple wine. Another half pound will give you up to 12,5 percent. I arrived at these figures by using the Pearson Square, which will be discussed later in the section on fortified wines. At this point, I simply want you to know you don't have to do everything by rote.

If you are making wine with whole fruit, don't forget that there is sugar in the fruit! Always add the minimum amount of sugar at first, then, as the wine ferments, add a little more. Give the yeast a chance to make use of the sugar in the fruit.

There is no easy way to gauge this, of course, but the hydrometer gives you a pretty good chance. Generally, two and a half pounds of added sugar per gallon will give you a dry wine, and three pounds of added sugar per gallon will give you a sweet wine. Be sure you dissolve the sugar or honey well before you measure.

By the way, it is always easier to make a dry wine and sweeten it up than it is to hope that the yeast has eaten all the extra sugar you thought it might. Did it eat the sugar, and leave you with a sweet wine that has finished fermenting, for sure, or do you have a potential for cork blowing here because the fermentation stuck or the yeast wasn't quite up to par? Maybe there was more sugar in the fruit than you thought. Chances are it's OK, but chances are chances. Ferment it out, THEN sweeten.

When taking a reading of any must or wine, remove it from the main lot with a sanitized wine thief and use a thermometer to find out the temperature of the liquid.

Numbers can be our friends. Don't let them get a stranglehold, that's all. We are making wine, not the secret formula to cure the common cold (alas).

Don't put the wine or must back in the fermenter. Toss it out. There are just too many things that can go wrong between getting the wine out and measuring it. Better to waste half a cup or so than to contaminate your wine.

DON'T FORGET TO WRITE DOWN THE PA!

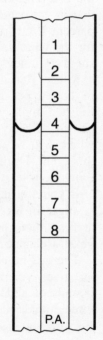

Water tension causes your reading to look higher than it really is. You want to look at where the water level is just to the sides of the stem. Otherwise you could be as much as one-half degree off. This is not really critical unless you are trying to decide if the fermentation is done, and then it is critical!

THERMOMETER

Very useful; not totally essential. They don't cost much. Get a cute little floating thermometer so you can tell how warm or cool your must is. This helps you make more accurate PA and SG readings (remember temperature of the must affects the reading), and it lets you know that the must has cooled down enough to add the yeast. It also helps you judge how warm the temperature is for your primary and secondary fermenting.

As always, keep it clean! Sanitize the thermometer before putting it in any must or wine. Rinse it off immediately afterward, as well.

SCALES

Scales are indispensable in winemaking.

A pound of sugar is roughly two cups. Easy to remember most of the time. However, it can get tricky when measuring out cups in practice and in your mind. The bigger the amount you are using, the more chance you will have of being off enough to create a result that is different from what you were expecting. Nothing like losing count in the middle of fifteen cups!

Fruit is not conveniently shaped. Some fruits have more juice than others, and are thus heavier. One batch of four cups of peaches might well weigh more or less than the next. This is why I always specify the weight of the fruit to use.

My winemaking life became much easier when I went out and bought a kitchen scale that can weigh items up to ten pounds. It cost fifteen dollars. I use it for cooking and canning, too. I highly recommend that you get one. A good hardware store or a good wine supply store will carry them. Don't get the tiny twelve-ounce postal scale, unless you want to measure chemicals (or letters).

MEASURING CUPS AND SPOONS

Use glass or plastic; avoid metal if you can. Try to keep your winemaking supplies separate from your cooking utensils. This is not so much out of concern about the poisonous aspects of any winemaking chemicals as about a strange roast beef or garlic flavor appearing in the wine.

CHEMICAL JARS and BOTTLES

You need a pint or quart bottle with a good lid to store your sulphite solution. My friend at the lab gave me a nice official-looking brown one. Be sure to label the bottle with the words

Mr. Ick

POISON and DO NOT DRINK, and put a Mr. Ick face on it if you have small children around.

Then keep it out of sight and out of reach of any children or pets or curious adults who might wander by. Do not put it in a food cupboard.

Keep your chemicals in plastic bags or bottles and keep them labeled and in a safe place, too. Don't take chances.

BOILING POT

If you have a nice five-gallon stainless steel pot, use it! You can use any steel or enamel pot to boil water and sugar in. If you have to do it in batches, well, that's OK. Don't use aluminum in winemaking: the acids in the fruits will react to it adversely.

LOCATION, OR WHERE AM I GOING TO PUT ALL THIS STUFF?

Bottled wine must be stored on its side to keep the cork from drying out and shrinking. You can get into all sorts of discussions about exactly what angle and all is right, but the most important thing is to keep it on its side. It needs to be kept cool (under 60°F is best), quiet, and away from direct sunlight and weird chemicals.

Fermenting wine should also be kept cool and away from light. You can always wrap a cloth around it, or put a heavy paper sack over it.

So where to put your wine, and all the other stuff that goes with it? That depends on how far you get into winemaking and how much space you have to begin with.

It's best to keep your equipment all in one place that is easy to get at, clean, and out of the way. I keep all my corks and small pieces (like hydrometers, packaged yeasts, and chemicals) in little plastic bins on a shelf in a hallway outside the kitchen. This is because I do most of my primary fermentation in the kitchen.

The big stuff and all the bottles and jugs are in the basement, because that's where I store and clean everything, and that's where the wine lives.

If you live in a small place, look for a cupboard or closet that is someplace quiet, to store supplies and equipment. It really doesn't take much space. Try to keep as much of them in one place as possible, and keep them away from pets, children, and other things that could contaminate them (like paint thinner).

Is there a door that is always open that has some space behind it? Put up a few shelves.

Bottles and fermenting wine do take up space. You can tuck fermenting wine behind doors, sofas, standing screens, or, if you use mostly one-gallon jugs, in an old cupboard. You can build or adapt an old canning cupboard in the basement by fitting it with sturdier shelves and a door or heavy curtain.

Empty wine bottles can be put in cardboard wine boxes and stacked in all sorts of places. It doesn't matter if the place is hot or cold.

For the finished wine itself, a basement is ideal, if you have one, and as long as it doesn't freeze.

Some people have beautiful temperature-controlled cellars fitted with thermometers and bins and cubes and racks. Others have workmanlike racks or stacks of individual cubes, which use space economically and look fine.

I have a series of wide shelves (which should be sturdier but aren't) on which I have cardboard wine cartons from the liquor

A modest array of five-gallon carboys and one-gallon jugs of various wines aging and waiting to be bottled, tucked into an unused corner of the basement. The pie cherry wine was the wine racked earlier, and needs topping up, whilst the three light-colored wines are vying for the honor of being used as the bad example. The peach wine won.

If any of these wines had still been fermenting, I would have them in a warmer place! Note the high tech record book close to hand for making notes and observations.

store lying on their sides. I lay the wine bottles in the separate compartments in the boxes. I don't dare stack them more than one box high. On the floor below, I have stacked large batches of bottles on their sides in wooden packing cases, bottle on top of bottle, the way I've seen it done in French cellars. I also keep my empties down near the floor, as well, sorted by size, color, and shape. The temperature of my cellar ranges from 45°F in the winter to 80°F (occasionally) in the summer. The temperature fluctuations are never rapid, because of the thick limestone foundation, so I just don't worry about it. One works with what one has.

Occasionally I find in a catalog a nice wine storage system made of dwelling or long rectangular bars, but when I calculate how much it will cost to take care of all the bottles in my cellar, my gorge rises.

One day I'll rev up the saw, measure everything in sight, and do something about it, or maybe hire or trade for a carpenter to do it.

I have lots of room to spare, so it really doesn't matter. Most people don't. But if you look at the photo, you will see that half of the area shown could fit in a closet quite easily.

To store wine in an apartment, the best way is to dedicate part of your coolest closet to sturdy wooden shelving, and use the cardboard wine box method. You can get sixty or more bottles in even a tiny closet and still hang winter coats and the like in front of them, as long as you hang a sheet of plastic in front of the bottles to protect the coats from the occasional spouting cork and gush of wine.

A cupboard near the floor also works, if you don't mind kneeling down and reaching back into it. Or you can create a false shallow cupboard in a wide hallway that will allow you to hide the wine from dust and light and still accommodate other things on top of it.

Part of my wine cellar. In the space between the two uprights, which is six feet by six feet, I have about 100 bottles of wine, a lot of empties, jugs, some beer, homemade liqueurs, mustard pickles which have edged over into the space, and my Art Deco bottle capper. There's a lot of wasted space, of course. Half that area, say three feet wide by six feet tall in a cupboard or closet, fitted with better shelves could hold almost the same amount, especially if you put the pickles and the beer elsewhere. Temperature fluctuates between 45° F and 80° F over the course of a year.

CHAPTER FOUR

Ingredients

Always use the best fruit, vegetables, herbs, flowers, grains, spices, you can afford. ALWAYS.

SUGARS AND OTHER SWEETENERS

When I say sugar, I mean either cane, or beet white sugar, or sucrose. There is no chemical difference between the two, and they both work fine. Always make sure to keep the sugar clean. A tin canister works best. Sugar kept in a sack can absorb "off" odors if kept near something else with a strong smell. I tend to stockpile sugar when it is on sale.

Invert sugar is a sugar that has been chemically changed to ferment out faster, and it is sometimes used in beermaking. It's expensive. Some yeasts don't react well to it. Some very advanced winemakers use it for special effects.

Corn sugar, or dextrose, is also a beermaking ingredient. It's

> NOTE: As an experiment you might try making the straight mead recipe, an all-honey wine with no fruit, herbs, or flowers in it. Then make a gallon of wine using only sugar, no fruit, herbs, or other flavoring. It will be interesting, and you'll learn a lot!

more expensive than regular sugar, but you can use it if you want to. Some winemakers like it better than cane or beet sugar. Use it just as you would plain sugar.

Corn syrups I've never used.

Brown sugar is merely white sugar with molasses added to it. It used to be unrefined white but is no longer. Use it by weight equal to the white sugar in a recipe, but realize that it will affect the taste and color of the wine considerably.

Molasses is what's left over from sugar refining. I've never used it in winemaking. It has a very strong flavor and color.

Raw sugar is expensive. I have never used it in winemaking, but there is no reason you can't, if you want to. Use it by weight.

HONEY

Honey is plant nectar refined by the digestive system of a bee. My partner claims it is bee vomit and won't eat it, except when it has been made into wine. It has traces of other matter in it, like pollen, wax, and bits of bee, occasionally. Different honeys have different flavors, depending on what the bees grazed on. Generally, lighter honeys have lighter flavors, and darker honeys have more assertive flavors.

I prefer to use local honey that I get from a beekeeper at the farmers' market rather than supermarket honey. Supermarket honey consists of blended honeys from many different places according to what was cheapest at the time and what tastes the most bland. However, sometimes one has no choice.

Honey has the disadvantage of being more expensive than sugar. It's also harder to handle, since it's liquid and sticky. I try to buy it from the beekeeper in jars that hold the right amount for a batch of wine—either one, two, three, or ten pounds of honey. That way

I can just warm up the closed jar in a pan of warm water to make it easier to pour into the boiling pot.

If I am adding just half a pound to some sugar, I eye the jar carefully and "bloop" it in by eye rather than mess up a measuring cup for weighing. I've gotten pretty good at it. A few ounces more or less won't hurt anything.

You can measure honey by warming it up in its container in some hot water and warming up a glass measuring cup in hot water. The honey will pour easily into the measuring cup and come out of the cup easily if you pour it back out quickly. If you let it cool, use a spatula to scrape out the full measure. DON'T use the old cooking trick of oiling the measuring cup! That's fine for cooking, but it will give you an unpleasant oil film in your wine.

More honey is needed to make a measurement equivalent to sugar. In the various recipes I will say, "2½ lbs. of sugar OR 3 lbs. of honey," give or take a quarter pound here and there. Sometimes I advise a little more or less depending on how much I think the honey affects the taste of the wine.

In ALL recipes feel free to use either honey or sugar, no matter what is specified.

If you use sugar for the most part, I also encourage you to substitute half a pound of honey for a half pound of the total amount of sugar used. Just do a straight swap, it's easier. Honey mellows out the flavor and gives more body to a wine, even if you add a small amount of it. In big batches of wine I might use half honey and half sugar and still think of it as a mead.

Honey adds its own taste to a wine. Some people like it and some don't.

Some people prefer honey over sugar for health reasons, but as far as I'm concerned, sugar is sugar. From an ecological point of view, though, I prefer honey. It doesn't deplete the soil, dirty the air, use much fuel, or have to be shipped vast distances. Instead, our crops are fertilized, local people have a lucrative hobby or actual jobs, and I get nice honey. Seems reasonable to me. Downtrodden, exploited proletariat worker bees might disagree.

MALT

You can use light malts in winemaking. I don't advise using ALL malt, unless you want to make a very beerlike wine. Yeast likes malt, and half a cup of light malt (dry or liquid) in a recipe in place of some of the sugar or honey can be very nice, particularly in the vegetable wines. It WILL change the flavor, though. Buy malt at the beer and wine supply store, not the expensive way in the health food store.

Different malts have different flavors. The darker a malt is, the more assertive it is. Measure it out the same way you do honey. Store any leftovers in the fridge.

GRAPE CONCENTRATE

Very sweet, and flavorful, of course! Half a pound or one pint of red or white substituted for half a pound of sugar or honey in a recipe will give you a wine with more body and flavor, though be aware that you won't always want the grape flavor. In some recipes you can also use grape concentrate in addition to sugar or honey if you want a higher alcohol content. Refrigerate any leftovers and use them as quickly as possible.

The variety you can get is astonishing. If you are buying grape concentrates to make a grape wine, buy the best you can afford. Always ask your supplier's advice on the different brands, and buy only fresh concentrates. If it comes out of the can brown, return it. In some wine supply places you can buy the concentrates in one-pound or one-quart cans.

FRESH GRAPE JUICE

If you can get it, use it! Fresh wine grape juice is sometimes available in grape-growing areas. A local wine supply store might be able to give you more information.

Aseptically packaged grape juice is also available and is wonderful stuff. It is packaged in mylar and plastic like some fruit juices, and it has been sterilized. You might have to mail order it.

NOTE: In any recipe, you can substitute some honey, malt, or grape concentrate for part of the sugar or honey. Only the honey should be used in quantities of more than half a pound.

ACID BLEND

Acid is necessary to give wine its "bite." It helps keep colors from fading or mudding out, and it helps preserve the wine. Acid blend is a blend of citric, malic, and tartaric acid, and is a good, balanced product to use. Sometimes it is merely labeled Acid Blend, and sometimes it has a commercial name. It is inexpensive and keeps very well. Older recipes sometimes didn't even include acid! If the fruit was high in acid, it didn't matter, though sometimes you got a very insipid wine.

Other recipes used mostly citric acid, which is OK. It works. Acid blend is better, though.

Did you ever notice there is acid in soda pop? Check it out.

NEVER USE VINEGAR as a substitute for acid.

LEMONS

You can substitute the juice of one lemon for one teaspoon of acid blend in most recipes. It adds a little flavor of its own. The problem is that lemons vary in size. They also vary in acidity. Most of the time this is no problem. Acid blend is cheaper and more accurate, however.

Zest, by the way, is the thin layer of colored skin on a citrus fruit, which can be pared off the bitter white pith below it for added flavor.

Old recipes sometimes specified "slice one lemon," never saying whether they meant the whole thing or just the fruit without the peel. From "bitter" experience, I suggest using only juice and zest.

GRAPE TANNIN

Tannin is an astringent compound that gives a dryness to the mouthfeel of a wine. This is very necessary, especially in red wines. Tannin also helps clear and stabilize the wine. Wine supply stores sell food-grade grape tannin. It doesn't take much per gallon for the effect; a quarter teaspoon to a teaspoon will do the trick. It also keeps well. Some fruits (like grapes, obviously!) come with their own tannin supply in their skins. Elderberries have plenty! Blueberries have some, as do blackberries.

Use grape tannin unless you are allergic to it. It comes in a powder form or a liquid form. I have given measurements for the dry form in my recipes. There is evidence that the liquid tannin gets used more efficiently by the wine, though. Traditionally, we add tannin to red fruit wines, and not to white fruit wines, but see how you feel about it. Tastes differ.

Older recipes either skipped it, since it wasn't readily available, or used tea, which has a form of tannin in it. "A half cup of strong tea" is what they usually recommended per gallon. This is OK by way of experiment or in case of emergency; however, teas vary in their tannin content, and "strong" isn't a very accurate measurement.

PECTIC ENZYME

This is an enzyme that eats pectin. Pectin is the stuff in some fruits that causes them to jell when cooked. In winemaking, it results in a haze. It's best to avoid hazy, jellylike wine.

Some fruits are high in pectin, others are very low. I usually use it out of sheer habit. The enzyme is killed off by heat, so always make sure your must is tepid before you add it. Give it twelve to twenty-four hours to work before you add the yeast.

Pectic enzyme comes in a granular form, and the standard amount is one teaspoon. It is also available in a liquid form that must be refrigerated. Seven to eight drops per gallon are used for fruit mixtures, and three teaspoons for grape juice. You can use either form, but for simplicity's sake I'll refer to the granular form in the recipes.

Pectic enzyme is cheap and saves you a lot of hassle, so use it!

YEASTS

Yeasts are living creatures, even if they don't look like it when they come out of the yeast packet. They eat sugar, reproduce, and colonize the must. Then when there are enough of them, they make alcohol and carbon dioxide. What a life!

When the alcohol content gets too high (as it were), or the yeast run out of food, most of them die off and fall to the bottom of the wine as lees, or sediment. There are always a few left over after the initial fermentation dies back, which is why you want to be sure that there is either no more sugar for them to eat or that you kill them off by adding extra alcohol or a chemical stabilizer before you bottle. I will tell you more about this a little later on. Yeasts can be very sneaky at reproducing.

Temperatures above 110°F will kill off wine yeasts. They work best at temperatures between 60° and 80°. Cold doesn't kill them, it just slows them down to almost no action. It's your job to make a happy little home for them long enough to produce wine. Most wine must ferments best at around 75°F. When you put the wine into the secondary fermenter, a temperature cooler than 75° is best.

There are thousands of kinds of yeasts on this planet. Back in the olden days, people threw the grapes into the vat and hoped for the best. Of course, they didn't really know about yeast as such. They only knew that something caused the wine to ferment, and it happened more reliably when they added the grape skins.

Then they started saving some of the living wine that turned out well, using it to inoculate the next batch of wine. Eventually, various strains of wines yeasts that gave a good clean fermentation, firm sediment, and high alcohol were isolated.

It was only recently that home winemakers began to have access to good wine yeasts. Granular Montrachet, Flor sherry, and champagne yeasts are pretty standard now and don't cost much. But

---

NOTE: In some climates, keeping the fermenting wine warm enough is a problem in the winter, and sometimes in the summer! The British books talk about fermenting cupboards, insulated cupboards built up against chimneys or fitted with an electric bulb for warmth. Electric mats made for heating seedings are a possibility, as are belt-type heating pads. Always be sure you are taking fire safety into consideration.

If you live off the power grid, there are various ways to keep your wine warm besides direct sunlight, which is NOT a good idea. Look for warm nooks around the house, behind the stove, next to a flue, etc. Take a tour of your house with a thermometer and see what you can do to boost the temperature in a small area. The idea of insulating a large cupboard or packing case isn't a bad one. If you have a passive solar area that gets really warm during the day, you can use bricks or stones against one side of the case to soak up daylight heat and radiate it out at night. Just be careful it doesn't get too hot during the day!

there are better wine yeasts available. They are liquid yeasts named after the various regions in which they originated. You have to use a starter to incubate them, which can take one to four days. They cost a little more but seem well worth it. The kinds available fluctuate from area to area, so I am not going to name them here. Talk to your local wine supply person or the yeast maven in your local winemaking club.

Any time I name a yeast in a recipe, feel free to substitute another kind. They will all work. Some, however, work better than others with various wine ingredients. Montrachets are usually standard for red wines, while champagne is for rosé or white wines. Sherry Flor is used for higher alcohol content, and actually needs more oxygen than other yeasts, so when you rack your wine it won't hurt to splash it around a bit and leave room in the fermenter for more air contact with the wine (but *don't* leave off the air lock!).

I do discourage you from using beer and bread yeasts in these recipes. They weren't bred to take the high levels of sugar and alcohol these wines demand, and they will result in off-tasting syrupy wines.

If you have a taste for fortified ports and sherries, you can make wine yeast produce more than 10 to 14 percent alcohol by keeping it very cool and feeding it small amounts of sugar syrups over a period of time. Too much sugar all at once will result in a stuck ferment.

A stuck ferment is a situation where the wine yeast stops working. The PA or SG has stayed at the same place for a couple of months with no change. This rarely happens.

Sometimes it's just dumb luck. Sometimes the must is at a cooler or hotter temperature than you thought and just isn't doing its job.

Other times the wine just needs some stirring up. Or there is too much sugar or too little.

To "unstick" the ferment, you can:

- check the temperature of the wine and adjust it if necessary
- simply rack the wine and let it splash a bit, adding a little oxygen
- check your original measurements and PA. Whoops, you think you added the sugar twice? Dilute the wine with water

that has been boiled and cooled to obtain a more reasonable PA.

- add some more yeast nutrient or yeast hulls or a little Marmite or Vegemite (⅛ tsp.)

- compare the PA and your original PA. If there is still sugar in the must, make up a starter bottle of new yeast, get it going, and add it to the must

If all else fails, shrug and start over.

YEAST NUTRIENT

Yeast needs other food besides sugar and fruit. Yeast nutrient is basically urea—highly purified! You can buy it at a wine supply store or from a mail order wine supply house.

You use only a small amount (one teaspoon), but it makes the yeast so happy! Think of it as the yeast's vitamin pill. It is especially important in making mead. Yeast nutrient is cheap and keeps well.

Some people are currently advocating the use of "yeast hulls," or "yeast skeletons," or "yeast extract." It is made from the dehydrated remains of yeast sediment. Many people are enthusiastic about it, using it to fix stuck fermentations, and in some cases (particularly in meads) in place of yeast nutrient. It is very inexpensive and is available at wine and beer supply stores, and through the mail. Use half a teaspoon per gallon instead of regular yeast nutrient. So far, I can't see any difference between regular yeast nutrient and yeast hulls.

STABILIZER

Potassium sorbate is used to prevent the yeast from growing again after you are satisfied with the alcohol content of the wine and want to sweeten it (it doesn't kill the yeast completely, though). It is available at wine supply stores and through the mail.

You need half a teaspoon per gallon. Rack the finished wine into a sanitized primary fermenter. Just before bottling, mix the stabilizer with a cup or so of the finished wine in a sanitized container, until dissolved, then add to the rest of the wine. Wait half an hour to one hour, add the sugar syrup to sweeten, stir well, then bottle.

Some people don't like the taste of stabilizer in their wines. It also isn't a good idea to use it in a wine you are going to keep a long time, because it can develop off tastes.

SULPHITE

Campden tablets contain one half gram of sulphite (aka metabisulphite). It is also available in crystal form. For sanitizing, use a stock solution of one quarter ounce or nine grams in a pint of water. That would be about thirteen Campden tablets.

To purify a must before adding the yeast, use one Campden tablet or the equivalent, and wait twenty-four hours before adding the yeast. Heat destroys sulphites, so the must needs to be cool before you add the tablet.

When you rack the wine (after secondary fermentation is done), you can also use one crushed Campden tablet per gallon to help stabilize the wine. This is optional but recommended by many experts.

To completely stabilize a wine before bottling, use two to three tablets.

When you sanitize your bottles, drain them well, but don't rinse them unless you are sensitive to sulphites. This extra bit will help stabilize the wine.

For most people, sulphites are safe, especially in the small amounts we are using here. I am moderately sensitive to them. (Eating at salad bars used to make me sick before regulations were passed to forbid using sulphites to keep the lettuce from turning brown. Cheap wines can make my stomach upset, too, and I suspect they are heavily sulphited.)

I use Campden tablets to sanitize, in some of my apple wines, and in a few others. I don't rinse the sulphite from my fermenters or bottles when I sanitize them, and it works out fine for me.

Take a cautious sniff of your sanitizing solution to make sure it is still good, but for heaven's sake don't take a big lungful. It irritates the lungs and eyes in that concentration. Always keep sulphites labeled, and out of the reach of pets, children, and anyone else who might not know any better.

If you are sensitive to sulphites, don't use them.

OTHER SANITIZERS

Wine supply stores and mail order sources sell several varieties of equipment sanitizers, that are marketed under various brand names. They cost more than Campden tablets and cannot be used in the wine itself. Each brand comes with its own directions for use.

I continue to use metabisulphite because I know I understand what's in it and how it works, though I have used some of the other sanitizers. They work well and are probably easier to use for people who make large amounts of wine.

GLYCERINE

Glycerine is a nonfermentable, nontoxic substance that will give body and a bit of sweetness to a finished wine. In fact, some companies call it Wine Finisher or Wine Conditioner. Use one ounce of food-grade glycerine per gallon. You can buy it at any wine supply store or through the mail. You can also buy it in some drug stores.

COLORING

Most of the time, I don't color my wine. But now and then one comes up with a "white" wine that needs a little help. It's best to use a natural winemaking ingredient to give color, like some red fruit or lightly toasted bread. Or, in a pinch, you can decant the wine just before serving and add a drop or two (not very much!) of food coloring or red fruit juice concentrate.

I have colored my mint wine green once or twice just for the effect. It was nice for Saint Patrick's Day.

CHALK

Chalk is food-grade calcium carbonate. Available at wine supply stores and by mail order, it is used to reduce acid in a wine. Use an acid test kit to determine the acid content of the wine. The wine is racked off into a primary fermenter, and two to six teaspoons is stirred in per gallon. It is stirred every few hours for twenty-four hours, then the wine is racked carefully off the sediment back into a sanitized secondary fermenter. Two teaspoons reduces the acid 0.1–1.15 percent. Never add more than six teaspoons per gallon.

There are also commercial products available at wine supply stores to reduce acid; these products come with complete instructions.

CHAPTER FIVE

Fresh Fruit Wines

Here we go, real fruit wines. Remember that I am assuming you have read the previous chapters. Also remember to read the recipe all the way through before starting. There are lots of little details that you won't want to miss.

Be sure to obtain the best fresh fruits you can for your wine, fruits that are ripe and sound. It's better to use a little less good fruit than a lot of dubious fruit.

Look for local fruit if you can. It is almost always better than fruit brought in to your area. The less it's been hauled around, the better. Local fruit is usually cheaper, too.

You can find fruit in many places besides the grocery store. Look for special fruit and vegetable stores, farmers' markets, road-side stands, and pick-your-own farms, where you can pick your own fresh fruit and pay less than you would in the stores. Your local state or county offices might have a listing of such places. Very useful!

Nonlocal fruits can be quite good, too. If you check out the farmers' markets or fruit and vegetable stores, you can get some bargains with fruit that is dead ripe and won't hold for another day or so. Check carefully for mold or rot, especially on the bottom of the case. Be picky. Tell them you want it for wine. This usually catches the sellers' interest, and they are more likely to make sure you get good fruit.

Sometimes buying by the lug or case is cheaper, though not always. It's best to know what the going price is for fruits you are interested in. I've gotten some good bargains by showing up at the end of the day at the farmers' market. I've also missed some choice fruits that went fast because I wasn't there earlier. You never know.

Sometimes ethnic grocery stores carry interesting fruits. When I lived in the Mission District in San Francisco, we could buy enormous pieces of sweet papaya by the pound.

Wild fruits are good as long as you aren't breaking any laws by gathering them or aren't picking them on private property without permission. Also, be very sure you know WHAT you are picking. Don't just take someone's word for it. Look it up in a wild plant field guide.

Admittedly it's hard to mistake raspberries or strawberries for anything else that will harm you. Blueberries are pretty easy, too, or so I thought. Recently I discovered that friends of mine were making wine from what they said were blueberries. I looked at the berries and the plants they came from. Doubt crept over me. I had a horrible feeling the berries were nightshade. We discussed it at length. They had been eating these berries all summer, and hadn't gotten ill from them.

I went to the reference section of the university library and did some careful checking with a sample of the leaves, flowers, and berries. Common nightshade!

As a matter of fact, common nightshade berries are quite good and are marketed as garden huckleberries or Wonderberries. One of these friends had grown up in the country, and they had always called these berries blueberries. I, who thought I knew what a blueberry was, felt quite shaken by the experience.

Deadly nightshade is much nastier.

ALWAYS double-check if you have the slightest doubt.

When you get the fruit, wash it and make it into wine as soon as possible. Slightly overripe fruit is OK. Rotten fruit is not OK. Any bits of mold should be cut away, as should bruises. Underripe fruit shouldn't be used because it isn't ripe. You won't get a good flavor from it. Ripe fruit smells fragrant.

Sometimes people will cheerfully give you fruit. Maybe their trees or bushes overproduce. Ask around. Make friends with gardeners. Of course, you can always grow your own fruit, if you have a garden. I have only a small city lot, but I have tucked in many gooseberry and currant bushes.

Freezing fresh fruit seems to help release the juice. If you have a freezer, take advantage of this. Be sure you know the proper methods of freezing, of course. When your primary fermenters are busy, and the fruit is coming in too fast, you can simply freeze the surplus for future use.

The following recipes will make one-gallon batches. Make the wine in a one- or two-gallon batch the first time around to make sure you like it. Then, if you care to make bigger batches, multiply everything by five EXCEPT the yeast. Easy.

Let's start with a wine that will run you through the basic steps of making a fresh fruit wine. Remember to read the recipe through, and to pay attention to sanitation. Tsp.=teaspoon, Tbls.=tablespoon, by the way. Use measuring spoons.

☜FURST RASPBERRY WINE☞

No, it's not a typo. I have named this wine after the person who brought me that first bottle of homemade raspberry wine.

This is my favorite wine, bar none. I make some every year and guard it jealously. It is served only to special guests, and given away only to people I really like and respect. Made well, this wine is fragrant, subtle, dry, and goes with anything except heavy tomato and meat dishes.

It tastes of the fruit, but not overwhelmingly so. Put all thoughts of raspberry soda far from your mind and think of tart, warm berries picked in a lightly shaded meadow by a running stream. Chill it slightly, and sip. There, you see?

Raspberries are expensive. I usually go to a pick-your-own place and suffer mosquitoes and heat rash for this wine. I want perfect, flavorful, fresh berries. To heck with the scars. Then I drive home as fast as I legally can and start the wine ASAP. Raspberries will start to mold within hours of picking.

It is true that sometimes I make a second batch with frozen berries from the store if my fresh berry supply hasn't let me make the amount I want. Some raspberry wine is better than none, and more raspberry wine is better than a little.

For the El Primo stuff I use only the best. Wild raspberries, especially wild black raspberries, would probably kick me up into raspberry heaven.

I use sugar when I make this wine. Honey is OK, but to me it mars the taste. Other people might like it just fine, or even better.

3¾ quarts water
2¼ lbs. sugar or 2½ lbs. mild honey
3–4 lbs. fresh or frozen raspberries
½ tsp. acid blend
⅛ tsp. tannin
1 tsp. yeast nutrient
1 Campden tablet, crushed (optional)
½ tsp. pectic enzyme
1 packet Montrachet or champagne wine yeast

Wash your hands. Put the water mixed with the sugar or honey on the stove to boil. Pick over the berries carefully, discarding any that are not up to par. Rinse lightly. Put the berries into a nylon straining bag and tie the top tightly.

Wash your hands again, rinsing especially well, and put the bag of fruit into the bottom of your primary fermenter and crush the berries within the bag. You can use a sanitized potato masher if you prefer, but hands are the best (besides, they are easy to clean).

Now pour the hot sugar water over the crushed berries. This sets the color. If you prefer, you can chill and reserve half the water beforehand; if you've done so, you can pour it now to bring the temperature down quickly in the primary fermenter. Add the acid, tannin, and yeast nutrient. Cover and fit with an air lock. Wait till the temperature comes down to add the Campden tablet if you use it. Twelve hours after the Campden tablet, add the pectic enzyme. If you don't use the tablet, then merely wait until the must cools down to add the pectic enzyme.

After you add the pectic enzyme, check the PA and write it down. Remember, you can always sweeten later. Put the lid on the primary fermenter and install a rubber bung fitted with an air lock. Make sure the lid is on firmly.

Another twelve hours later, add your yeast simply by sprinkling it on the top of the must (unfermented fruit and sugar water). Don't stir it in. You want the fermentation to start right away. If you scatter the yeast, it will take too long for it to get going.

Once the fermentation gets going, sanitize a large plastic spoon or spatula and carefully stir the contents of the primary fermenter once a day, being careful to maintain the cleanliness of the fermenter lid when you remove and replace it. Be sure the air lock still contains the proper amount of liquid.

After the first excitement of the yeast is over (it takes about one week for all the froth and bubbling to die down to a quiet but obvious activity), remove the bag (don't squeeze). After the sediment has settled down again, check the PA. If it is still above 3 to 4 percent, let the wine ferment for another week, stirring daily, and then rack it into your glass fermenter. Bung and fit with an air lock.

Rack it at least once during secondary fermentation. You don't want any off flavors. Be sure to keep it in a dark jug, or put something over it to keep the light from stealing the color.

In four to six months, check the PA again. Taste the wine. I like it dry, but you might want to sweeten it. Not too much! Add some stabilizer and 2 to 4 ounces of sugar dissolved in water. Bottle, label, let it rest a year, then open and enjoy it. Serve lightly chilled.

OK, so now you get the basic idea. There are a lot of different kinds of fruit out there. Mostly what is going to change is how you process the fruit, the acid content, and the sugar. There are also some small differences in handling the fruit here and there.

NOTE: If you have black raspberries, thimbleberries, salmonberries, or any other raspberry-like wild berry use this recipe. The color will be darker or lighter, depending on the berries. You can also use a mixture of these berries.

~RICH APPLE WINE~

You might use this wine as a base wine with other flavorings in the future. It's endlessly useful and inexpensive. This is really just a fancier version of the simple apple wine from the first section.

> *water to make up the gallon, as needed*
> *2 lbs. sugar or 2¼ lbs. mild honey*
> *8 lbs. crushed or chopped apples or 24 oz. frozen apple concentrate*
> *1 tsp. acid blend (only ½ tsp. if you have tart apples)*
> *¼ tsp tannin*
> *1 tsp. yeast nutrient*
> *½ tsp. pectic enzyme*
> *1 Campden tablet, crushed (optional)*
> *1 packet champagne wine yeast*

Put the water mixed with the sugar or honey on the stove to boil. If you are using crushed or chopped fruit, process it as quickly as possible, stirring in the crushed Campden tablet. Tart apples mixed with sweeter apples are better than using all sweet dessert apples. Peels are OK, but it's best to get rid of the seeds if you can. Put the crushed or chopped fruit into a nylon straining bag and put it in the bottom of your primary fermenter.

Now pour the hot sugar water over the apples or the frozen apple juice in the primary fermenter. If you prefer, you can chill and reserve half the water beforehand; if you've done so, you can pour it now to bring the temperature down quickly. Add the acid, tannin, and yeast nutrient, but wait till the temperature comes down to add the Campden tablet if you choose to. Cover and fit with an air lock. Twelve hours after the Campden tablet, add the pectic enzyme. If you don't use the tablet, then merely wait until the must cools down to add the pectic enzyme.

Check the PA and write it down.

Twenty-four hours later, add your yeast. Stir daily. After about one week, remove the bag (don't squeeze). After the sediment has settled down again, check the PA. If it is still above 3 to 4 percent PA, let it ferment another week or so, then rack it into your glass fermenter. Bung and fit with an air lock.

Rack the wine at least twice during secondary fermentation.

In four to six months, check the PA to see if it has fermented out. Taste it, too. You might want to sweeten it. Add some stabilizer and 2 to 4 ounces of sugar dissolved in water. Bottle, label, let it rest a year, then open and enjoy it. Serve chilled.

NOTE: You can use this recipe for **crab apple** wine, but use only half the amount of apples, and skip the acid blend, unless they are remarkably sweet crab apples. In many areas, crab apples can be had for the asking, since many people plant them as ornamentals. The varieties with red skins will give you a nice pink color. The teeny tiny ones can be used, too. Always wash the fruit carefully.

⌘CIDER APPLE WINE⌘

1 gallon fresh pressed cider or apple juice, no preservatives
1 quart water
1½ lbs. sugar or 2 lbs. honey
1 tsp. acid blend (½ tsp. if apples are tart)
¼ tsp. tannin
1 tsp. yeast nutrient
½ tsp. pectic enzyme
1 Campden tablet, crushed (optional)
1 packet champagne wine yeast

Put aside 1 quart of the apple juice or cider to drink later. Put the water mixed with the sugar or honey on the stove to boil.

Now pour the hot sugar water over the apple cider. You can do this in a secondary container if you use a funnel and are careful. The cool cider will bring the temperature down quickly. Add the acid, tannin, and yeast nutrient, but wait until the temperature comes down to add the Campden tablet if you choose to. Cover and fit with an air lock. Twelve hours after the Campden tablet, add the pectic enzyme. If you don't use the tablet, then merely wait until the must cools down to add the pectic enzyme.

Check the PA and write it down. It should be within a reasonable range (10 to 13 percent, depending on how sweet the cider was).

Twenty-four hours later, add the yeast. Stir daily for about two weeks. Check the PA. When it is down to 3 to 4 percent, rack the wine into another glass fermenter.

Rack at least twice during secondary fermentation. It might take a while to clear. Keep for at least six months. Serve chilled.

⧫APRICOT OR PEACH WINE⧫

Get the ripest fruit you can and wash it well. It should be soft and fragrant. Hard, underripe apricots or peaches are useless except for baseball practice. No need to peel the fruit, but remove the pits and any bruises. You can also use frozen peaches or apricots. Just put them, frozen, into the straining bag.

1 gallon water
2¼ lbs. sugar or 2½ lbs. mild honey
3 lbs. ripe apricots or peaches
1½ tsp. acid blend OR juice and zest of 2 lemons
¼ tsp. tannin
1 tsp. yeast nutrient
1 Campden tablet, crushed (optional)
½ tsp. pectic enzyme
1 packet champagne wine yeast

Put the water mixed with the sugar or honey on the stove to boil. Put the halved fruit into a nylon straining bag and put in the bottom of your primary fermenter. Wash your hands and crush the fruit as much as you can. It will be really gloppy. (Your hands will be gloppy, too. It's good for the complexion.)

Now pour the hot sugar water over the fruit. If you prefer, you can chill and reserve half the water beforehand; if you've done so, you can pour it in now to bring the temperature down quickly. Add the acid, tannin, and yeast nutrient, but wait till the temperature comes down to add the Campden tablet if you choose to. Cover and fit with an air lock. Twelve hours after the Campden tablet, add the pectic enzyme. If you don't use the tablet, then merely wait until the must cools down to add the pectic enzyme.

Check the PA and write it down. It might seem a bit high because of the pulp escaping the nylon bag.

Twenty-four hours later, add the yeast. Stir daily. After about one or two weeks remove the bag (don't squeeze). After the sediment has settled down again, check the PA. If it is above 3 to 4 percent PA, let it go another week or so, then rack it into your glass fermenter. Bung and fit with an air lock. You might have to make up the gallon with a little water to make up for the sediment.

Rack the wine at least twice during secondary fermentation. You don't want any off flavors.

In six months, check the PA to see if it has fermented out. Taste it. You might want to sweeten it. Add some stabilizer and 2 to 4 ounces of sugar dissolved in water. Bottle, label, let it rest a year, then open and enjoy it. Serve chilled.

NOTE: You can probably use this recipe for fruits such as mango, loquat, and papaya. They aren't much different in general flavor or water content than peaches or apricots. It's best to peel mangos and papayas, but loquats don't need peeling. Remove any seeds.

⟡BODACIOUS BANANA⟡

Use organically grown bananas for this wine, because the skin of nonorganic bananas has a lot of pesticide residue on it. You can use bananas that have been ripened and frozen. They keep well. Banana wine sounds a little funny, but it's amazingly good and is a nice blending wine (I'll explain later). Do not use plantains for this wine.

1 gallon water
3 lbs. very ripe (black but not rotten) bananas
2 lbs. sugar or 2¼ lbs. mild honey
3 tsp. acid blend OR juice of 3 large lemons
½ tsp. pectic enzyme
¼ tsp. tannin
1 tsp. yeast nutrient
1 packet champagne wine yeast
1 Campden tablet, crushed (optional)

Put half the water on to boil. Wash and slice the bananas, skins and all. Put them in a nylon straining bag and simmer for half an hour in the water. Remove and reserve the nylon straining bag. Pour the liquid into the primary fermenter. Add the straining bag. Boil the sugar or honey with the rest of the water and skim if necessary.

Pour the hot sugar water over the contents of the primary fermenter. Add the acid, tannin, and yeast nutrient, but wait until the temperature comes down to add the Campden tablet if you choose to. Cover and fit with an air lock. Twelve hours after the Campden tablet, add the pectic enzyme. If you don't use the tablet, then merely wait until the must cools down to add the pectic enzyme.

Check the PA and write it down. It might seem a bit high because of the pulp escaping the nylon bag. Don't worry if it looks alarming.

Twenty-four hours later, add the yeast.

Stir daily. Check the PA. (What should it say?) After the froth has died down, you can put it into a secondary fermenter. You might have to top up the gallon with a little water to make up for the sediment. Bung and fit with an air lock.

Rack the wine at least twice during secondary fermentation.

In six months, check the PA to see if it has fermented out. Taste the wine. You might want to sweeten it. Add some stabilizer and 2 to 4 ounces of sugar dissolved in water. Bottle, label, let it rest a year, then open and enjoy it. Serve chilled.

☙VICTORY BLACKBERRY❧

San Francisco Bay Area gardeners curse the blackberry. The thorny vines seem to grow even through concrete. Legend has it that blackberries were planted widely during World War Two in Victory Gardens, and they got away: a thorny victory.

All up and down the West Coast you can find huge clumps of plump, rich blackberries guarded by dense thorns, free for the picking and flesh wounds. Always be sure to pick wild berries away from roads and industrial areas. (Alas, those are blackberry vines' favorite hangouts.)

3¾ quarts water
2¼ lbs. sugar or 2½ lbs. mild honey
3–4 lbs. fresh or frozen blackberries
2 tsp. acid blend
1 tsp. yeast nutrient
1 Campden tablet, crushed (optional)
½ tsp. pectic enzyme
1 packet Montrachet yeast

Put the water mixed with the sugar or honey on the stove to boil. Pick over the berries carefully, discarding any that are not up to par. Rinse lightly. Put the berries into a nylon straining bag and tie the top tightly.

Put the bag of fruit into the bottom of your primary fermenter and crush the berries within the bag. You can use a sanitized potato masher if you prefer, but hands are the best. (You might want to wear clean rubber gloves to avoid staining your skin.)

Pour the hot sugar water over the crushed berries. You can chill and reserve half the water beforehand; if you've done so, you can pour it now to bring the temperature down quickly. Add the acid and yeast nutrient, but wait till the temperature comes down to add the Campden tablet if you choose to. Cover and fit with an air lock. Twelve hours after the Campden tablet, add the pectic enzyme. If you don't use the tablet, merely wait until the must cools down to add the pectic enzyme.

Check the PA and write it down.

Twenty-four hours later, add the yeast. Stir daily. After about one week, remove the bag (don't squeeze). After the sediment has settled down again, check the PA. If it is above 3 to 4 percent, give it another week or so, then rack the wine into your glass secondary fermenter. Bung and fit with an air lock.

Rack at least once during secondary fermentation. You don't want any off flavors. Be sure to keep the wine in a dark jug, or to put something over it to keep the light from stealing the color.

In four to six months, check the PA. Taste it, too. I like it dry, but you might want to sweeten it. Not too much! Add some stabilizer and 2 to 4 ounces of sugar dissolved in water. Bottle, label, let it rest a year, then open and enjoy it at room temperature.

NOTE: Follow this recipe for Marionberries, loganberries, and any other blackberry-like bramble berry.

ꚍSAL'S BLUEBERRY WINEꙎ

Remember that children's book, *Blueberries for Sal*? I think of those illustrations every time I make this.

So let's try that noble fruit, the blueberry. Obviously, if you can get wild blueberries, do so! However MAKE SURE THEY ARE ACTUALLY BLUEBERRIES! Sometimes you can get wild blueberries frozen.

Tame blueberries make a fine wine, as well. I like the ones that come from Oregon and Washington the best. They seem to have more flavor. If you can get fresh local blueberries, do so.

3³/₄ quarts water
2¹/₂ lbs. sugar or 3 lbs. mild honey
2–3 lbs. fresh or frozen blueberries
2 tsp. acid blend
¹/₈ tsp. tannin
1 tsp. yeast nutrient
1 Campden tablet, crushed (optional)
¹/₂ tsp. pectic enzyme
1 packet Montrachet yeast

Put the water mixed with the sugar or honey on to boil. Pick over the berries carefully. Watch for mold. Discard anything that looks odd. Wash the berries in cool water and drain.

Put the berries in a nylon straining bag and into the primary fermenter, then squish them with your clean hands or a sanitized potato masher. You have to be sure to press them well before you pour the hot water over them. Don't be chagrined by the sickly green color that comes out before you add the hot water. (This makes a good "magic" trick to surprise a child with.) If you cut a fresh blueberry in half with a knife, you'll frequently find that it's green inside. Heat and pressure release the wonderful red/blue that is more familiar.

Pour the hot sugar water over the crushed berries. This sets the color. If you prefer, you can chill and reserve half the water beforehand; if you've done so, you can pour it now to bring the temperature down quickly. Add the acid, tannin, and yeast nutrient, but wait till the temperature comes down to add the Campden tablet if you choose to. Cover and fit with an air lock. Twelve hours after the Campden tablet, add the pectic enzyme. If you don't use the tablet, then merely wait until the must cools down to add the pectic enzyme.

Check the PA and write it down.

Twenty-four hours later, add your yeast. Stir daily. After two weeks, remove the bag (don't squeeze). After the sediment has settled down again, rack the wine into your glass fermenter. Bung and fit with an air lock.

Rack the wine at least once during secondary fermentation. You don't want any off flavors. Be sure to keep it in a dark jug, or put something over it to keep the light from stealing the color.

In four to six months, check the PA. Taste it. When you bottle this one, you might want to sweeten it. Use stabilizer, and add 2–6 ounces of sugar boiled in water. Keep it for a year before drinking, if you can. This is one of those wines that is hard to resist when you want to introduce friends to homemade wines. It has a lovely fragrance and looks like a light red grape wine in the glass. Serve at room temperature or lightly chilled.

In Part Three I'll show you a few ways of dolling this one up. But for now, you might want to add a little more sugar to start with to make a wine that is slightly higher in alcohol, or use another half pound of berries for a richer, stronger wine. Watch the PA so you don't end up with something too sweet.

☜DENNY'S PIE CHERRY WINE☞

No, this doesn't have little crumbs of pastry in it. Pie cherries are the sour cherries in pies. You almost never see them in the stores, because they aren't usually eaten raw like sweet cherries.

If you live in a temperate or northern area, check out the local fruit farms to see if you can get these fresh. They usually ripen around July, and the season is short. Otherwise, you might luck out in the frozen fruit section of fancier grocery stores. If all else fails, see the section (page 125) on canned fruits. Pie cherries are worth any trouble you have to go to to get them; they make a superb wine.

I can never decide if this wine is a dark rosé or a light red, but I don't care!

3¾ quarts water
2½ lbs. sugar or 3 lbs. mild honey
3 lbs. fresh or frozen pie cherries
1 tsp. yeast nutrient
⅛ tsp. tannin
1 Campden tablet, crushed (optional)
½ tsp. pectic enzyme
1 packet Montrachet yeast

Put the water and sugar or honey on the stove to boil.

Pick over the cherries carefully. Watch for mold. Discard any bad ones. Stem. You don't have to pit these if you are careful not to break the pits when you squish them. Broken pits will make the wine bitter. Cherry pits are very sturdy, though. Wash the cherries in cool water and drain.

Put the cherries in a nylon straining bag and into the primary fermenter, then squish with your clean hands. They are a firm fruit, so do a good job. Don't they smell wonderful?

Pour the hot sugar water over the crushed cherries. This sets the color. If you prefer, you can chill and reserve half the water beforehand; if you've done so, you can pour it in now to bring the temperature down quickly. Add the yeast nutrient and tannin, but wait till the temperature comes down to add the Campden tablet if you choose to. Cover and fit with an air lock. Twelve hours after the Campden tablet, add the pectic enzyme. If you don't use the tablet, then merely wait until the must cools down to add the pectic enzyme.

Check the PA and write it down.

Twenty-four hours later, add your yeast. Be prepared for a lot of foam. Stir down daily. After two weeks, remove the bag (don't squeeze). After the sediment has settled down again, rack the wine into your glass fermenter. Bung and fit with an air lock.

Rack the wine once or twice during secondary fermentation. Be sure to keep it in a dark jug, or put a piece of cloth around it to keep out light.

In four to six months, check the PA. Taste it. I prefer this wine dry, but you might want to sweeten it. Use stabilizer, and add 2 to 4 ounces of sugar boiled in water. Keep it for a year. Very special! Make as much as you can afford to! Heck, says my partner, make more than you can afford—you won't be sorry! Serve lightly chilled.

NOTE: You can use the pie cherry recipe for wild cherries and choke-cherries. You might need to use half a pound more sugar.

⚜SWEET CHERRY WINE⚜

As always, local is best, but most of us depend on cherries shipped from Washington or Michigan. Any kind of sweet eating cherry will do. Be sure to get good ripe ones. The dark red ones give the best color, of course. Don't be afraid to mix several kinds. Sweet cherry wine isn't as fragrant as pie cherry wine is, but it is certainly worth making!

Back in the Depression my Grandmother Scearcy worked all day picking cherries for a farmer in exchange for some of the cherries. My grandfather got hold of them and tried to make wine, but failed. My mother says grandmother never forgave him. Maybe she would have if he had used this recipe.

3¾ quarts water
2 lbs. sugar or 2½ lbs. mild honey
4–5 lbs. fresh or frozen sweet cherries
2 tsp. acid blend OR juice and zest of 2 lemons
¼ tsp. tannin
1 tsp. yeast nutrient
1 Campden tablet, crushed (optional)
½ tsp. pectic enzyme
1 packet Montrachet yeast

Put the water and sugar or honey on the stove to boil. Pick over the cherries carefully. Watch for mold. Discard any bad ones. Stem. You don't have to pit these either. Wash the cherries in cool water and drain. If you like, reserve a few of the pits, unbroken, to add to the fruit.

Put the cherries in a nylon straining bag and into the primary fermenter, then squish them with your hands. They are a firm fruit, so do a good job. The color should be great.

Pour the hot sugar water over the crushed cherries. You can chill and reserve half the water beforehand; if you've done so, you can pour it in now to bring the temperature down quickly. Add the acid, tannin, and yeast nutrient, but wait till the temperature comes down to add the Campden tablet if you choose to. Cover and fit with an air lock. Twelve hours after the Campden tablet, add the pectic enzyme. If you don't use the tablet, then merely wait until the must cools down to add the pectic enzyme.

Check the PA and write it down.

Twenty-four hours later, add your yeast. Be prepared for a lot of foam. If it foams up into the air lock, scoop some of the foam out with a sanitized scoop, and clean out the air lock. Stir down daily. After two weeks remove the bag (don't squeeze). After the sediment has settled down again, check the PA. If it is above 3 to 4 percent, let the must ferment for another week or so before racking the wine into your glass fermenter. Bung and fit with an air lock.

Rack the wine once or twice during secondary fermentation. Be sure to keep it in a dark jug, or put a piece of cloth around it to keep out light.

In four to six months, check the PA. Taste it. I prefer this wine dry, but you might want to sweeten it. If so, use stabilizer, and add 2 to 6 ounces of sugar boiled in water. Keep it for a year. Lovely. Serve lightly chilled.

☜CHEERFUL CRANBERRY WINE☞

Cranberries are almost always available in the frozen food section; freezing helps release the juice. You can use lingonberries for this recipe, too, if you can get them. Sometimes Scandinavian specialty stores carry them around Christmas. Expensive, but nice. This wine is on the thin side, hence the optional raisins.

3 lbs. fresh or frozen cranberries or lingonberries
3¾ quarts water
3 lbs. sugar or 3½ lbs. mild honey
1 lb. golden raisins (optional)
¼ tsp. tannin
½ tsp. acid blend
1 tsp. yeast nutrient
1 Campden tablet, crushed (optional)
½ tsp. pectic enzyme
1 packet Montrachet yeast

Pick over the berries. Discard any bad ones. Put them in some water and bring them *just* to the boil, then dump them into a nylon straining bag and let them cool down a bit in the primary fermenter.

Put the rest of the water and the sugar or honey on the stove to boil. If you are using the raisins, soak them overnight and chop them up and put them in the bag with the cranberries. Mash the fruit with a sanitized potato masher.

Pour the hot sugar water over the crushed berries. You can chill and reserve half the water beforehand; if you've done so, you can pour it in now to bring the temperature down quickly. Add the tannin, acid blend, and yeast nutrient, but wait till the temperature comes down to add the Campden tablet if you choose to. Cover and fit with an air lock. Twelve hours after the Campden tablet, add the pectic enzyme. If you don't use the tablet, then merely wait until the must cools down to add the pectic enzyme. Be sure to use the pectic enzyme! You don't want cranberry jelly.

Check the PA and write it down.

Twenty-four hours later, add the yeast. Stir down daily. After about one week, remove the bag (don't squeeze). After the sediment has settled down again, check the PA. If it is above 3 to 4 percent, let the must ferment for another week or so before racking the wine into your glass fermenter. Bung and fit with an air lock.

Rack the wine once or twice during secondary fermentation. Be sure to keep it in a dark jug, or put a piece of cloth around it to keep out light.

In four to six months, check the PA. Taste it. I prefer this wine dry, but you might want to sweeten it. Use stabilizer, and add 2 to 6 ounces of sugar boiled in water. Keep it for a year. Serve chilled. Wonderful for the holidays!

⌘CURRENTLY CURRANT WINE⌘

Currants deserve more notice in gardens than we give them. They are very popular in Europe. You rarely find them in stores in the U.S. or even in farmers' markets, though they are easy to grow and make good wine or jelly if you have enough of them. Two or three bushes will produce a lot. You can grow white, red, and black currants. The white are sweet, the red tart, and the black, tart with a musky blackberry taste. Currants are very high in vitamin C.

The following recipe is for red and white currants.

1 gallon water
3 lbs. sugar or 3½ lbs. mild honey
3 lbs. ripe currants (don't use more, as they are a high acid fruit)

no acid
⅛ tsp. tannin
½ tsp. pectic enzyme
1 Campden tablet, crushed (optional)
1 packet Montrachet yeast

Boil the water and sugar or honey, and skim, if necessary.

Pick over the berries carefully. Discard any bad ones. Put them in a nylon straining bag and crush with clean hands or a sanitized potato masher.

Pour the hot sugar water over the crushed berries. The color should be very pretty if you have used red currants. You can chill and reserve half the water beforehand; if you've done so, you can pour it in now to bring the temperature down quickly. Add the tannin and yeast nutrient, but wait till the temperature comes down to add the Campden tablet if you choose to. Cover and fit with an air lock. Twelve hours after the Campden tablet, add the pectic enzyme. If you don't use the tablet, then merely wait until the must cools down to add the pectic enzyme. Be sure to use the pectic enzyme!

Check the PA and write it down.

Twenty-four hours later, add your yeast. Stir down daily. After one week, remove the bag (don't squeeze). After the sediment has settled down again, check the PA. If it is above 3 to 4 percent, let the must ferment for anther week or so and rack the wine into your glass fermenter.

Rack the wine once or twice during fermentation. Be sure to keep it in a dark jug.

In four to six months, check the PA. Taste it, too. I prefer this wine dry, but you might want to sweeten it. Use stabilizer, and add 2 to 6 ounces of sugar boiled in water. Keep it for a year. The color and flavor should be very nice. Serve lightly chilled. Good with poultry, fish, etc.

NOTE: If you can find a small amount of currants in a market somewhere, you can always add them to some cranberries and use either recipe.

☜BLACK CURRANT WINE☞

Black currants are REALLY hard to get in the United States unless you grow them yourself. Although they used to be banned because they carried a rust that affected pine trees, new varieties have been developed, and they're OK now. Just in case, here's a recipe, because I know people out there are growing more and more of this tasty fruit, and some of our Canadian friends might be reading this.

> 1 gallon water
> 2½ lbs. sugar or 3 lbs. mild honey
> 2½ lbs. black currants (high acid fruit)
> no acid
> no tannin
> 1 tsp. yeast nutrient
> 1 Campden tablet, crushed (optional)
> ½ tsp. pectic enzyme
> 1 packet Montrachet yeast

Boil the water and sugar or honey, and skim, if necessary.

Pick over the berries carefully. Discard any bad ones. Put them in a nylon straining bag and crush with clean hands or a sanitized potato masher. Black currants will stain.

Pour the hot sugar water over the crushed berries. If you prefer, you can chill and reserve half the water beforehand; if you've done so, you can pour it in now to bring the temperature down quickly. Add the yeast nutrient, but wait till the temperature comes down to add the Campden tablet if you choose to. Cover and fit with an air lock. Twelve hours after the Campden tablet, add the pectic enzyme. If you don't use the tablet, merely wait until the must cools down to add the pectic enzyme. Be sure to use the pectic enzyme!

Check the PA and write it down.

Twenty-four hours later, add your yeast. Stir down daily. After the first excitement of the yeast is over (about one week), remove the bag (don't squeeze). After the sediment has settled down again, check the PA. If it is above 3 to 4 percent, let the must ferment for another week or so and rack the wine into your glass fermenter. Bung and fit with an air lock.

Rack the wine once or twice during secondary fermentation. Be sure to keep it in a dark jug, or put a piece of cloth around it to keep out the light.

In four to six months, check the PA. Taste it, too. I prefer this wine dry, but you might want to sweeten it. It's very fragrant. Use stabilizer, and add 2 to 6 ounces of sugar boiled in water. Keep it for a year. Serve lightly chilled.

> NOTE: For a more portlike wine you can make this wine with more berries and more sugar by following the red currant wine recipe—but don't use more than three pounds of fruit.

⌐HISTORICAL MONUMENT ELDERBERRY WINE↬

Elderberry wine is steeped in so much history that it seems like an institution to be preserved for posterity, and rightly so. Recipes are mentioned in many old cookbooks. There are references to elderberry wine all through American literature (Remember *Arsenic and Old Lace*?) Elderberry juice was used for dye and even ink, as well as for wine, jam, and pie.

Unless you grow them yourself, elderberries are only available in the wild. BE SURE YOU KNOW WHAT YOU ARE PICKING! Pick only ripe, dark elderberries, away from roads and industrial wastelands. They grow over much of North America.

The first time I saw anyone attempt to make homemade wine, my friend simply put a whole bunch of elderberries and some sugar and water in a jug and set it in the sun. It was a disaster! It turned into primordial soup, and we dumped it into the storm drain rather than inflict it upon the compost heap. You can do better, if you are lucky enough to have these fine berries. They have plenty of flavor and tannin but very little sugar. They also make good jelly. Like mulberries, a raw elderberry is pretty boring, but cooked or made into wine, they are transformed!

1 gallon water
2½ lbs. sugar or 3 lbs. mild honey
3 lbs. ripe elderberries
2 tsp. acid blend

1 tsp. yeast nutrient
1 Campden tablet, crushed (optional)
½ tsp. pectic enzyme
no tannin
1 packet Montrachet yeast

Put the water and sugar or honey on the stove to boil. Pick over the berries carefully. Take them off the stems. Discard any bad ones. Put them in a nylon straining bag and crush them with clean hands in sanitized rubber gloves or with a sanitized potato masher. They stain like all get out.

Now pour the hot sugar water over the crushed berries. If you prefer, you can chill and reserve half the water beforehand; if you've done so, you can pour it in now to bring the temperature down quickly. Add the acid and yeast nutrient, but wait until the temperature comes down before adding the Campden tablet if you choose to. Cover and fit with an airlock. Twelve hours after the Campden tablet, add the pectic enzyme. If you don't use the tablet, then merely wait until the must cools down to add the pectic enzyme. Be sure to use the pectic enzyme.

Check the PA and write it down.

Twenty-four hours later, add the yeast. Stir down daily. This can froth quite a bit. After two weeks, remove the bag (don't squeeze). After the sediment has settled down again, check the PA. If it is above 3 to 4 percent, let the must ferment for another week or so and then rack the wine into your glass fermenter. Bung and fit with an air lock.

Rack the wine once or twice during secondary fermentation. Be sure to keep it in a dark jug, or put a piece of cloth around it to keep out the light.

In four to six months, check the PA. Taste it, too. I prefer this wine dry, but you might want to sweeten it. Use stabilizer, and

NOTE: Elderberries might throw a dark stain on the insides of your wine bottle. Don't worry, just decant carefully before serving. Later on, in Part Three, I'll show you how to make a portlike wine out of these great berries.

add 2 to 6 ounces of sugar boiled in water. Keep it for a year. Isn't that a lovely color? Serve at room temperature.

❧GRANDMA'S GOOSEBERRY WINE❧

Another wine your great-grandmother might have made, from an old-fashioned fruit normally available only in home gardens. More people are planting them, though, because they are pretty, though prickly, bushes, and the berries are good for wine, desserts, and jam. A fine example of edible landscaping.

The first time I had gooseberries almost turned me off them for life. I was on a youth hostel hike in Wales, and for dessert we got canned gooseberries served with English custard sauce (made from a box, ugh). I wouldn't touch gooseberries for years.

Then I had a friend who grew them, and I tasted them fresh. They were OK. THEN I had some gooseberry wine! Now THAT was a good use for these fruits!

Gooseberries also grow wild in many areas. The leaves are very distinctive, but MAKE SURE you know what you are picking. Pick only ripe, sweet gooseberries. (My partner wants to know why gooseberries—why not chickenberries or duckberries?)

1 gallon water
2½ lbs. sugar or 3 lbs. mild honey
3 lbs. gooseberries (high acid fruit)
no acid blend
no tannin
1 tsp. yeast nutrient
1 Campden tablet, crushed (optional)
½ tsp. pectic enzyme
1 packet champagne yeast

Boil the water and sugar or honey, and skim, if necessary. Pick over the berries carefully. Take off the stems. You can leave the tails. Discard any bad berries. Put them in a nylon straining bag and crush them with clean hands or a sanitized potato masher.

Pour the hot sugar water over the crushed berries. If you prefer, you can chill and reserve half the water beforehand; if you've done so, you can pour it in now to bring the temperature down quickly. Add the yeast nutrient, but wait until the temperature comes down to add the Campden tablet if you choose to. Cover and fit with an air lock. Twelve hours after the Campden tablet, add the pectic enzyme. If you don't use the tablet, then merely wait until the must cools down to add the pectic enzyme. Be sure to use the pectic enzyme!

Check the PA and write it down.

Twenty-four hours later, add your yeast. Stir down daily. After about one week, remove the bag (don't squeeze). After the sediment has settled down again, check the PA. If it is above 3 to 4 percent, let the must ferment for another week or so and then rack the wine into your glass fermenter. Bung and fit with an air lock.

Rack the wine once or twice during secondary fermentation.

In four to six months, check the PA. Taste it, too. I prefer this wine dry, but you might want to sweeten it. Use stabilizer, and add 2 to 6 ounces of sugar boiled in water. Keep it for a year. Excellent with poultry, fish, and grain dishes. Serve chilled.

⌘ GRAPEFRUIT WINE ⌘

During the winter, grapefruit goes on sale. Take advantage of it and make some grapefruit wine! More a social wine than a table wine, it's dry and refreshing. Use white or pink grapefruit that are heavy with juice. I recommend organic grapefruit if you can get them, because you will want to use some of the zest, or thin peelings. Also, I think it is a good idea to add a can of frozen white grape juice to this wine to give it some body. Or you can use one pound of golden raisins.

3¾ quarts water
2 lbs. sugar or 2¼ lbs. light honey (clover is good)
6 big juicy grapefruit, pink or white
1 12 oz. can frozen white grape juice or 1 lb. golden raisins
    or 1 pint white grape concentrate from wine supply store
no acid
1 tsp. yeast nutrient
¼ tsp. tannin
1 Campden tablet, crushed (optional)
½ tsp. pectic enzyme
1 packet champagne yeast

Boil the water and sugar or honey, and skim, if necessary. Prepare the zest of two or three of the grapefruits. Then peel

NOTE: if you are one of those people who find grapefruit bitter (apparently it's a genetic trait), you won't like this wine.

the grapefruits and section them, getting rid of as much white pith as you can. Put the segments and the zest (and soaked, cut-up raisins, if you use them) in a nylon straining bag, and put it in the bottom of a primary fermenter. Mash with very clean hands or a sanitized potato masher.

If you aren't using raisins, add the grape juice or grape concentrate now. Pour the hot sugar water over the crushed fruit. If you prefer, you can chill and reserve half the water beforehand; if you've done so, you can pour it in now to bring the temperature down quickly. Add the yeast nutrient and tannin, but wait till the temperature comes down to add the Campden tablet if you choose to. Cover and fit with an air lock. Twelve hours after the Campden tablet, add the pectic enzyme. If you don't use the tablet, then merely wait until the must cools down to add the pectic enzyme. Be sure to use the pectic enzyme.

Check the PA and write it down.

Twenty-four hours later, add your yeast. Stir down daily. After about one week, remove the bag (don't squeeze). After the sediment has settled down again, check the PA. If it is above 3 to 4 percent, let the must ferment for another week or so, and rack the wine into your glass fermenter.

Rack the wine once or twice during fermentation.

In four to six months, check the PA. Taste it. You might want to sweeten it. Use stabilizer, and add 2 to 6 ounces of sugar boiled in water. Keep it for six months to a year before drinking. Serve chilled, maybe even with ice. It should have a light, pleasant fragrance.

YES! GRAPE WINE

If you can obtain real, ripe grapes, you can make real grape wine with no sugar. If you can get only a few pounds, turn to page 108.

Grapes grow almost everywhere in the United States. In the

South, the grapes are a native American kind called Muscadine, which has a musky sort of flavor but makes a tasty wine. You have to thin it down and add sugar, as you also have to do with wine made from Concord grapes and Catawba wine.

Wild grapes, sometimes called fox grapes, also have an intense, distinctive flavor, but they don't have enough sugar to make wine on their own.

Other varieties are grown for table use and wine use. Your local wine shop might be able to get shipments of wine grapes from various places. You might ask around to see if there is a nearby vineyard willing to sell you grapes or fresh wine grape juice.

Garden grapes are grown for wine and fruit. There are many different kinds. Check out local pick-your-own places and farmers' markets. Ask at your local wine supply place, county extension office, or agricultural college. Someone is bound to know!

❧WINE GRAPE RED WINE❧

This is just a basic recipe with no frills. You need a lot of grapes and a lot of time, but hey, we're having fun, right?

Equipment:

A BIG nylon straining bag or two smaller bags
18 lbs. of red wine grapes (I told you it was a lot)
1 Campden tablet, crushed (highly recommended)
1 packet Montrachet yeast

Sounds simple, huh? Check over the grapes, remove any moldy ones, stems, leaves, bugs, etc.

Put the grapes into a nylon straining bag (or two, if you can't get a really big one) and crush the grapes in the bottom of the primary fermenter. Use very clean hands, or a big sanitized potato masher. Squish the daylights out of the grapes, turning the bag or bags around and around. (If you have a grape crusher, or can borrow one, use it, of course.) You should have juice up to the one-gallon mark and somewhat over, because of the fruit pulp.

Let the juice settle out a bit and check the PA of a clear sample. You are aiming for 10 to 12 percent PA. If there is less than that, then your grapes weren't as sweet as they should have been.

You'll have to add some sugar dissolved in a little water to make it up.

If the PA is higher, well, it's OK up to 13 to 14 percent. If it is more than THAT, remove some juice and add water to make it up and thin out the sugar from the grapes.

If you happen to know how to use an acid test kit (not difficult, they come with instructions), check the acid and adjust that, too, to 65 to 70 percent. If you don't, then don't worry about it. Everything is probably OK.

Stir in the Campden tablet and cover the mixture for twenty-four hours. Add the yeast. After fermentation starts, stir daily, squashing the grape pulp in the bag. When the PA gets down to about 4 percent, lift out the bag and let the juice settle. Should smell pretty good!

Rack the wine into a secondary glass container, topping up with a little water or fresh juice if necessary. Bung and fit with an air lock. After another four weeks, check the PA and rack off into a clean secondary fermenter.

Now let it sit for a few months, racking it maybe once. Wait till it clears and ferments out dry. Bottle it and keep it for six months before trying. There you have it! The flavor will depend on the grapes, of course, but it will be real grape wine!

ᑫWINE GRAPE WHITE WINEᑭ

Did you know that you can make white wine from red grapes? The biggest difference between the two kinds is that you never ferment the white wine "on the skins." You press the juice and get rid of the pulp and skins immediately. There are, of course, white wine grapes that start out white, but you still don't use the skins. So, get the best you can and let's go for a ride.

Equipment:

  a BIG nylon bag AND an extra primary fermenter
  16–18 lbs. wine grapes
  1 Campden tablet, crushed (highly recommended)
  1 packet champagne or Montrachet yeast

Check over the grapes, get rid of any moldy ones, get rid of stems, leaves, bugs, stray satyrs and their panpipes, etc.

Put the grapes into a nylon straining bag (or two, if you can't get a really big one), and crush the grapes into the bottom of the extra primary fermenter. Use very clean hands, or a big sanitized potato masher. Squish the daylights out of the grapes, turning the bag or bags around and around. (If you have a grape crusher, or can borrow one, use it, of course.) Add the Campden tablet now. You should have juice up to the one-gallon mark and somewhat over, because of the fruit pulp.

Pour out the grape juice into the second primary fermenter and squeeze or press the remaining pulp as best you can (a grape press would be nice, but not too many people have one lying around).

Let the juice settle out a bit and check the PA of a clear sample. You are aiming for 10 to 12 percent PA. If it is less than that, then your grapes weren't as sweet as they should have been. You'll have to add some sugar dissolved in a little water to make it up.

If it's more than that, it's OK, up to 13 percent. If it is more than THAT, take some juice out and add water to make it up and thin out the sugar from the grapes.

If you know how to use an acid test kit, then check the acid and adjust that, too, to 70 percent. If you don't, then don't worry about it. Everything is probably OK.

Cover for 12 hours and fit with an air lock. Add the yeast. After fermentation starts, stir daily. When the PA gets down to about 4 percent, let the juice settle. It might be pinkish, but that's OK. Many white wines are.

Rack the wine off into a secondary glass container, topping up with a little water or fresh juice if necessary. After another four weeks, check the PA and rack off into a clean secondary fermenter. Bung and fit with an air lock.

NOTE: Discard the pulp, or save it in the fridge and use it in the next couple of hours to help ferment and flavor a grape concentrate wine, or grape wine made with fewer grapes and added sugar. This is a pleasant trick as old as the hills. It's called making a "second" wine. You can just use sugar and water and the pulp, fermenting out on the pulp. There's still sugar in there. Use your hydrometer to help you figure it out.

Now let it sit for a few months, racking maybe once. Wait till it clears and ferments out dry. Bottle it and keep it for six months before trying.

NOTE: The above method is OK for a few gallons, but if you are making any more than ten, you need proper equipment (which I discuss in Part Three on page 181) and more knowledge. Check the bibliography for books that get more serious about grape wines than I do in this book, and consult with people who are also serious.

☙ WHOLE GRAPE TABLE GRAPE WINE ❧

Table grapes aren't as sweet as wine grapes are. But you can still make "whole grape" wine with them by adding a little sugar and a little acid.

Follow the above recipes, and simply add enough sugar to achieve the proper PA. It probably won't need much . . . say, half a pound to one pound extra sugar and a teaspoon of acid blend. If you are using white or light red table grapes, add ½ teaspoon tannin to the must. Dark red grapes use ¼ teaspoon.

Thompson-like grapes will be a little bland; you might want to sweeten them at bottling time.

☙ CONCORD, ETC. GRAPE WINE ❧

Heavily flavored grapes like Concord and Muscadine will produce a heavily flavored wine. You can attempt to make them without sugar if you want to, but the acid will be way off and the flavor too much for most people. So compromise. Use half the amount of grapes, add water to make up to the gallon, and check the PA to see how much sugar you need—probably about a pound. Be sure to add half a teaspoon pectic enzyme, 1 teaspoon yeast nutrient, and a Campden tablet. Use a Montrachet yeast.

☙ DRAGON LADY WILD GRAPE WINE ❧

I've named this after a friend who loves dragons, and gives me wild grapes from her property every year. We think they are actually Foch grapes gone feral, but it's hard to be sure.

Wild grapes and semiwild grapes vary drastically in sugar content, even from year to year. Flavor will, too. Gather them dead ripe. You can also use this recipe for other grapes when you have only a limited amount. If you have only a handful of wild grapes, make up the difference with tame grapes.

1 gallon water
2½ lbs. sugar or 3 lbs. mild honey
3 lbs. wild or other grapes
1 tsp. acid blend
¼ tsp. tannin
1 tsp. yeast nutrient
1 Campden tablet, crushed (highly recommended)
½ tsp. pectic enzyme
1 packet Montrachet yeast

Boil the water and sugar or honey, and skim, if necessary. Pick over the grapes carefully. Take them off the stems. Discard any bad ones. Put them in a nylon straining bag and crush with clean hands or a potato masher. They stain like all get out.

Pour the hot sugar water over the crushed grapes. If you prefer, you can chill and reserve half the water beforehand; if you've done so, you can pour it in now to bring the temperature down quickly. Add the acid, tannin, and yeast nutrient, but wait till the temperature comes down to add the Campden tablet and the pectic enzyme. Be sure to use the pectic enzyme. Cover and fit with an air lock.

Check the PA and write it down.

Twenty-four hours later, add your yeast. Stir down daily. After the first excitement of the yeast is over (about one week), remove the bag (don't squeeze). After the sediment has settled down again, check the PA. If it is above 3 to 4 percent, let the must ferment for another week or so, remove the bag, and rack the wine into your glass fermenter.

Rack the wine once or twice during secondary fermentation. Bung and fit with an air lock. Be sure to keep it in a dark jug, or put a piece of cloth around it to keep out the light.

In four to six months, check the PA. Taste it. I prefer this wine bone dry, but you might want to sweeten it when you bottle it. Use stabilizer, and add 2 to 6 ounces of sugar boiled in water. Keep it for a year. If you get a dark stain on the sides of the bottle, don't worry—it's the nature of some dark fruits with lots of color. Serve at room temperature if red, and chilled if white.

NOTE: You can use this recipe for Oregon grape, which is not a grape at all, but nice in its own way. Beautiful foliage, as well.

GRAPE CONCENTRATE WINES AND KITS

These wines are easy and fun. SO many varieties are available! *This* is how you make a Chablis, if you want Chablis! You make them in five-gallon batches. Usually, it takes two to three cans to make the wine if you use the concentrates. Follow the directions given by the various companies, but double-check with your wine supplier. He or she might have other ideas, from vast experience. You can make SO many classic varieties, and they usually turn out well. However, they aren't cheap to make. The more you pay, the better quality you get.

During the height of winemaking season, it isn't a bad idea to keep an open can of red or white concentrate in the refrigerator to help give some of your thinner wines body, as discussed earlier.

⬥KIWI WINE⬥

Kiwis are easier to get and much cheaper than they used to be. They make a very nice white wine, as well. I'm talking about kiwifruit, not the small flightless bird from New Zealand. Those make lousy wine.

3³⁄₄ quarts water
2¹⁄₄ lbs. sugar or 2¹⁄₂ lbs. mild honey
3 lbs. fresh kiwifruit
1 tsp. acid blend OR juice and zest of one small lemon
¹⁄₈ tsp. tannin
1 Campden tablet, crushed (optional)
1 tsp. yeast nutrient
¹⁄₂ tsp. pectic enzyme
1 packet champagne wine yeast

Put the water mixed with the sugar or honey on the stove to boil. Peel and chop the kiwifruit, put it into a nylon straining bag, and tie the top tightly. Put the bag of fruit into the bottom of your primary fermenter, and use your clean hands or a sanitized potato masher to crush the fruit.

Pour the hot sugar water over the crushed fruit. If you prefer, you can chill and reserve half the water beforehand; if you've done so, you can pour it in now to bring the temperature down quickly. Add the acid, tannin, and yeast nutrient, but wait till the temperature comes down to add the Campden tablet if you choose to. Cover and fit with an air lock. Twelve hours after the Campden tablet, add the pectic enzyme. If you don't use the tablet, then merely wait until the must cools down to add the pectic enzyme.

Check the PA and write it down.

Twenty-four hours later, add the yeast. You want the fermentation to start right away. Stir daily.

After about one week remove the bag (don't squeeze). After the sediment has settled down again, check the PA. If it is above 3 to 4 percent, give it another week or so, and rack the wine into your glass secondary fermenter. Bung and fit with an air lock.

Rack the wine at least once during fermentation.

In four to six months, check the PA. Taste it, too. You might want to sweeten it. Add some stabilizer and 2 to 4 ounces of sugar dissolved in water. Bottle it, label it, let it rest six months, then open and enjoy it. A nice table wine, served lightly chilled.

⚜MEAD⚜
(FOR TERRY PRATCHETT)

This is where honey comes into its blessed own. Use the best local honey you can get, light or dark. In some areas you can get honey from bees used to pollinate various fruit and grain crops. These include citrus blossom, apple blossom, clover blossom, alfalfa, and buckwheat. There are wildflower honeys galore. Each one has its own character. If you live in a place where it's feasible, you might investigate keeping your own little herd of bees. It's a fascinating hobby, with bountiful results. (Training the beedogs to herd them, however, is a bit of a pain.) Check your local agricultural extension service.

Fruit wine made with honey is called melomel. Pyment is grape and honey, Metheglyn is herb and honey. Cyser is apple and honey. But honey and honey is mead! Simple.

There is currently a lot of discussion about using yeast nutrient in mead. Some people feel it gives an "off" taste, and they are using an all-natural product called yeast extract or yeast hulls. The following recipe works just fine with them. Charlie Papazian talks about mead in *The NEW Complete Joy of Home Brewing,* and there are whole books on the subject. Check out the bibliography.

Try this for a start. It makes a light, pleasant mead.

3 lbs. honey, light or dark
water to make up the gallon, about 3 quarts
3 tsp. acid blend
1 tsp. yeast nutrient
1 crushed Campden tablet (optional)
1 packet mead yeast (if you can get it), or champagne yeast

Boil the honey with quarts of the water. Skim if necessary. Pour into primary fermenter. Cool, and add acid blend and nutrient. You can add the Campden tablet here, if you use it. Cover and fit with an air lock. Twenty-four hours later add yeast. Stir daily. Check the PA in a few days. When it gets down to 3 to 4 percent, rack the mead into a secondary glass fermenter. Bung and fit with an air lock. A few weeks later rack it again. When it ferments out dry and clear, stabilize and sweeten if you like, and bottle.

Mead takes a while to age. I've seen books recommending five years! But you don't have to wait *that* long. Try it in a year, then two years, and see how it comes along.

NOTE: For a sweeter mead, start with three pounds of honey, and then add another one half pound to one pound when you rack it into the secondary container the first time, keeping track of your original PA and how much sugar you are adding. You will have to remove a little of the original must. This gives the yeast a chance to cope with all that sweetness. It will take longer to ferment out, and probably won't ferment out all the way. When you think it is done, stabilize and bottle it. It takes longer to age, but it keeps for a good long time. You will be drinking a little piece of history.

☜MEG'S MELON WINE☞

I was muttering about making melon wine and fussing about the recipes I had, so my sister said, "Well, just do it!" And I did. There are as many different kinds of melons as there are instruments in an orchestra. Every area has its favorite, which comes ripe late in the summer and is bought cheaply. Whatever kind of melon you use, make sure it is completely ripe and flavorful. Melons can't always be frozen for eating, but they all can be frozen for wine. I like to use them absolutely fresh if I can, though, to make sure to capture the wonderful flavor and aroma. They make a thin wine, and it comes out different than you would expect. Try a few types to see how you feel about it. My favorites are watermelon, and the local muskmelon, a kind of cantaloupe that nearly falls apart when you cut into a ripe one. The scent is like perfume ought to be and isn't.

You'll have to decide for yourself if it is a table wine or a social wine.

3½ quarts or so of water
2 lbs. of sugar or 2 lbs. light honey (highly recommended)
3–4 lbs. very ripe melon from the centers of the melons
2 tsp. acid blend
1 tsp. yeast nutrient
1 Campden tablet, crushed (optional)
1 packet champagne yeast

Boil the water and sugar or honey, and skim, if necessary. Cut the melon in chunks and put them in a fine nylon straining bag and into the bottom of a primary fermenter. With clean hands or a sanitized potato masher, squish the melon. Don't worry about seeds.

Pour the hot sugar water over the crushed fruit. If you prefer, you can chill and reserve half the water beforehand; if you've done so, you can pour it in now to bring the temperature down quickly. Add the acid, tannin, and yeast nutrient, but wait till the temperature comes down to add the Campden tablet if you choose to. Cover and fit with an air lock. Twelve hours after the Campden tablet, add the pectic enzyme. If you don't use the tablet, then merely wait until the must cools down to add the pectic enzyme.

After a week, lift out what remains of the melon, and let the bag drain into the primary fermenter. Don't squeeze. When the wine settles, check the PA. If it is above 3 to 4 percent, let it continue for another week or so, then rack the wine off into a glass secondary fermenter. Bung and fit with an air lock. A couple of weeks after that, do it again, making up the level with a little boiled water if you have to.

Rack the wine again in the next two to six months, and wait for it to ferment out and clear. This is better when sweetened a little, so stabilize, and add 2 to 6 ounces of sugar in a bit of water, and bottle. Keep it six months to a year. Serve chilled.

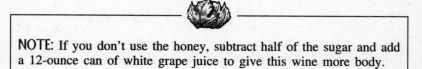

NOTE: If you don't use the honey, subtract half of the sugar and add a 12-ounce can of white grape juice to give this wine more body.

☙MULBERRY REVENGE❧

Mulberry trees produce a huge amount of fruit, which falls when it darned well pleases and makes a mess. Birds and squirrels love them, but they should be planted well away from houses. If anyone out there is really interested in a renewable resource, mulberries are it; they set seed all over the place and grow like lightning.

White mulberries taste insipid. The black or red mulberries have a nice, if mild, flavor. Our neighbor's tree overhung part of our yard, and drove us crazy by dropping fruit all over the path to the garage.

One year I spread a tarp and knocked a lot of the pesky fruit off the branches over the course of a week, then froze it, and made this wine. It was pretty darned good! When our neighbors finally got rid of the tree, I gave them a bottle. They laughed at the label and drank the wine.

3³/₄ quarts water
2¹/₄ lbs. sugar or 2¹/₂ lbs. mild honey
3–4 lbs. fresh or frozen mulberries
1 tsp. acid blend OR juice and zest of one small lemon
¹/₈ tsp. tannin
1 tsp. yeast nutrient
1 Campden tablet, crushed (optional)
¹/₂ tsp. pectic enzyme
1 packet Montrachet or champagne wine yeast

Put the water mixed with the sugar or honey on the stove to boil. Pick over the berries carefully, discarding any that are not up to par. Rinse lightly. Put the berries into a nylon straining bag and tie the top tightly.

Put the bag of fruit into the bottom of your primary fermenter and crush the berries within the bag. You can use a sanitized potato masher if you prefer, but hands in sanitized rubber gloves are best.

Pour the hot sugar water over the crushed berries. You can chill and reserve half the water beforehand; if you've done so, you can pour it in now to bring the temperature down quickly. Add the acid, tannin, and yeast nutrient, but wait till the temperature comes down to add the Campden tablet if you choose to. Cover and fit with an air lock. Twelve hours after the Campden tablet, add the pectic enzyme. If you don't use the tablet, merely wait until the must cools down to add the pectic enzyme.

Check the PA and write it down.

Twenty-four hours later, add the yeast. Stir daily. After two weeks, remove the bag (don't squeeze). After the sediment has settled down again, check the PA. If it is above 3 to 4 percent, give it another week or so, and rack the wine into your glass secondary fermenter. Bung and fit with an air lock.

Rack the wine at least once during fermentation. Be sure to keep it in a dark jug, or put something over it to keep the light from stealing the color.

In four to six months, check the PA. Taste it, too. I like it dry, but you might want to sweeten it. Add some stabilizer and 2 to 4 ounces of sugar dissolved in water. Bottle it, label it, let it rest a year, then open and enjoy it. A nice table wine, served lightly chilled. It's a good one on which to start people new to fruit wines.

⚜ORANGE WINE⚜

This wine, like grapefruit wine, is more of a social wine, for sipping in the garden or in the evening with friends. Get organic oranges, since you will be using some of the zest. Otherwise wash them well before scraping the zest.

3¾ quarts water
2 lbs. sugar or 2¼ lbs. light honey (orange blossom is good!)
10 heavy juice oranges

no acid
¼ tsp. tannin
1 tsp. yeast nutrient
1 Campden tablet, crushed (optional)
½ tsp. pectic enzyme
1 packet champagne yeast

Boil the water and sugar or honey, and skim, if necessary. Use the zest of four or five of the oranges. Then peel the fruits, and section them, getting rid of as much white pith as you can. Put the segments and the zest in a nylon straining bag, and put it in the bottom of a primary fermenter. Mash with very clean hands or a sanitized potato masher.

Pour the hot sugar water over the crushed fruit. If you prefer, you can chill and reserve half the water beforehand; if you've done so, you can pour it in now to bring the temperature down quickly. Add the yeast nutrient and tannin, but wait till the temperature comes down to add the Campden tablet if you choose to. Cover and fit with an air lock. Twelve hours after the Campden tablet, add the pectic enzyme. If you don't use the tablet, merely wait until the must cools down to add the pectic enzyme. Be sure to use the pectic enzyme.

Check the PA and write it down.

Twenty-four hours later, add the yeast. Stir down daily. After about one week, remove the bag (don't squeeze). After the sediment has settled down again, check the PA. If it is above 3 to 4 percent, let the must ferment for another week or so and rack the wine into your glass fermenter. Bung and fit with an air lock.

NOTE: Use this recipe for tangerine wine, too, using as many tangerines or mandarin oranges as oranges. You should add 1 teaspoon acid blend, because these fruits aren't as high in acid as oranges.

For lemon or lime wine, use only six to seven lemons or limes, with zest from three of them.

Fresh homegrown lemons or limes are the best. If you live in California or Florida, you'll probably be able to get them from friends or your own tree. Worth doing, if you can manage it. Nice especially in punches and coolers.

Rack the wine once or twice during secondary fermentation.

In four to six months, check the PA. Taste it. You might want to sweeten it when you bottle it. Use stabilizer, and add 2 to 6 ounces of sugar boiled in water. Keep it for six months to a year before trying. Serve chilled, maybe even with ice.

⚓MATCHED PEAR⚓

Use ripe pears only. You might have to buy them unripe and ripen them, which is easy to do in a brown paper bag. Pears make a pleasant mild wine; people have been making pear wine for a long time.

3½ quarts or so of water
2 lbs. of sugar or 2 lbs. light honey (highly recommended)
4 lbs. ripe pears
1 Campden tablet, crushed (recommended)
2 tsp. acid blend
1 tsp. yeast nutrient
¼ tsp. tannin
½ tsp. pectic enzyme
1 packet champagne yeast

Boil the water and sugar or honey, and skim, if necessary. Wash the pears well, remove the stems, cut them in half, and take out the cores. No need to peel. Cut the pears in chunks and put them in a fine nylon straining bag and into the bottom of a primary fermenter. With a sanitized potato masher, mash the pears with the Campden tablet.

Pour the hot sugar water over the crushed fruit. If you prefer, you can chill and reserve half the water beforehand; if you've done so, you can pour it in now to bring the temperature down quickly. Add the yeast nutrient and tannin, but wait till the temperature comes down to add another Campden tablet if you choose to. Cover and fit with an air lock. Twelve hours after the Campden tablet, add the pectic enzyme. If you don't use the tablet, merely wait until the must cools down to add the pectic enzyme. Be sure to use the pectic enzyme. Stir daily.

After a week, lift out the pear pulp, and let the bag drain into the primary fermenter. When the wine settles, check the PA. If it is above 3 to 4 percent, let it continue for another week or so, then rack the wine off into a glass secondary fermenter. Bung and fit with an air lock. A couple of weeks after that, do it again, making up the level with a little boiled water if you have to.

Rack the wine again in the next two to six months, and wait for it to ferment out and clear. Bottle the wine. This is better when sweetened a little, so stabilize it, and add 2 to 6 ounces of sugar in a bit of water, if you like. Keep six months to a year. Serve chilled.

NOTE: To make perry, which is like hard apple cider, use only ¾ to 1 pound of sugar. It will take less time to ferment out and clear, and it will have less alcohol. Bottle when done and try in two months. I actually like this better than pear wine.

If you know how to bottle beer, you can bottle it in capped beer bottles or in capped champagne bottles, with 1½ tablespoons of sugar per gallon to make it sparkle. DO NOT USE REGULAR WINE BOTTLES for this. Read ahead in the sparkling wine section (page 229) to learn how to bottle this way if you don't know how.

⬥HAWAIIAN PINEAPPLE WINE⬥

Our beautiful fiftieth state produces superb pineapples, which are shipped fresh to us less fortunates. It takes a bit of shopping to find a truly ripe pineapple. When you do, they are frequently on sale, so grab a couple of good ones and zip home with them. Pineapples are ripe when they are fragrant, a little sticky, and the top knot of leaves is loose. Don't buy them if they are over the hill, because they've started fermenting on their own!

3½ quarts or so of water
2 lbs. of sugar or 2 lbs. light honey (highly recommended)
3–4 lbs. ripe pineapples
½ tsp. acid blend
¼ tsp. tannin
1 tsp. yeast nutrient
1 Campden tablet, crushed (recommended)
½ tsp. pectic enzyme
1 packet champagne yeast

Boil most of the water and all the sugar or honey, and skim, if necessary.

Remove the leaves and skin the pineapple, saving any juice you lose. Watch out for stickers! Don't worry if you don't get all the knots out of the skin. Cut the pineapple in half, and take out the core, then cut the fruit into small pieces over a bowl, saving the juice. Put it in a nylon straining bag and into the bottom of a primary fermenter. With a sanitized potato masher, mash the pineapple with the Campden tablet.

Pour the sugar water over the fruit. See if you need to add the rest of the water to make up the gallon, allowing for the bulk of the fruit, of course. When cooled, add acid, tannin, yeast nutrient, and another Campden tablet if you choose to. Cover and fit with an air lock. Twelve hours after the Campden tablet, add the pectic enzyme. If you don't use the tablet, merely wait until the must cools down to add the pectic enzyme.

Twenty-four hours later add the yeast. Stir daily.

After a week, lift out what remains of the pineapples, and let the bag drain into the primary fermenter (don't squeeze). When the wine settles, check the PA. If it is above 3 to 4 percent, let it continue for another week or so, then rack the wine off into a glass secondary fermenter. Bung and fit with an air lock. A couple of weeks after that, do it again, making up the level with a little boiled water if you have to.

Rack the wine again in the next two to six months, and wait for it to ferment out and clear. Pineapple wine is better when sweetened a little, so stabilize it, and add 2 to 6 ounces of sugar in a bit of water, and bottle. It should be very fragrant. Keep six months to a year. Serve chilled and think of Hawaii. Ukeleles optional.

☜PLUM OR NECTARINE WINE☞

There are many different kinds of plums and nectarines, which are a cross between peaches and plums. Plums are yellow, red, nearly black, and even green. Get what tastes the best and is ripest. Fresh prune plums are good, too. Plums are grown in much of the United States and Canada.

Wild plums are lower in sugar and higher in acid, so use fewer of them and add a half pound more sugar or honey.

Plum or nectarine wine is mild and tends to be thin, but it has a rightful place in home winemaking, since plums are so easy to grow. Plum wine is a favorite in Japan and China.

3½ quarts or so of water
2 lbs. of sugar or 2 lbs. light honey (highly recommended)
4 lbs. ripe sweet plums or nectarines or 3 lbs. wild plums
1½ tsp. acid blend (none for wild plums)
⅛ tsp. tannin
1 tsp. yeast nutrient
1 Campden tablet, crushed (recommended)
½ tsp. pectic enzyme
1 packet champagne or Montrachet yeast

Boil most of the water and all of the sugar or honey, and skim, if necessary.

Wash, stem, and pit the plums. No need to peel them. Then cut them into small pieces over a bowl, saving the juice. Put it in a nylon straining bag and into the bottom of a primary fermenter. With a sanitized potato masher, mash the fruit.

Pour the water and sugar over the fruit. See if you need to add the rest of the water to make up the gallon, allowing for the bulk of the fruit, of course. When cooled, add acid, tannin, yeast nutrient, and the Campden tablet if you choose to. Cover and fit with an air lock. Twelve hours after the Campden tablet, add the pectic enzyme. If you don't use the tablet, merely wait until the must cools down to add the pectic enzyme.

Twenty-four hours later, add the yeast. Stir daily.

After a week, lift out what remains of the fruit, and let the bag drain. When the wine settles, check the PA. If it is above 3 to 4 percent, let it continue for another week or so, then rack the wine off into a glass secondary fermenter. Bung and fit with an air lock. A couple of weeks after that, do it again, making up the level with a little boiled water if you have to.

Rack the wine again in the next two to six months, and wait for it to ferment out and clear. Plum wine is better when sweetened a little, so stabilize it, and add 2–6 ounces of sugar in a bit of water, and bottle. Keep it six months to a year. Serve chilled.

☙ RHUBARB RHUBARB RHUBARB ❧

In high school drama class we were told to murmur *rhubarb* over and over during crowd scenes. I still can't say it more than twice in a row without stuttering and smelling greasepaint.

Rhubarb grows all over the United States, in cities and out in the country. If you are driving around in the country and see a big patch of rhubarb out in a field on its own, you know there was once a farmhouse on the site. Rhubarb is a vegetable, not a fruit, although we use it as a fruit.

Use ONLY the stalks of rhubarb, never the leaves, which are highly poisonous. In the spring, you can buy rhubarb in grocery stores and farmers' markets. Rhubarb is a high-acid fruit, so don't use more than 3 pounds to a gallon, unless you are willing to use precipitate chalk to take down the acid contents. It makes a fine wine.

1 gallon water
2½ lbs. of sugar or 3 lbs. light honey (highly recommended)
3 lbs. rhubarb stalks, the redder the better, fresh or frozen
1 6 oz. can frozen apple or white grape juice, optional
no acid blend
⅛ tsp. tannin
1 tsp. yeast nutrient
1 Campden tablet, crushed (optional)
½ tsp. pectic enzyme
1 packet champagne or Montrachet yeast

Boil the water and sugar or honey, and skim, if necessary. Wash and cut the rhubarb stalks into small pieces. Put them in a nylon straining bag and into the bottom of a primary fermenter. With a sanitized potato masher, mash the fruit.

If you use the apple juice or white grape juice, leave out ¼ lb. sugar or honey. Pour the hot water and sugar over the fruit. Let it cool a bit, then mash it again, and add the apple or grape juice if you are using them. When cooled, add the tannin, yeast nutrient, and the Campden tablet if you choose to. Cover and fit with an air lock. Twelve hours after the Campden tablet, add the pectic enzyme. If you don't use the tablet, merely wait until the must cools down to add the pectic enzyme.

Twenty-four hours later, add the yeast. Stir daily.

After three to four days, lift out what remains of the fruit, and let the bag drain. Don't squeeze. When the wine settles, check the PA. If it is above 3 to 4 percent, let it continue for another week or so, then rack the wine off into a glass secondary fermenter with a little boiled water if you have to. Bung and fit with an air lock.

Rack the wine again in the next two to six months, and wait for it to ferment out and clear. Rhubarb wine is good dry, but you might like it better sweetened a little. If so, stabilize it, add 2 to 4 ounces of sugar in a bit of water, and bottle it. Keep it six months to a year. Serve chilled. Very nice with poultry, fish, and grain dishes.

⚜LIPS LIKE STRAWBERRY WINE⚜

The above bit of song lyric always kept me wondering as a kid. My first kiss fell considerably short of that ideal.

Strawberries never fail. Local strawberries are best, because they don't have to be bred to withstand shipping, like the ones from California. Local strawberries will make a sweeter, redder wine. But the commercial California berries will make a good wine, too. Be picky about what you get; sometimes you can get a flat of berries that are dead ripe and cheap because they won't hold another day. For the freshest and best, go to a pick-your-own farm.

This wine doesn't have a lot of body, but it's very nice. Some use it as a table wine.

If you can get wild strawberries, well, you are a very lucky person, and you should invite me over.

3½ quarts or so of water
2 lbs. of sugar or 2 lbs. light honey (highly recommended)
4 lbs. ripe sweet strawberries, fresh or frozen
1 tsp. acid blend OR juice of one large lemon
⅛ tsp. tannin
1 tsp. yeast nutrient
1 Campden tablet, crushed (optional)
½ tsp. pectic enzyme
1 packet champagne or Montrachet yeast

Boil most of the water and all of the sugar or honey, and skim, if necessary.

Wash and stem the berries. Pick them over and cut out any bad parts. Put them in a nylon straining bag and into the bottom of a primary fermenter. Squash the strawberries with your clean hands or a sanitized potato masher. You'll get a frothy pink substance.

Pour the hot water and sugar over the fruit. See if you need to add the rest of the water to make up the gallon, allowing for the bulk of the fruit, of course. When cooled, add acid, tannin yeast nutrient, and the Campden tablet if you choose to. Cover and fit with an air lock. Twelve hours after the Campden tablet, add the pectic enzyme. If you don't use the tablet, merely wait until the must cools down to add the pectic enzyme.

Twenty-four hours later, add the yeast. Stir daily.

After a week, lift out what remains of the fruit, and let the bag drain. Do not squeeze the bag. When the wine settles, check the PA. If it is above 3 to 4 percent, let it continue for another week or so, then rack the wine off into a glass secondary fermenter, with a little boiled water if you have to. Bung and fit with an air lock.

Rack the wine again in the next two to six months, and wait for it to ferment out and clear. I like strawberry wine very dry. If you would prefer it sweetened a little, then stabilize it, add 2 to 6 ounces of sugar in a bit of water, and bottle it. Keep it six months to a year. Serve chilled. Excellent for Saint Valentine's Day.

⌘TOMATO WINE⌘

Tomatoes are fruits, not vegetables. Use tomatoes that are dead ripe and locally grown—otherwise, don't bother. I make no guarantees on this one, because some people just can't get beyond the idea of tomato wine, but hey, you might be surprised.

3½ quarts or so of water
2 lbs. of sugar or 2 lbs. light honey
4 lbs. ripe tomatoes, red or yellow
2 tsp. acid blend
⅛ tsp. tannin
1 tsp. yeast nutrient
1 Campden tablet, crushed (optional)
½ tsp. pectic enzyme
1 packet champagne or Montrachet yeast

Boil most of the water and all of the sugar or honey, and skim, if necessary.

Wash the fruit. Look the tomatoes over and cut out any bad

parts as you cut them into chunks over a bowl. Put them in a nylon straining bag and into the bottom of a primary fermenter with any juice caught in the bowl. Squash the fruit with your clean hands or a sanitized potato masher.

Pour the hot water and sugar over the fruit. See if you need to add the rest of the water to make up the gallon, allowing for the bulk of the tomatoes, of course. When cooled, add acid, tannin, yeast nutrient, and the Campden tablet if you choose to. Cover and fit with an air lock. Twelve hours after the Campden tablet, add the pectic enzyme. If you don't use the tablet, merely wait until the must cools down to add the pectic enzyme.

Twenty-four hours later, add the yeast. Stir daily.

After a week, remove what remains of the fruit, and let the bag drain into the primary fermenter. Don't squeeze. When the wine settles, check the PA. If it is above 3 to 4 percent, let it continue for another week or so, then rack the wine off into a glass second-ary fermenter, with a little boiled water if you have to.

Rack the wine again in the next two to six months, and wait for it to ferment out and clear. The color of the wine varies from a red gold to gold. Tomato wine is better when sweetened a little, so stabilize it and add 2 to 4 ounces of sugar in a bit of water, and bottle. Keep six months to a year. Serve chilled.

A GENERAL NOTE ON FRUIT WINES

You can find all sorts of fruits I haven't mentioned here, many of them wild. By now, you should get the general gist of things. Decide which of these recipes uses a fruit most like the one you have, remembering that sweetness and acid content are the most important things. Then use that recipe for whatever fruit you have picked. You can't go very wrong, honest.

DESSERT WINES

Almost any of the above recipes can be made into a dessert wine. Dessert wines are thicker, fruitier, and sweeter than regular table or social wines. The darker, richer fruits are better in this mode, but the heavier light fruits can be good too.

Use a half pound to one pound extra fruit in the recipe, and when you get ready for the secondary fermenter, add a half pound more sugar or honey. You'll have to rack the wine an extra time before it clears. Stabilize and sweeten it when you bottle it.

CHAPTER SIX

Wines from Canned Fruits, Concentrates, and Dried Fruits

A very good thing about canned fruits is that they are available all year round. If you have missed part of the fresh fruit season or can't get a particular fruit in your area, canned fruit might be an option for you once in a while. Another plus is that the fruit has already been processed for you. There is no pitting, seeding, or peeling involved. You don't have to clean up a mess afterward. Recycle your cans, please.

While wine made with canned fruit won't taste as fresh and vibrant as wine made with fresh or frozen fruit, it will still be good.

Much depends on how good the fruit was when it went into the can in the first place. A peach isn't just a peach. There are many varieties of peach. Some are better suited to tasting good in a can. Some are more suited to looking good in a can. The ripeness of the fruit, how it has been handled, and the quality of the processing at the cannery all have a lot to do with the result.

I used to buy peaches and pears from an orchard near my house that had been rejected by the cannery as too big for its machinery. My canned peaches and pears were superb (at ten cents a pound). So was the brand that bought the orchard's output. They always picked at the perfect time, and the cannery was only a few miles away. Alas, time has passed, and the orchard and cannery are no more. I sure wish I had known how to make wine in those days!

In most cases there are two ways to go: to the grocery store or to the wine supply store.

FRUIT WINE BASES AND CONCENTRATES

Most wine supply houses have what they call fruit wine bases and concentrates. These usually consist of ripe fruit canned in its own juices or in water. One can is usually enough to make five gallons of wine. It was canned with winemaking in mind and comes with instructions right on the label. I've made a few of these, and they came out just fine (although the starting PA frightened me a bit.) Some fifteen to twenty varieties are available.

So far, blackberry, marionberry, and gooseberry are my favorites because those fruits are hard to get in my area. If you aren't paying postage, the price is quite reasonable.

GROCERY STORE CANNED FRUITS

The grocery store has fruits and juices in an amazing array. You can buy little tiny cans of fruit and giant food service–sized cans. You can buy fruit canned in its own juices or in water.

Generally, I would say that using canned juices isn't worth the trouble. I prefer to work with frozen juices, which we covered back in chapter 2. Sometimes, though, canned juices might be all that's available. If so, refer back to chapter 2.

Be open to experiment. For one thing, you don't have to make batches bigger than one gallon if you don't want to. You might find good wine fodder on sale. ("No one wants these plums, let's try putting them out dirt cheap!" Bingo!)

There are a few things to keep in mind. If the canned fruit on sale is a brand you aren't familiar with, buy one can and taste it. If it is mostly syrup and not much fruit, you won't get much flavor in the resulting wine. If it's high in fruit content and you like the taste, check the PA or SG carefully. Figure out what kind of dilution and additional sugar you will need to make a gallon. Remember that suspended fruit particles can make the SG seem much higher than it really is.

Also remember that can sizes vary seemingly at the whim of the Can Fairy. Can sizes used to be fairly standard. Nowadays you will find cans of fruit that look at first glance to hold 16 ounces, only to discover upon further examination (right after you open all the cans, most likely) that the can really contains 15½ ounces or 14, or even 19.

Don't worry. A few ounces here and there won't make much of a difference. If the portions you buy are a slightly different size from what I talk about here, it's OK!

The "Oregon" brand that is usually in the fancy part of the canned fruit section is just about the best you can buy for "small" fruits such as berries. The price can take your breath away, but even so, two tins will make a remarkably good gallon of wine.

There are some very interesting imported canned fruits, though you should *ALWAYS* taste before using. I've eaten canned lychee fruit quite cheerfully, but I have never made wine from it. For all I know it would be delish, but I just have a bad feeling that canned lychees were not meant to be made into wine. Ditto for durian.

Sometimes the canning standards in other countries aren't up to what you might be used to. The U.S. government inspects shipments that come into the States, but they can't check every can. So that's your job. If you don't like the way it smells or looks, don't use it.

Avoid canned fruit that is labeled "pie filling." It has less fruit, more sugar, and thickeners that are best avoided.

Always read the label. I fully expect one day to find something

NOTE: If you want to make more than one gallon, go ahead—multiply everything but the yeast by the number of gallons you plan to make (one packet of yeast is good for one to five gallons). It's a good idea to write the amounts in pencil or on a separate piece of paper so you don't forget to multiply one or two ingredients, as I have frequently done.

labeled "pineapple" in large letters and in teeny-tiny letters under it: "Shaped rings of solidified food starch with pineapple and other natural flavors in a syrup of imitation sugar with even more natural flavors augmented with unnatural flavors and a vitamin in every can."

Also, please note that I don't require you to boil the water and sugar or honey in these recipes. This is because the fruit already has a cooked taste. Use very hot but not boiling water to dissolve the sugar or honey.

Let's start out with:

☜PEACHY CAN DEW WINE☞

water, about 3½ quarts
2 16 oz. (or so) cans of peach slices or halves in light syrup
2 lbs. sugar (if fruit is canned in its own or something else's juices, add about another ¼–½ lb. of sugar)
1 cup fresh squeezed or frozen orange juice (optional)
2 tsps. acid blend
1 tsp. yeast nutrient
¼ tsp. tannin
1 Campden tablet, crushed (optional)
½ tsp. pectic enzyme
1 packet champagne yeast

Heat the water. Drain the syrup from the fruit. Place the fruit into a nylon straining bag and put it in the bottom of a sanitized primary fermenter. Add the orange juice if you wish. It helps perk up the taste.

Measure out 3½ quarts of warm water to start with, and add the fruit syrup. Add 1½ pounds of the sugar and stir until dissolved. Be sure it is dissolved. Check the PA. For this wine you want about 12 percent potential alcohol.

You can never tell about fruit syrups. Supposedly there are standards as to how much sugar is in them, but with fruit solids and volume and all that, it's best to check.

If the PA is below 12 percent (and it probably will be), stir in the other half pound of sugar. Stir it in well and check the PA again. Don't worry if it is a degree off. This is art, not science. You could go up to 14 percent and a little beyond if you wanted to, but this is best as a medium sort of wine. The fruit still has sugar in it, too, don't forget.

Pour the water and sugar/syrup mixture over the fruit, and add the acid, yeast nutrient, and tannin. If you don't have a little over a gallon of must in the fermenter, add another couple of cups of water and check the PA again.

After the mixture cools down, add a crushed Campden tablet, if you choose to use one. Cover and fit with an air lock. Twelve hours after the Campden tablet, add the pectic enzyme. If you don't use the tablet, merely wait until the must cools down to add the pectic enzyme.

Twenty-four hours later, add the yeast.

Let ferment for five days, stirring daily. When the PA falls to 3 to 4 percent, remove the fruit. Drain it well, but don't squeeze; it will simply turn to fine pulp that will end up displacing the wine. Let the wine settle, then rack into a gallon jug. Bung and fit with an air lock.

Rack the wine once or twice over the next three to six months. Sometimes this ferments out quite quickly, depending on the weather and the reaction of the yeast and fruit.

When the fermentation is done, taste the wine and decide how you like it. If you've gotten good canned peaches, it should taste pretty good, though you'll probably be able to tell that it needs to sit in the bottle for a while. If the peaches weren't the best, it might taste rather harsh. Fear not. Add stabilizer, sweeten it up a bit with a couple of ounces of dissolved sugar or boiled honey, and sit back and let the bottle and time do their magic.

NOTE: Canned pears can be used in place of the peaches in the recipe above. Also, if you run across some canned tropical fruits you'd like to try, such as mangoes, guavas, or papayas, they'll work too.

❦CANNED BLUEBERRY OR
BLACKBERRY WINE❧

This comes out very well. If you can find canned wild blueberries, use them!

water, about 3½ quarts
2 16 oz. (or so) cans of blueberries or blackberries in light
   syrup
2 lbs. sugar (if fruit is canned in heavy syrup, subtract another
   ¼ lb. of sugar)
2 tsp. acid blend OR zest and juice of 2 large lemons
⅛ tsp. tannin
1 tsp. yeast nutrient
1 Campden tablet, crushed (optional)
½ tsp. pectic enzyme
1 packet Montrachet yeast

Heat the water. Drain the syrup from the fruit. Place the fruit (and zest if you are using it) into a nylon straining bag and put it in the bottom of a sanitized primary fermenter.

Measure out 3½ quarts of warm water to start with and add the fruit syrup. Add 1½ pounds of the sugar and stir till dissolved. Be sure it is dissolved. Check the PA. For this wine you want about 12 percent potential alcohol.

If the PA is below 12 percent (and it probably will be), stir in the other one half pound of sugar well and check the PA again. Don't worry if it is a degree off. The fruit still has sugar in it, too, don't forget.

Pour the water/sugar/syrup mixture over the fruit and add the acid, yeast nutrient, tannin, and lemon juice if you are using it instead of the acid. After the must cools, add a crushed Campden tablet, if you choose to use one. Cover and fit with an air lock. Twelve hours after the Campden tablet, add the pectic enzyme. If you don't use the tablet, merely wait until the must cools down to add the pectic enzyme.

Twenty-four hours later, add the yeast.

Let the wine ferment for five days, stirring daily. When the PA falls to 3 to 4 percent, remove the fruit. Drain it well, but don't squeeze; it will turn to fine pulp that will displace the wine. Let the wine settle, then rack it into a gallon jug. Bung and fit with an air lock.

Rack the wine once or twice more over the next three to six months. When the fermentation is done, taste it and decide how you like it. If you want it sweeter, stabilize it and sweeten it up a bit with a couple of ounces of dissolved sugar or boiled honey, and bottle it.

☜CANNED PIE CHERRY WINE☞

Another good one. Be sure you don't get cherry pie *filling*. Some stores have pie cherries and others don't. Check around.

water, about 3½ quarts
2 16 oz. (or so) cans pie cherries in light syrup
2 lbs. sugar (if fruit is canned in heavy syrup, subtract another
   ¼ lb. of sugar; if in water, add ¼ lb.)
1 tsp. acid blend
1 tsp. yeast nutrient
1 Campden tablet, crushed (optional)
½ tsp. pectic enzyme
1 packet Montrachet yeast

Heat the water. Drain the syrup from the fruit. Place the fruit into a nylon straining bag and put it in the bottom of a sanitized primary fermenter.

Measure out 3½ quarts of warm water to start with, and add the fruit syrup. Add 1½ pounds of the sugar and stir till dissolved. Be sure it is dissolved. Check the PA. For this wine you want about 12 percent potential alcohol.

If the PA is below 12 percent (and it probably will be), stir in the other half pound of sugar well and check the PA again. Don't worry if it is a degree off. The fruit still has sugar in it, too, don't forget.

Pour the water and sugar syrup mixture over the fruit, and add the acid, yeast nutrient, and tannin. After the must cools, add a crushed Campden tablet, if you choose to use one. Cover and fit with an air lock. Twelve hours after the Campden tablet, add the pectic enzyme. If you don't use the tablet, merely wait until the must cools down to add the pectic enzyme.

Twenty-four hours later, add the yeast.

Let it ferment for five days, stirring daily. When the PA falls to 3 to 4 percent, remove the fruit. Drain it well, but don't squeeze;

it will simply turn to fine pulp that will displace the wine. Let the wine settle, then rack it into a gallon jug. Bung and fit with an air lock.

Rack the wine once or twice over the next three to six months. When the fermentation is done, taste and decide how you like it. If you want it sweeter, stabilize it, and sweeten it up a bit with a couple of ounces of dissolved sugar or boiled honey, and bottle it.

NOTE: To make this wine with canned sweet eating cherries, use Bings or some other red sweet cherry, and add 2 teaspoons of acid blend, following the above recipe. If you want to live dangerously, you could try using a can of both kinds of cherries.

ᴄ᎒CANNED PINEAPPLE WINEᴇ᎒

Canned pineapples make a pretty good wine—and you don't have to worry about their ripeness or getting the rind off. Use a good brand, not a cheapie. Try to use pineapple canned in its own juice, because you get more pineapple flavor that way.

water, about 3½ quarts
2 16 oz. (or so) cans of pineapple, crushed in juice
2 lbs. sugar (if fruit is canned in syrup, subtract another
    ¼ lb. of sugar) or 2 lbs. light honey
1 tsp. acid blend
1 tsp. yeast nutrient
1 Campden tablet, crushed (optional)
½ tsp. pectic enzyme
1 packet champagne yeast

Heat the water. Drain the juice from the fruit, place the fruit into a nylon straining bag, and put it in the bottom of a sanitized primary fermenter. (The fruit is already crushed.)

Measure out 3½ quarts of warm water to start with, and add the fruit juice. Add 1½ pounds of the sugar and stir till dissolved. Be sure it is dissolved. Check the PA. For this wine you want about 12 percent potential alcohol.

If the PA is below 12 percent (and it probably will be), stir in the other ½ pound of sugar well and check the PA again. Don't worry if it is a degree off.

Pour the water and sugar syrup mixture over the fruit in the fermenter and add the acid, yeast nutrient, and tannin. After the must cools, add a crushed Campden tablet, if you choose to use one. Cover and fit with an air lock. Twelve hours after the Campden tablet, add the pectic enzyme. If you don't use the tablet, merely wait until the must cools down to add the pectic enzyme.

Twenty-four hours later, add the yeast.

Let it ferment for five days, stirring daily. When the PA falls to 3 to 4 percent, remove the fruit. Drain it well, but don't squeeze; it will simply turn to fine pulp that will displace the wine. Let the wine settle, then rack it into a gallon jug. Bung and fit with an air lock.

Rack the wine once or twice over the next three to six months. When the fermentation is done, taste it and decide how you like it. It's nice dry. If you want it sweeter, stabilize it and sweeten it up a bit with a couple of ounces of dissolved sugar or boiled honey, and bottle it.

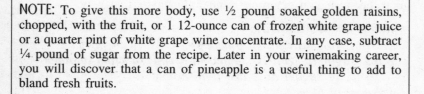

NOTE: To give this more body, use ½ pound soaked golden raisins, chopped, with the fruit, or 1 12-ounce can of frozen white grape juice or a quarter pint of white grape wine concentrate. In any case, subtract ¼ pound of sugar from the recipe. Later in your winemaking career, you will discover that a can of pineapple is a useful thing to add to bland fresh fruits.

☙CANNED PLUM WINE☙

water, about 3½ quarts
2 16 oz. (or so) cans of plums, any kind, in light syrup
2 lbs. sugar (if fruit is canned in heavy syrup, subtract another
    ¼ lb. of sugar; if canned in water, add ¼ lb.)
2 tsps. acid blend OR juice and zest of 2 lemons
⅛ tsp. tannin
1 tsp. yeast nutrient
1 Campden tablet, crushed (optional)
½ tsp. pectic enzyme
1 packet Montrachet yeast

Heat the water. Drain the syrup from the fruit. Take out any pits, and place the fruit (and zest if you are using it) into a nylon straining bag. Put it in the bottom of a sanitized primary fermenter.

Measure out 3½ quarts of warm water to start with, and add the fruit syrup. Add 1½ pounds of the sugar and stir till dissolved. Be sure it is dissolved. Check the PA. For this wine you want about 12 percent potential alcohol.

If the PA is below 12 percent (and it probably will be), stir in the other ½ pound of sugar. Stir it in well, and check the PA again. Don't worry if it is a degree off. The fruit still has sugar in it, too, don't forget.

Pour the water and sugar syrup mixture over the fruit, and add the lemon juice, if you are using it, or the acid, yeast nutrient, and tannin. After the must cools, add a crushed Campden tablet, if you choose to use one. Cover and fit with an air lock. Twelve hours after the Campden tablet, add the pectic enzyme. If you don't use the tablet, merely wait until the must cools down to add the pectic enzyme.

Twenty-four hours later, add the yeast.

Let it ferment for five days, stirring daily. When the PA falls to 3 to 4 percent, remove the fruit. Drain it well, but don't squeeze; it will simply turn to fine pulp that will displace the wine. Let the wine settle, then rack into a gallon jug. Bung and fit with an air lock.

Rack the wine once or twice over the next three to six months. When the fermentation is done, taste it and decide how you like it. If you want it sweeter, stabilize it and sweeten it up a bit with a couple of ounces of dissolved sugar or boiled honey, and bottle it.

GENERAL NOTE: If you think most of these recipes look alike, you're right. You can adapt almost any canned fruit to these recipes with very little risk. Explore!

DRIED FRUIT

Dried fruit has all the advantages and disadvantages of canned fruit, though in a slightly different way.

Canning fruit preserves the fruit, but it changes the color, flavor, and texture because the fruit has been cooked for sterilization.

Similar changes occur when fruit is dried, although the fruit is heated rather than cooked. It is not necessarily sterilized. Preserving fruit by removing most of the moisture both takes away and replaces some of the fruit's original qualities.

While canned fruits rarely have chemical preservatives in them, many dried fruits have been treated with sulfur, glycerin, and other additives. This may or may not be a plus, depending on your tastes. For example, a sulfured apricot retains its orange color and has a brighter flavor than an unsulfured apricot. It's softer and plumper, and easier to get the flavor and sugars to release. This method of preservation is considered safe; however some people prefer to avoid any preservatives.

Most dried fruit can be reconstituted by soaking it in water, but it will never come close to resembling the fruit in its fresh state.

However, dried fruit has a rich, dark flavor of its own: the natural sugar of the fruit is very concentrated. A small amount of dried fruit added to a regular fresh fruit recipe can change its character considerably. It provides more body and a warmer, perhaps deeper, tone of flavor, as well as extra sugar. Raisins are especially good for producing this effect. Yeasts love raisins and all that nice grape sugar. We'll get further into the nuances in the advanced section in chapter 10.

Think of what a fresh Thompson grape tastes like (Thompsons are commonly sold in supermarkets as "green" grapes). Now think about what a normal raisin tastes like. Very different, yet still related. Just as you can find different kinds of grapes in the market, you can find different kinds of raisins. There is the regular sort of raisins, generically labeled "raisins." There are golden raisins, made from white grapes; muscat raisins made from the sweet, luscious muscat grapes; and currants. Unless you have currant bushes and dry them yourself, I'm sorry to say you can't get real dried currants. The "currants" you buy in the grocery are merely small raisins.

It's also easy to find prunes (dried prune plums), apricots, peaches, apples, dates, pears, pineapples, and sometimes mango, sweet and sour cherries, blueberries, and cranberries. In fancy grocery stores I've also seen dried star fruit and kiwi. Beware: some of these last fruits have sugar and oil added to them to improve their flavor and to soften them. The sugar is OK, but the oil is not!

It's best to read the label carefully and be cautious. Don't use any dried fruit that has oil added to it. For instance, most dried bananas have a LOT of oil added to them because they are fried. Any amount of oil will show on the top of your wine and may go rancid.

I've used organic and nonorganic, sulfured and unsulfured dried fruits, and I have had good results with all of them. So suit yourself. Do remember to buy the best-quality dried fruit you can. Elderly, dusty fruit isn't going to be any better as wine. Fresh, tender dried fruit is preferable to wizened and hard. Always rinse the fruit lightly and check for foreign substances or the very occasional sign of insect damage.

To get untreated fruit you usually have to go to a whole foods store or a co-op. You will probably find both sulfured fruit and unsulfured fruit, as well as organic. The choice is yours. You can buy the fruit in bulk and get exactly as much as you need, sometimes at a much cheaper price than you'd pay for the boxed stuff at a normal grocery store.

Another way to obtain dried fruit is to dry it yourself. In hot, dry climates this is easy. For the rest of us there are inexpensive home dehydrators.

You can dry almost anything, it turns out, but it's best to plan in advance how you'll use the fruit.

Many people have a fruit tree or two that cheerfully overproduces. If you have a surplus of fruit, not much freezer space, and all your wine bins are going, you might want to consider drying some of your excess fruit for future use.

Another place to get dried fruit is the wine supply store. Most carry dried elderberries, rose hips, and dried banana flakes. The dried banana flakes sold in wine supply houses have no oil in them. Dried elderberry wine is a treasure.

A wine made with dried fruit tastes something like sherry to most people. True sherry is made by a special process, with a special yeast, in the Jerez area of Spain. It is fortified with extra alcohol so that it will keep for the longer period of time necessary to age it properly. The Flor yeasts used to make sherry also have an effect different from that of most other wine yeasts, tolerating a slightly higher level of alcohol before they are killed off by their own by-product. The barrels of wine are stored for long periods of time in huge open sheds in the hot, dry climate. Unlike just about every other wine in the world, sherries do their best when they get some air.

The grapes for sherry might come from many different vineyards of the area. There are light, dry sherries called fino, and dark, richer sherries called oloroso, and lots of variations in between. Blending and aging involve complicated processes that only experts can achieve.

Here in the United States we also make some pretty good sherries, but they are nothing like the wines from the Jerez region. Do yourself a favor and taste a really good one if you haven't already.

I might call some of the wines we are making sherry, but I really mean sherry-like. Sherry-like wines also have a place in the world, so let's make some.

The sherry-like taste we get with dried fruit wines comes from the slightly oxidized condition of the fruit, mimicking the long fermentation of the true sherry wine. Not all dried fruits produce this effect, but most of them do. Dried fruit wine keeps for a long time and ages well. I use it for sipping socially and for cooking, particularly in Chinese recipes. Never cook with something you won't drink!

Here are two raisin wines to start out with. Raisins are hard to chop, but chop you must to release the sugar and flavor. Buy tender ones to start with. I've had best success with rinsing and soaking the raisins overnight, then processing them with some of the water in a food processor, or, alternatively, with soaking them overnight and running them through an ordinary meat grinder. If you don't have either of these machines, soak them all night, drain, then go at your raisins with a heavy cleaver. I use my Chinese cleaver (carefully cleaned to avoid any stray onion or garlic, of course) for small amounts. Be sure to use a very clean chopping board. Use your soaking water in the recipe.

☞GOLDEN RAISIN WINE☜

1 gallon of water
2 lbs. ordinary raisins or golden raisins
2 lbs. sugar or 2½ lbs. light or dark honey
1 tsp. acid blend
1 tsp. yeast nutrient
¼ tsp. tannin

1 Campden tablet, crushed (optional)
½ tsp. pectic enzyme
1 packet Flor sherry yeast or Montrachet

Boil the water and sugar or honey together on the stove, and skim, if necessary.

Chop the raisins as suggested above. Be careful to keep them clean. Put them in a nylon straining bag and place them in the bottom of the primary fermenter. Pour the water and sugar or honey hot as possible, over the raisins. (Some recipes suggest boiling the raisins, but I find this gives the wine a Christmas pudding flavor best left to Christmas puddings.)

Cool the mixture to tepid, add the acid, tannin, and yeast nutrient, and the Campden tablet, if you choose. Cover and fit with an air lock. Twelve hours after the Campden tablet, add the pectic enzyme. If you don't use the tablet, merely wait until the must cools down to add the pectic enzyme.

Check the PA and add the Flor sherry yeast. Stir daily. The fermentation will be vigorous. When the PA gets down to 2 to 3 percent, rack the wine into a glass secondary fermenter. Bung and fit with an air lock.

When you remove the raisins, let the bag drip, but don't squeeze. Rack the wine again during the next three to six months. When the wine is fermented dry, bottle it. This makes a medium, light-colored sherry-like wine that needs to age at least a year. The color will range from light gold to a medium amber, depending on what kind of raisins you used to make it.

NOTE: If you want to make this wine sweeter, do so on your next batch, or sweeten only half the bottles and compare. Aging this wine will bring some pleasant surprises which are good to learn and depend on your personal taste.

☙FAT NUDE RAISIN SHERRY WINE❧

Look Ma, no sugar! Yup, that's right. This wine takes a lot of raisins! I made this for the first time when I received a lot of leftover raisins from a group who had been making vast quantities of gorp for a party. Otherwise, this is an investment, but a good one.

I call it Fat Nude because it comes out the color of the skin of an old acquaintance who is tan, plump, and shared with me the joys of a hot tub and a glass of excellent old wine. So this wine is for fat nudes everywhere!

> *1 gallon of water*
> *6–8 lbs. of raisins, any kind*
> *3 tsps. acid blend*
> *1 tsp. yeast nutrient (mostly for good luck)*
> *no tannin*
> *1 Campden tablet, crushed (optional)*
> *½ tsp. pectic enzyme*
> *1 packet Flor sherry or Montrachet yeast*

Boil the water. Process the raisins as above. Place the raisins in a nylon straining bag and put them in the bottom of the primary fermenter. Pour the hot water over the raisins. Cool to tepid, add the acid, nutrient, and the Campden tablet, if you choose to use one. Cover and fit with an air lock. Twelve hours after the Campden tablet, add the pectic enzyme. If you don't use the tablet, merely wait until the must cools down to add the pectic enzyme.

Check the PA, add the yeast, cover, and let it ferment. Stir daily.

Checking the PA on this one might be a bit tricky because of the solids from the raisins, but do your best. Lift the bag of raisins out after five or six days, and let it drip and settle. Then check the PA again. If it seems a bit high, put the raisins back in and let them ferment a few more days, maybe up to another week. Then rack the wine into a secondary fermenter. Bung and fit with an air lock.

Rack the wine once or twice in the next six months or so. When it's nice and clear and done fermenting, bottle it. If you used 6 pounds of raisins, this will be a dry, but full-flavored, sherry. If you used a greater amount, it will be sweeter. If you have any doubt about whether or not it's still fermenting, use some stabilizer, or let it stay in the secondary fermenter a few months longer. This is not a wine that should be hurried.

Store one or two years before sampling. I've kept this up to seven years, so far. It just keeps on getting better!

⟐REFINED ELDERBERRY WINE⟐

Elderberries are rich in tannin and flavor, but not in sugar. How this comes out—sherry-like or like a red wine—depends on the quality of the dried elderberries you use. Buy your dried elderberries from a wine supply place whose stock turns over rapidly, or pick and dry your own, making sure, of course, that you know that what you are picking are elderberries. Note that it doesn't take many dried elderberries to make a gallon of wine.

1 gallon water
2½ lbs. sugar or 3 lbs. light honey
¼–⅓ lb. dried elderberries
1 tsp. acid blend or juice of 1 lemon
1 tsp. yeast nutrient
no tannin or pectic enzyme
1 Campden tablet, crushed (optional)
1 packet Montrachet yeast

Boil the water with the sugar or honey and skim. Rinse the elderberries under cool running water in a sieve. They are very small, so be careful not to lose any! Check for and remove pebbles, twigs, etc. Put the berries in a nylon straining bag, which you place in a primary fermenter.

Pour the hot water and sugar over the elderberries. When cooled enough, add acid, yeast nutrient, and the Campden tablet, if you choose to use one. Cover and fit with an air lock. If you don't use the tablet, merely wait until the must cools down to add the yeast.

Add the yeast, cover, and let it ferment, stirring daily—mashing the berry bag occasionally. When the PA goes down to 2–3 percent, remove, squeeze, and drain the fruit. (Yes, you get to squeeze the fruit this time! Use sanitized plastic gloves because elderberries stain.) Rack the wine into a glass secondary container. Bung and fit with an air lock.

NOTE: You can add ¼ pound of chopped raisins to this recipe to improve the body if you don't use honey. Don't be tempted to use more elderberries than are listed in the recipe. Remember, they are high in tannin, and the wine will be, too.

During the next three to six months, rack the wine again. When the wine ferments out dry, bottle it. Elderberry wine is best dry.

Sometimes the color is a nice red, sometimes it is a rich amber. Keep it a year at least, and enjoy.

⌒◥SAHARA PEACH OR APRICOT WINE◤⌒

This is a light golden wine, usually, depending on the quality of the dried fruit you use. Sulfured apricots or peaches will produce a lighter wine, and unsulfured fruit will make a darker one. In any case it tends to be thin, so I recommend using all honey or part honey and part sugar.

> *1 gallon water, plus extra for soaking if you use sulfured fruit*
> *2–3 lbs. of dried peaches or apricots*
> *1½ lbs. sugar and 2 lbs. light honey OR 3½ lbs. honey*
> *1 cup fresh or frozen orange juice (optional)*
> *2 tsp. acid blend*
> *1 tsp. yeast nutrient*
> *no tannin*
> *1 Campden tablet, crushed (optional)*
> *1 tsp. pectic enzyme*
> *1 packet champagne yeast*

Rinse and soak the fruit overnight. Discard the soaking water if you have used sulfured fruit. Put the water and sugar and honey on to boil. Chop the fruit finely. Put it in a nylon straining bag, and place the bag in the bottom of your primary fermenter. Add the orange juice if you wish (I think it helps things along).

Pour the hot water and sugar and honey over the fruit. Cool to tepid, add acid and yeast nutrient, and add the crushed Campden tablet, if you choose to use one. Cover and fit with an air lock. After twelve hours, add the pectic enzyme. Check the PA.

Twenty-four hours later, add the yeast. Stir daily.

Ferment on the fruit for a week, stirring daily. When the PA is 2 to 3 percent, lift out the bag and drain, but don't squeeze. Discard the fruit. When the wine settles again, rack it into a glass secondary fermenter, bung, and fit with an air lock. Let it go on fermenting for three to six months, racking once or twice. When fermented out dry, taste it and decide if you want to sweeten it a bit. If so, stabilize and bottle it. Keep it for a year before sampling. Then try it again a year after that and see how you feel about it.

> NOTE: For some people, apricots have a stronger taste than peaches do. If you don't like apricots, don't use them. If you use peaches, use three pounds of dried fruit. Half apricots and half peaches is fine, too.
>
> I've never done it, but you could try using dried mango or papaya in this recipe instead of the apricots and peaches.

⌗MOHAVE APPLE OR PEAR WINE⌗

I'm including this recipe on the general principle that someone somewhere might want to try it, though I personally feel that fresh or frozen apples and pears yield a superior result. But you never know, there might be no better use for an attic full of dried apples, or pears, so here we go.

1 gallon water, plus extra for soaking if you are using sul-
fured fruit
3 lbs. dried apples and/or pears
2½ lbs. sugar or 3 lbs. light honey
1 gallon water
2 tsp. acid blend
1 tsp. yeast nutrient
no tannin
1 Campden tablet, crushed (optional)
½ tsp. pectic enzyme
1 packet champagne yeast

Rinse and soak the fruit overnight. Discard the soaking water if you used sulfured fruit. Put the water and sugar and honey on to boil. Chop the fruit finely, discarding any stems or pips. Put the fruit in a nylon straining bag and place it in the bottom of your primary fermenter.

Pour the hot water and sugar and honey over the fruit. Cool to tepid, add the acid and yeast nutrient, and add the crushed Campden tablet, if you choose to use one. Cover and fit with an air lock. After twelve hours, add the pectic enzyme. Check the PA.

Twenty-four hours later, add the yeast. Stir daily.

Ferment on the fruit for a week, stirring daily. When the PA is 2 to 3 percent, lift out the bag and drain, but don't squeeze. Discard the fruit. When the wine settles again, rack it into a glass secondary fermenter and bung and fit with an air lock. Let it go on fermenting for three to six months, racking once or twice. When fermented out dry, taste it and decide if you want to sweeten it a bit. If so, stabilize and bottle it. Keep it for a year before sampling.

NOTE: I've never tried this with mixed apples and pears, but I bet it would be very nice.

☙LATE KING TUT DATE WINE❧

I mostly like to eat dates or cook with them, but they make an acceptable wine, too. You don't have to pit them, nor do you have to soak them. They are very high in sugar, although low on flavor. If you make this wine with honey, you can dream perhaps of the ancient Egyptians making this wine and drinking it under the palms on a moonlit night. Or not.

1 gallon water
3–4 lbs. dates
2½ lbs. sugar or 3 lbs. light honey
2 tsp. acid blend
1 tsp. yeast nutrient
⅛ tsp. grape tannin
1 Campden tablet, crushed (optional)
½ tsp. pectic enzyme
1 packet champagne yeast

Boil the water and sugar or honey, and skim if necessary.

Rinse the fruit. Put the fruit in a nylon straining bag, squashing the dates a bit with your very clean fingers to loosen them up and break the skins; put the bag into the bottom of your primary fermenter. Pour the hot sugar water over the fruit.

Cool to tepid, add acid, tannin, yeast nutrient, and the Campden tablet, if you choose to use one. Cover and fit with an air lock. Twelve hours after the Campden tablet, add the pectic enzyme. If you don't use the tablet, merely wait until the must cools down to add the pectic enzyme.

Check the PA. Twenty-four hours later, add the yeast. Cover. Ferment on the fruit for a week, stirring daily. When the PA is 2 to 3 percent, lift out the bag and drain it, but don't squeeze. When the wine settles again, rack it out into a glass secondary fermenter, bung, and fit with an air lock. Let it go on fermenting for three to six months, racking it again once or twice. When the wine is fermented out dry, taste it, and decide if you want to sweeten it a bit. If so, stabilize and bottle it. Keep for six months to a year before trying. Aw, go ahead and think of moonlight and palms while you're at it.

☙WENDY ROSE HIP WINE❧

I'm naming this after my favorite poet, Wendy Rose, who's pretty hip. If you have access to fresh rose hips, use them!

1 gallon water
1/3–1/2 lb. dried rose hips or 2 lbs. fresh, unsprayed
2 1/2 lbs. sugar or 3 lbs. light honey
1 tsp. acid blend or juice of 1 lemon
1 tsp. yeast nutrient
no tannin
1 Campden tablet, crushed (optional)
1/2 tsp. pectic enzyme
1 packet Montrachet yeast

Rinse the dried rose hips under cool running water in a sieve. Check for and remove any pebbles, twigs, etc. Soak overnight and drain the rose hips. Put them in a nylon straining bag in a primary fermenter. Mash them lightly with your clean hands or a sanitized spoon.

If you are using fresh rose hips, rinse them under cool water, checking for insects. Put them in a blender and coarsely chop them before you place them in the bag. It is not necessary to soak them overnight.

Boil the water with the sugar or honey, and skim. Pour over the hips. When tepid, add acid, yeast nutrient, and the Campden tablet, if you choose to use one. Cover and fit with an air lock. Twelve hours after the Campden tablet, add the pectic enzyme. If you don't use the tablet, merely wait until the must cools down to add the pectic enzyme.

Twenty-four hours later, add the yeast, cover, and let it ferment, stirring daily—mashing the nylon bag. When the PA goes down to 2 to 3 percent, remove the bag and squeeze it using sanitized plastic gloves. Discard the fruit. Rack the wine into a glass secondary container. Bung and fit with an air lock. During the next three to six months, rack the wine again. When the wine ferments out dry, stabilize it and sweeten, then bottle it. This wine is best sweetened, as it is better as a social wine. Serve chilled.

✎DRIED BANANA WINE✎

Dry your own or get them at the wine supply store. They might have flakes instead of chips, but that's OK. A lot of us are more flaky than chipper . . .

1 gallon water
1 lb. golden raisins
½ lb. dried bananas
2 lbs. sugar or 2½ lbs. light honey
3 tsp. acid blend or juice of 3 lemons
¼ tsp. tannin
1 tsp. yeast nutrient
1 Campden tablet, crushed (optional)
½ tsp. pectic enzyme
1 packet Montrachet yeast

Soak the raisins overnight and chop them finely. Put the raisins and bananas in a nylon straining bag in a primary fermenter.

Boil the water with the sugar or honey and skim. Pour the sugar water over the fruit. When tepid, add acid, tannin, yeast nutrient, and the Campden tablet, if you choose to use one. Cover and fit with an air lock. Twelve hours after the Campden tablet, add the pectic enzyme. If you don't use the tablet, merely wait until the must cools down to add the pectic enzyme.

Twenty-four hours later, add yeast, cover, and let it ferment, stirring daily and mashing the nylon bag. The must might get thick and nasty looking, but don't worry. The dried banana flakes cause this temporarily.

When the PA goes down to 3 to 4 percent, remove the fruit

and let it drain. Rack the wine into a glass secondary container. Bung and fit with an air lock.

A few weeks later, rack it again. During the next three to six months, rack again, and when the wine ferments out dry, taste it. I feel this wine is best sweetened. Stabilize and sweeten with 2–6 ounces of sugar syrup, and bottle it. This is best as a social wine rather than a table wine. Serve chilled.

☜ SPECULATION DRIED FRUIT WINE ☞

This recipe is for all those interesting but usually expensive dried fruits that have been partially candied and dried, such as cranberries, cherries, pineapple, kiwi, blueberries, etc. The darker fruits tend to have more flavor, the lighter ones less. As I mentioned earlier in this chapter, be sure the dried fruit has no oil in it! It's best to use fruit you have dried yourself in a dehydrator or in the hot sun. Don't worry about exact amounts of fruit in this recipe. A little more or less won't hurt anything.

> *1 gallon water*
> *6–8 ozs. dried dark specialty fruit or 12–16 ozs. light dried fruit*
> *2 lbs. sugar or 2½ lbs. honey*
> *1 tsp. citric acid*
> *¼ tsp. tannin*
> *1 tsp. yeast nutrient*
> *1 Campden tablet, crushed (optional)*
> *½ tsp. pectic enzyme*
> *1 packet champagne yeast*

Rinse whichever fruit you are using and soak overnight. Chop the fruit finely. Put it in a nylon straining bag, and place in the bottom of your primary fermenter.

Boil the water and sugar and honey, and skim if necessary. Pour the hot sugar water over the fruit. Cool to tepid, add acid, yeast nutrient, tannin, and the Campden tablet, if you choose to use one. Cover and fit with an air lock. Twelve hours after the Campden tablet, add the pectic enzyme. If you don't use the tablet, merely wait until the must cools down to add the pectic enzyme.

Check the PA.

Twenty-four hours later, add yeast. Cover. Ferment on the fruit for a week, stirring daily. When the PA is 2 to 3 percent, lift out the bag and drain it, but don't squeeze. When the wine settles again, rack it out into a glass secondary fermenter, and let it go on fermenting for three to six months, racking it once or twice. When fermented out dry, taste it, and decide if you want to sweeten it a bit. If so, stabilize and bottle. Keep for six months to a year before sampling. Good luck.

CHAPTER SEVEN

Vegetable Wines

DRINK your vegetables?

Yes, in a way, but you still have to eat your vegetables, as well. Vegetable wine is no excuse for skipping good nutrition!

My first batch of vegetable wine was made out of curiosity and carrots. I was going through CJJ Berry's *First Steps in Winemaking,* and I thought, why not? It's winter, and carrots are cheap.

So I went out and got the five pounds of carrots required for a gallon and did it. As you might remember from the introduction, I wasn't impressed with the results, at first. I discovered the wonderful world of vegetable wines, thanks to time and the optimism of my brother.

Nearly all of the recipes I have adapted and used over the years have some fruit in them. In the older recipes, it is usually lemons, obviously included for the acid. Having made vegetable wines with and without citrus fruits, I must say I prefer wines that use them. They help round out the flavors. Some recipes have you add some malt, or raisins, or grape concentrate. These also help give the wine more body. But don't leave out the vegetables. They really are important!

Recommended vegetables: carrots, potatoes, beets, pea pods, parsnip, squash, sweet potatoes

Possibilities: celery, green beans, lettuce, sweet corn, onion, garlic, spinach, swiss chard

Not recommended: zucchini, cabbage, broccoli, cauliflower, kale, mushrooms

This first recipe should give you the basic idea. I've never had trouble with the dreaded "starch haze" mentioned in older books, particularly the British ones. Most recipes recommend that when using potatoes and carrots you use old vegetables, even withered ones (NOT rotten). I've done that, but I've also used nice, new, sweet vegetables and never had a problem in either case. It may be that overcooking or hard boiling causes the starch haze, but I don't do either of those, either.

So, pull up your suspenders of belief, and make a batch of:

☞OPTIMISTIC SIBLING CARROT WINE☜

1 gallon water (plus a little bit more, because you lose some in steam)
5 lbs. carrots (I prefer organically grown)
juice and zest of 3 oranges
juice and zest of 2 lemons or 4 tsps. acid blend
2½ lbs. sugar or 3 lbs. honey
1 tsp. yeast nutrient
¼ tsp. tannin
1 Campden tablet, crushed (optional)
½ tsp. pectic enzyme
1 packet champagne yeast
optional: 10 bruised peppercorns (more about peppercorns in the Big Time section)

Put the water on the stove to heat.

Scrub the carrots well. DO NOT PEEL, except for stubborn bits of stuff that won't come off. Slice fine, as for soup, by hand or with a food processor, working in batches.

Simmer the carrots in the water (add the peppercorns, if you want to try them) just until tender, 30–45 minutes. DO NOT BOIL!

Remove the zest from the citrus fruit (no white pith), and squeeze the juice. Place the zest in a small nylon straining bag.

Strain the carrots (and peppercorns) from the water. You can use the carrots as food, if you wish. Remove about a quart of the water to add back later if you don't have enough. It's hard to say how much you will have lost in steam while cooking. Add the sugar or the honey, and simmer until the sugar is dissolved. If using honey, simmer 10–15 minutes, stirring, and skim any scum.

Pour the hot water into a sanitized primary fermenter over the zest. Add the fruit juices. (You can reserve a bit of the orange juice and extra carrot water to start the yeast later, if you like.) Check to see if you have a gallon of must. If not, make it up with the reserved water. Add yeast nutrient, tannin, and acid blend if you didn't use lemons. Let the must cool, then add the Campden tablet, if you choose to use one. Cover and fit with an air lock. Twelve hours later, add the pectic enzyme.

Twenty-four hours later, check the PA and add the yeast.

Stir daily. In two weeks or so, check the PA. Lift out the bag of zest and let it drain back into the container. Do not squeeze. Discard the zest. Let the wine settle, and rack it into a secondary fermenter. Bung and fit with an air lock. Rack as necessary in the next six months or so. Check the PA. When it ferments out, bottle the wine. You can sweeten it if you like by adding stabilizer and 2 to 4 ounces of sugar syrup per gallon. I prefer it dry, and used as a table wine. Keep for two years at least.

☞POTABLE POTATO WINE☜

3 lbs. old potatoes (organically grown preferred)
1 gallon water
2½ lbs. sugar or 3 lbs. honey
juice and zest of 3 oranges
juice and zest of 2 large lemons or 4 tsps. acid blend
1 tsp. yeast nutrient
¼ tsp. tannin
1 Campden tablet, crushed (optional)
½ tsp. pectic enzyme
1 packet champagne or white wine yeast
10 bruised peppercorns (optional)

Potatoes appropriate for mashed potatoes or french fries are best. You can use potatoes that are sprouting if you break off the sprouts. The wine will be fine. Get rid of ANY green skin and discolored spots on the potatoes. DO NOT PEEL. Scrub well. Potatoes with red skins will give a nice "blush" color.

Slice the potatoes into the gallon of cool water, turn on the heat, and simmer till just tender, 30–45 minutes. DO NOT BOIL.

Remove the zest from the citrus fruit (no white pith), and squeeze the juice. Place the zest in a small nylon straining bag.

Strain the potatoes (and peppercorns) from the water. You can use the potatoes in a casserole if they were nice to begin with.

Remove about a quart of the water to add back later if you don't have enough. It's hard to say how much you will have lost in steam while cooking. Add the sugar or the honey, and simmer until the sugar is dissolved. If using honey, simmer 10–15 minutes, stirring, and skim any scum.

Pour the hot water into a sanitized primary fermenter over the zest. Add the fruit juices. (You can reserve a bit of the orange juice and extra potato water to start the yeast later, if you like.) Check to see if you have a gallon of must. If not, make it up with the reserved water. Add yeast nutrient, tannin, and acid blend if you didn't use lemons. Cover, and attach an air lock. Let the must cool, then add the pectic enzyme. Twenty-four hours later, check the PA and add the yeast.

Stir daily. In two weeks or so, check the PA. Lift out the bag of zest and let it drain back into the container. Do not squeeze. Discard the zest. Let the wine settle, and rack it into a secondary fermenter. Bung and fit with an air lock. Rack as necessary in the next six months or so. Check the PA. When it ferments out, bottle it. I prefer this wine dry. You can sweeten the wine if you like before bottling by adding stabilizer and 2 to 4 ounces of sugar syrup per gallon. Keep for two years at least. Use it as a table or social wine. As you will see in the advanced section, this wine is very useful for blending.

☙ RUBY SIPPER WINE ❧

This wine is great fun. The color, alas, isn't always stable; it sometimes fades to a deep tawny color. If you make pickled beets, and if you want a lighter wine, you can use the water in which you cooked the beets. Otherwise, you can make a deeper, more flavorful wine by fermenting on the beets.

I like the taste of this wine a lot. Some people find it a bit earthy. Maybe I'm just charmed by the idea of using such a "backyard" vegetable for wine. It's unexpected and beautiful, and reminds me of the Land of Oz in a way, hence the name. Cheers, Dorothy!

3 lbs. beet roots
1 gallon water
2½ lbs. sugar or 3 lbs. honey
10 bruised peppercorns (optional)
zest and juice of 3 oranges
juice and zest of 2 large lemons or 3 tsps. acid blend
⅛ tsp. tannin
1 tsp. yeast nutrient
1 Campden tablet, crushed (optional)
½ tsp. pectic enzyme
1 packet Montrachet or red wine yeast

Scrub the beets well, and cut off the tops and the root ends. Chop, slice or shred into the cool water, then heat. SIMMER, do not boil, for 45 minutes.

Remove the zest from the citrus fruit (no white pith), and squeeze the juice. Place the zest in a small nylon straining bag in the bottom of the primary fermenter.

Strain the beets (and peppercorns, if you used them) from the water. You can use the beets for food if you choose.

Remove about a quart of the water to add back later if you don't have enough. It's hard to say how much you will have lost in steam while cooking. Add the sugar or the honey, and simmer until the sugar is dissolved. If using honey, simmer 10–15 minutes, stirring, and skim any scum.

Pour the hot water into a sanitized primary fermenter over the zest. Add the fruit juices. (You can reserve a bit of the orange juice and extra beet water to start the yeast later, if you like.) Check to see if you have a gallon of must. If not, make it up with the reserved water. Add yeast nutrient, tannin, and acid blend if you didn't use lemons. Cover, and attach an air lock. Let the must cool, and add the Campden tablet, if you choose to use one. Twelve hours after the Campden tablet, add the pectic enzyme. If you don't use the tablet, merely wait until the must cools down to add the pectic enzyme. Twenty-four hours later, check the PA and add the yeast.

Stir daily. In two weeks or so, check the PA. Lift out the bag of zest and let it drain back into the container. Do not squeeze. Discard the zest. Let the wine settle, and rack it into a secondary fermenter. Bung and fit with an air lock. Rack as necessary in the next six months or so. Check the PA. When it ferments out, bottle it. I prefer this wine dry. You can sweeten the wine if you like before bottling by adding stabilizer and 2 to 4 ounces of sugar syrup per gallon. Keep for two years at least. This makes a nice social or table wine. I like it with beans or stew.

I see that there are golden beets in the seed catalogs these days. Now that should be interesting to try. Golden Sipper wine?

> NOTE: As an alternative to this recipe you might want to treat beets as you would a fruit to get a deeper color. After simmering the beets, put them in a nylon straining bag with the zest, and proceed with the rest of the recipe.

☙VEGETABLE SOUP WINE❧

Sorry, but I had to do it. You can never tell about the color, but it's always interesting. The shock value of the name alone makes it worth while.

2 lbs. carrots
2 lbs. potatoes
2 lbs. beets
1 gallon water
2½ lbs. sugar or 3 lbs. honey (I like dark honey with this)
zest and juice of 3 oranges
zest and juice of 2 lemons or 3 tsps. acid blend
¼ tsp. tannin
10 peppercorns (optional)
1 tsp. yeast nutrient
1 Campden tablet, crushed (optional)
½ tsp. pectic enzyme
1 packet Montrachet yeast

Scrub the vegetables well, cutting off the tops and the root ends. Chop, slice, or shred into the cool water, then heat. SIMMER, do not boil, for 45 minutes.

Remove the zest from the citrus fruit (no white pith), and squeeze the juice. Place the zest in a small nylon straining bag in the bottom of the primary fermenter.

Strain the vegetables (and peppercorns, if you used them) from the water. You can use the vegetables for food if you choose.

Remove about a quart of the water to add back later if you don't have enough. It's hard to say how much you will have lost in steam while cooking. Add the sugar or the honey, and simmer until the sugar is dissolved. If you're using honey, simmer 10–15 minutes, stirring, and skim any scum.

Pour the hot water into a sanitized primary fermenter over the zest. Add the fruit juices. (You can reserve a bit of the orange juice and extra vegetable water to start the yeast later, if you like.) Check to see if you have a gallon of must. If not, make it up with the reserved water. Add yeast nutrient, tannin, and acid blend if you didn't use lemons. Cover, and attach an air lock. Let the must cool, and add the Campden tablet, if you choose to use one. Twelve hours after the Campden tablet, add the pectic enzyme. If you don't use the tablet, merely wait until the must cools down to add the pectic enzyme. Twenty-four hours later, check the PA and add the yeast.

Stir daily. In two weeks or so, check the PA. Lift out the bag of zest and let it drain back into the container. Do not squeeze. Discard the zest. Let the wine settle, and rack it into a secondary fermenter. Bung and fit with an air lock. Rack as necessary in the next six months or so. Check the PA. When it ferments out, bottle it. I prefer this wine dry. You can sweeten the wine if you like before bottling by adding stabilizer and 2 to 4 ounces of sugar

NOTE: As you can see, whatever vegetable you use, it's best not to boil or overcook it. If you want to, you can add half a pound of raisins or some grape concentrate to these wines to give them a bit more body, but try them without, first. A half pound of light malt can also be used, and it is quite nice.

syrup per gallon. It ages for the same amount of time as the other root vegetable wines. I've always been tempted to add a few onions and call it Vegetable Stew, but I have not had the courage.

⟋VENERABLE PARSNIP WINE⟍

This is very traditional. It's also delicious. Parsnips are quite expensive in the store, so the only way you are likely to make it is if you grow the vegetables yourself or find some in the farmers' market. Parsnips are best after a heavy frost.

If you use store-bought parsnips, remove the wax coating that is sometimes applied to them—otherwise, you'll have a waxy mess. Scrape and peel thoroughly.

> *6 lbs. parsnips*
> *1 gallon water*
> *2½ lbs. sugar or 3 lbs. honey*
> *10 bruised peppercorns (optional)*
> *zest and juice of 3 oranges*
> *juice and zest of 2 large lemons or 3 tsps. acid blend*
> *1 tsp. yeast nutrient*
> *¼ tsp. tannin*
> *1 Campden tablet, crushed (optional)*
> *½ tsp. pectic enzyme*
> *1 packet Montrachet or sherry yeast*

Scrub the parsnips well, cutting off the tops and the root ends. Chop, slice or shred into the cool water, then heat. SIMMER, do not boil, for 45 minutes.

Remove the zest from the citrus fruit (no white pith), and squeeze the juice. Place the zest in a small nylon straining bag in the bottom of the primary fermenter.

Strain the parsnips (and peppercorns, if you used them) from the water. You can use the parsnips for food if you choose.

Remove about a quart of the water to add back later if you don't have enough. It's hard to say how much you will have lost in steam while cooking. Add the sugar or the honey, and simmer until the sugar is dissolved. If using honey, simmer 10–15 minutes, stirring, and skim any scum.

Pour the hot water into a sanitized primary fermenter over the zest. Add the fruit juices. (You can reserve a bit of the orange juice and extra vegetable water to start the yeast later, if you like.) Check to see if you have a gallon of must. If not, make it up with the reserved water. Add yeast nutrient, tannin, and acid blend if you didn't use lemons. Cover, and attach an air lock. Let the must cool, and add the Campden tablet, if you choose to use one. Twelve hours after the Campden tablet, add the pectic enzyme. If you don't use the tablet, merely wait until the must cools down to add the pectic enzyme. Twenty-four hours later, check the PA and add the yeast.

Stir daily. In two weeks or so, check the PA. Lift out the bag of zest and let it drain back into the container. Do not squeeze. Discard the zest. Let the wine settle, and rack it into a secondary fermenter. Bung and fit with an air lock. Rack as necessary in the next six months or so. Check the PA. When it ferments out, bottle it. I prefer this wine dry. You can sweeten the wine if you like before bottling by adding stabilizer and 2 to 4 ounces of sugar syrup per gallon.

Keep for a year before drinking. If you add one pound of raisins, you'll get a sherry-like wine.

☙MAGICIAN TURNIP WINE☙

To be honest, you might not like this wine, though many people do. It has a sort of peppery taste, but others say it tastes like cabbage. Either way I like it.

One of my favorite magicians, Arthur Murata, had a lemon and a turnip in his act. They were easier to care for than a rabbit. At one point during the act, the turnip would appear unexpectedly. "Oh," he'd say innocently, "I didn't think that would turn up." Arthur is still notorious for his puns.

As with parsnips, store-bought turnips and rutabagas may come with a waxy coating that must be removed. Scraping and peeling is the only way to do it. Get young, fresh turnips and rutabagas for this wine.

6 lbs. turnips or rutabagas
1 gallon water
2½ lbs. sugar or 3 lbs. honey
zest and juice of 3 oranges
juice and zest of 2 large lemons or 3 tsps. acid blend
1 tsp. yeast nutrient

¼ tsp. tannin
1 Campden tablet, crushed (optional)
½ tsp. pectic enzyme
1 packet champagne or sherry yeast

Scrub the turnips well, cutting off the tops and the root ends. Chop or slice them into the cool water, then heat. SIMMER, do not boil, for 45 minutes.

Remove the zest from the citrus fruit (no white pith), and squeeze the juice. Place the zest in a small nylon straining bag in the bottom of the primary fermenter.

Strain the turnips (and peppercorns, if you used them) from the water. You can use the parsnips for food if you choose.

Remove about a quart of the water to add back later if you don't have enough. It's hard to say how much you will have lost in steam while cooking. Add the sugar or the honey, and simmer until the sugar is dissolved. If using honey, simmer 10–15 minutes, stirring, and skim any scum.

Pour the hot water into a sanitized primary fermenter over the zest. Add the fruit juices. (You can reserve a bit of the orange juice and extra vegetable water to start the yeast later, if you like.) Check to see if you have a gallon of must. If not, make it up with the reserved water. Add yeast nutrient, tannin, and acid blend if you didn't use lemons. Cover, and attach an air lock. Let the must cool, and add the Campden tablet, if you choose to use one. Twelve hours after the Campden tablet, add the pectic enzyme. If you don't use the tablet, merely wait until the must cools down to add the pectic enzyme. Twenty-four hours later, check the PA and add the yeast.

Stir daily. In two weeks or so, check the PA. Lift out the bag of zest and let it drain back into the container. Do not squeeze. Discard the zest. Let the wine settle, and rack it into a secondary fermenter. Bung and fit with an air lock. Rack as necessary in the next six months or so. Check the PA. When it ferments out, bottle it. I prefer this wine dry. You can sweeten the wine if you like before bottling by adding stabilizer and 2 to 4 ounces of sugar syrup per gallon.

You can decide if this wine is magic or not!

☞ONION WINE☜

Truth be told I have never made this. Some people say it's interesting and good for marinating meat. Onions do have some sugar in them. I'm throwing it in for the daredevils. I am told that you can also make garlic wine. It's a free country.

½ lb. onions
½ lb. potatoes OR carrots
½–1 lb. golden raisins
1 gallon water
2½ lbs. sugar or 3 lbs. honey
juice and zest of 2 large lemons or 3 tsps. acid blend
1 tsp. yeast nutrient
½ tsp. pectic enzyme
1 packet champagne or sherry yeast

Soak the raisins overnight. Chop them and put them in a nylon straining bag with the zest from the citrus fruit. Place the bag in the bottom of a primary fermenter. Squeeze the juice from the fruit.

Scrub the vegetables well and cut off the tops and the root ends. Leave the peels on the onions. Chop or slice them into the cool water, then heat. SIMMER, do not boil, for 45 minutes.

Strain the vegetables from the water. You can use the vegetables for food if you choose.

Remove about a quart of the water to add back later if you don't have enough. It's hard to say how much you will have lost in steam while cooking. Add the sugar or the honey, and simmer until the sugar is dissolved. If using honey, simmer 10–15 minutes, stirring, and skim any scum.

Pour the hot water into a sanitized primary fermenter over the zest and raisins. Add the fruit juices. (You can reserve a bit of the orange juice and extra vegetable water to start the yeast later, if you like.) Check to see if you have a gallon of must. If not, make it up with the reserved water. Add yeast nutrient, tannin, and acid blend if you didn't use lemons. Cover, and attach an air lock. Let the must cool, and add the Campden tablet, if you choose to use one. Twelve hours after the Campden tablet, add the pectic enzyme. If you don't use the tablet, merely wait until the must cools down to add the pectic enzyme. Twenty-four hours later, check the PA and add the yeast.

Stir daily. In two weeks or so, check the PA. Lift out the bag of zest and raisins and let it drain back into the container. Do not squeeze. Discard the zest and raisins. Let the wine settle, and rack it into a secondary fermenter. Bung and fit with an air lock. Rack as necessary in the next six months or so. Check the PA. When it ferments out, bottle it. My instincts suggest that this wine is best dry. Leave it in the bottle for at least a year.

> NOTE: Winter squash or pumpkin makes an interesting wine, but it might be an acquired taste. Follow the carrot wine recipe; instead of peppercorns, use 5 or 6 fresh cinnamon sticks, NOT cinnamon powder. Pare the rind from the squash carefully before simmering.
>
> I've tried zucchini and hated it. No one I know really liked it, although my partner claimed to be able to tolerate it. Might be his Norwegian blood.

⟆PEA POD WINE⟆

If you have a large garden, you might want to try pea pod wine, after you finish shucking the peas. Snap beans, snow peas, and sugar snap peas can also be used, as well as any green leafed vegetable, if you want to experiment. The wine isn't to everyone's taste, but what the heck.

There was a British comedy show called *Good Neighbors* in the United States and *The Good Life* in Britain, about a couple of people who prided themselves on self-sufficiency. One of the staple jokes on the show was pea pod burgundy. It was shown as white and cloudy, but the characters drank it regularly. I wish the writers could have had the decency to call it pea pod Chablis, or something besides burgundy, a red wine. It would have been just as funny. Humph. Our recipe will go into the world unadorned, unbowed, and quite clear.

1 gallon water
3–4 lbs. pea pods, snap beans, or snap peas
2½ lbs. sugar or 3 lbs. light honey
3 tsp. acid blend
1 tsp. yeast nutrient

½ tsp. tannin
1 Campden tablet, crushed (optional)
1 tsp. pectic enzyme
1 packet champagne yeast

Rinse the pea pods or bean pods well. Put them in the cool water and turn on the heat. Simmer for about 10 minutes in the water, then lift them out and put them in the nylon straining bag and place in a sanitized primary fermenter.

Add the honey or sugar to the water and boil, skimming if necessary.

Pour the hot sugar water over the nylon straining bag.

Add yeast nutrient, tannin, and acid blend if you didn't use lemons. Let the must cool, and add the Campden tablet, if you choose to use one. Cover and fit with an air lock. Twelve hours after the Campden tablet, add the pectic enzyme. If you don't use the tablet, merely wait until the must cools down to add the pectic enzyme. Twenty-four hours later, check the PA and add the yeast.

Stir daily. In two weeks or so, check the PA. Lift out the bag of pea pods and let it drain back into the container. Do not squeeze. Discard the pea pods. Let the wine settle, and rack it into a secondary fermenter. Bung and fit with an air lock. Rack as necessary in the next six months or so. Check the PA. When it ferments out, bottle it. Keep for one year, and see how you like it. Do not call it burgundy.

A TRUE STORY

A friend of mine and I were once giving a demonstration about making home brew and homemade wines. Of course we brought samples.

People tried the dark ale and the light ale, and the stout disappeared entirely. The raspberry wine was well on its way to gone, but no one would touch the carrot. Too weird.

But it's good, I insisted. I knew for a fact that some of these very people had eaten Spam Mousse only a few years before. How could they be afraid of mere carrot wine?

Then a very brave woman stepped forth and tried the carrot wine. She exclaimed with pleasure. In five minutes it was gone, after the rest of the room rushed to try it.

Moral: If your audience contains no classy people, hire a ringer.

CHAPTER EIGHT

Herb, Flower, Seed, and Grain Wines

On a hot summer evening, there's nothing quite like a glass of chilled mint wine. Dandelion wine in the winter brings back some of the promise of spring, and basil wine reminds me that summer will come again. Caraway seed wine makes simple cheese and crackers seem more of a celebration of the richness of life.

Herb, flower, seed, and grain wines are usually made light and dry and are best served as aperitif or social wines. The flavors are very pleasant but usually too distinctive for the table. Although I rarely make more than a gallon of a kind at a time, they are an important part of my cellar.

I have a garden and grow fresh herbs and flowers; however, there is no reason not to try the dried variety. If you want to try using dried herbs, make sure they are (and this will sound a little silly) FRESH dried herbs. Do not use the can of dried parsley Aunt Hilda left you in her will. Do not use dried herbs that have faded in color or lost their scent. If it smells like musty hay, it will taste like musty hay. Co-ops are a good place to buy dried herbs cheaply and in bulk, where you can smell them to see if they are fresh and have flavor.

HERBS

Particularly recommended herbs are parsley, pineapple sage, regular sage, basil (particularly the purple basils, which come out pink), oregano, thymes in all their varieties, lemon balm, mints in all their varieties, and sweet woodruff, the herb in May Wine. I also recommend trying rosemary, bay leaves, catnip, dill, hyssop, and marjoram.

Not recommended are chives, garlic chives, or any herb you cannot identify for sure. Always make sure you know EXACTLY what you are working with. Check herb and weed and wildflower books to make sure you are not using something that could be poisonous. Some medicinal herbs are OK in small amounts, but not in the large amounts you would be using in winemaking. When in doubt, DON'T.

FLOWERS

Some flowers are poisonous. Don't take chances. Be very careful about what you are picking.

In all flower recipes, gather the flowers after the morning dew has dried off but before the heat of the day has set in. Remove all green parts. Use only the blossoms. Lavender is an exception to this rule; the stems and leaves are also very fragrant. Roses sometimes have a bitter white part where the stem connects to the flower. Be sure to snip this part off.

Recommended flowers are dandelions, elderflowers, rose petals, lavender, chamomile, nasturtiums, calendula (pot marigolds), apple blossoms, citrus blossoms, pansies, Johnny-jump-ups, violets, day lilies, borage, broom, goldenrod (honest!), hawthorn, honeysuckle, and primrose.

Poisonous flowers include most lilies (except day lilies), rhododendrons, azaleas, aconite, buttercups, clematis, crocuses, daffodils, delphiniums, lily of the valley, lupin, peonies, and poppies. There are more poisonous flowers than not. I have consulted several lists, and I have concluded that the only flowers I can safely recommend are the ones I have mentioned above. Some lists say, for instance, that lilacs are poisonous, while others say they are fine. I would rather err on the side of caution, especially with wildflowers.

Allergies should also be considered. I never make elderflower wine because the blossoms make me sneeze. However, most people have no ill effects with elderflower wine, and it has been popular for centuries.

When gathering herbs and flowers in the wild, be sure it is legal to gather in the spot you want to gather in. Don't rely on a vague memory. Find out for sure. Don't pick wildflowers that are protected or rare. If they are on private property, ask permission. That might be someone else's favorite dandelion patch! On the other hand, the owner might well be thrilled that a) you asked, and b) you want to pick the dandelions.

When picking, be sure you know WHAT you are picking. I cannot emphasize this enough.

Don't destroy other plants in your zeal to get at the plants you want. Be nice to Mother Nature. Be sure, too, that no one has either sprayed the area with pesticide or dumped toxic waste there. If you see old fertilizer bags or oilcans around, don't pick in that area. Old nuclear waste containers are also a turnoff.

Do not use flowers that have been dried for the decorative dried flower trade. You don't know where those flowers have been, how they have been handled, or what has been sprayed on them. Use only unsprayed flowers that you have dried yourself, or which are sold in herb shops or as dried tea meant for human consumption. Chamomile is a commonly available dried flower. Dried dandelion or elderflowers are sold in wine supply shops. Dried rose hips, which are really a fruit, are sometimes sold as tea.

For a gallon of wine, I use four to six cups of freshly picked herbs or flower petals, depending on the strength of the herb and its bulk. The herbs usually weigh about a pound. Some old recipes recommend as much as two pounds of an herb, like parsley or balm, but that sounds like far too much these days, and I suspect the result would be a strong medicinal wine. Of course, you might just adore it, who knows?

If you are using dried herbs and flowers, use two ounces. I am counting caraway seeds and the like as herbs.

I have used some herbal teas for flavoring wines, with great success. Sample the tea as a hot tea, then let it cool and see if you still like it. Some of the Celestial Seasonings teas I've used are Red Zinger, Roastaroma, Peppermint, and Sleepytime. Use one to two ounces of the tea, and steep it as you would for dried herbs.

The quantity of sugar used in making these wines is going to be a little more than you are used to, because there is no sugar in flowers or herbs. These wines are not usually drunk with a meal, so I make them with a high alcohol content so they will keep longer.

⌘BASIC HERB OR FLOWER RECIPE⌘

4–6 cups, packed lightly, of herbs or flowers
1 gallon water
3 lbs. sugar or 3½ lbs. honey
1 tsp. yeast nutrient
⅛ tsp. tannin
no pectic enzyme
3 tsps. acid blend or juice of 2 fresh lemons
1 Campden tablet, crushed (optional)
1 packet champagne or Montrachet yeast

Rinse off fresh herbs or flowers under cold running water to remove dust, dirt, insects, etc. For flower wines, use only the petals. Discard any green parts. For herb wines, remove any dead leaves or other plants that have gotten mixed in. For dried herbs, just make sure there are no pebbles or twigs mixed in.

Put the herbs or flowers into a 2 quart saucepan with a tight-fitting lid. Pour a quart of the water over them. Bring the water to a simmer, put on the lid, and turn the heat off. Let this mixture steep for one to two hours, or as many as six, depending on how strong or subtle you want the flavor to be. Remember, the flavor and fragrance of flowers are delicate, so don't steep the flowers too long.

In the meantime, boil the rest of the water with the sugar or honey (or half of each). Skim, if necessary, put a lid on it, and allow it to cool.

Strain the quart of herb water into a sanitized primary fermenter. Add the sugar/honey water, yeast nutrient, tannin, and acid or lemon juice. Add the Campden tablet after the mixture has cooled, if you choose to use one. Cover and fit with an air lock.

Twenty-four hours later, add the yeast.

Ferment 3–5 days in the primary fermenter until the PA reaches 3 to 4 percent, then rack the wine into a glass secondary fermenter, bung, and fit with an air lock.

Ferment the wine another month. Rack it again, then wait three to six months until fermented out, and bottle it. Stabilize and sweeten if you like. It's drinkable anywhere from three months to a year later, depending on the herb or flower. Dandelion takes a full year, other flower wines take less time. Herbal wines are usually ready to drink within three to six months. These wines usually keep very well, but you must be extra careful to keep them from light.

∾MELLOW MINT WINE∾

Here's my favorite herb wine. Mint is an example of an herb that offers a wonderful taste with a minimum amount of leaves. Any kind of mint will do, but apple mint and orange mint seem the best to me. I made spearmint wine once, and it tasted hauntingly like a popular chewing gum.

Use this wine in the summer, chilled in a wine cooler, or over ice with some extra sprigs of mint in it. I've used it as a base for punch many a time, even in winter. You can also use it instead of white wine in fruit cup. Delicious!

With this wine, the ferment has a tendency to stick or stop. See the troubleshooting section in the back of the book if this happens. Keep it warm while fermenting, and don't overload it with sugar.

4 cups, packed lightly, of fresh mint
1 gallon water
1 tsp. yeast nutrient
¼ tsp. tannin
3 tsps. acid blend
3 lbs. sugar or 3½ lbs. honey
1 packet champagne or Montrachet yeast

Follow the general method for herb wine on the previous page. Don't steep the mint too long—no more than an hour or so is needed. I use the acid blend in this recipe because I don't want a citrus taste. The wine is more versatile without it, I think, but you can use lemon if you want. I like this a bit sweet, but be very careful to keep it from coming out *too* sweet. I have added a tiny bit of green food coloring to this wine upon occasion, because sometimes it comes out a sickly yellow green that needs some help in the form of a drop or two. Keep a year before drinking.

☙RYE NOT KUMMEL WINE☙

If anyone in your family is from eastern Europe, you may already be familiar with the taste of this wine. Kummel, or caraway, as we know it in this country, is a popular flavoring for schnapps or sweet liqueurs in many European countries. In this country it ends up in rye bread and sauerkraut, but there are many other uses for this abundant seed. It is supposed to be very good for the digestion. Be sure to use fresh caraway.

2 ozs. caraway seed (kummel)
1 gallon water
1 tsp. yeast nutrient
¼ tsp. tannin
3 tsps. acid blend or juice of 2 fresh lemons
3 lbs. sugar or 3½ lbs. honey
1 Campden tablet, crushed (optional)
1 packet champagne or Montrachet yeast

Follow the general herb and flower recipe method on page 163. An alternative way to make this wine is to soak the seed for about four hours in a half cup of warmed brandy or vodka to extract the flavor, then strain out the seeds. You can either include the seeds in a fine straining bag for the initial fermentation, or throw them into a batch of bread.

Bottle the wine dry or slightly sweetened, depending on your taste. This keeps well.

Serve this wine warm, like sake, or very cold, as a social drink. Some people won't like it; others will rave about it. You never know. Other seeds you can use are dill and cumin.

☙BRADBURY DANDELION WINE☙

Ray Bradbury wrote a book called *Dandelion Wine*, which had a profound effect on me as a teen. It changed the way I read and the way I wrote. He also stepped on my foot in an elevator once, but I'm sure it was an accident, and no harm was done. Here's my chance to thank him for his contributions to my imagination.

6–8 cups dandelions, packed lightly
1 gallon water
3 lbs. sugar or 3½ lbs. honey
1 tsp. yeast nutrient
¼ tsp. tannin
3 tsps. acid blend or juice of 2 fresh lemons
1 Campden tablet, crushed (optional)
1 packet champagne or Montrachet yeast

Pick the dandelions in an area that is not polluted with car or dog exhaust. This might not be easy, because dandelions love disturbed ground like roadsides. Be very sure the dandelions haven't been sprayed with herbicide.

Gather these and all flowers when they are in full bloom and the dew of the morning has dried. That's when the fragrance is best.

They are kind of tedious to pick, as they are low to the ground, but put on some knee pads and go to it. The wine is worth it.

Most people don't realize how fragrant dandelions are. They are my favorite flower.

After you pick them, remove all the green parts, especially the stem, which is bitter. Process them as soon as you can, without washing, to preserve the delicate fragrance. The wine will not be yellow. A lot of people think it should be, but it isn't. In fact, the color is really not very wonderful at all. The taste is.

Keep dandelion wine a year before you drink it. I like it dry dry dry. Stabilize and sweeten if you think you'll feel different about it. Read Mr. Bradbury's books, but be careful about sharing an elevator with him.

GRAIN WINES

These go back a long way. Back in the olden days, if there were a peasant with some extra grain and honey that didn't go into beer or holiday bread, she would put it into wine as a good way of making festive use of the surplus before the Cossacks got it.

Beer and wine not only helped keep disease down by being safe to drink but they were also good medicine and a high-caloric food for people who were ill. In times of famine, beer and wine would satisfy more stomachs than gruel would, although the hangovers must have been terrible. Hmm, maybe that was the point. After a couple of days of imbibing, no one would WANT to eat.

Many of these wines are flavored with flowers, spices, and fruits.

Another use for grains, which we will get into later, is to use them to give body to other wines, as well as give them more color. In this section I will stick to very simple wines. In making some of the following recipes, you'll gain an appreciation of what grain can do for your wines, and what the flavors and colors are like.

QUALITY TIME!

You see a lot of ads and signs these days saying things like Quality Mattress Sale! or Quality Used Cars. My question is always, what kind of quality? Good, bad, indifferent? Quality doesn't just mean *good* quality. It is a noun that can be qualified many different ways.

The question applies to whole grains as well. Allow me to warn you that whole grains go rancid. That is why milling and white bread were invented. Take off that bothersome bran and pesky germ, and the grain keeps better because nothing can go bad. Much of the nutrition goes down the drain or to the pigs, but so what?

It's important to buy only good whole or freshly cracked grains to make these wines. Buy the *best* quality you can get. Don't pick up a box from an obscure corner of the grocery; it'll be stale for sure. Go to a co-op or whole foods store and buy grains by the pound. It will be fresher and cheaper.

Take a good sniff of the grain in the bin if you can. If it's fresh, it will smell great. If it's stale or even rancid, you'll know by the smell of rancid oil, or a metallic smell. If it doesn't smell good, don't buy it.

If you live in an area that doesn't have a food co-op, you can buy some pretty good brands in the health food section of the grocery, and you can also order whole grains by mail. Arrowhead Mills makes some nice products, and they date their packages, too. Alternatively, you can go to the local feed store and buy grain there, if they will sell it in small quantities.

Wine supply places don't generally carry grain unless they sell

> **NOTE:** In almost any of these recipes you can use lemon juice and zest instead of the acid blend. You can also add the juice and zest of two or three oranges. This livens up the flavor quite a bit. It's also very traditional. Just add the orange juice and zests into the straining bag before you pour the hot sugar water over everything, and be sure to use pectic enzyme.

beermaking supplies as well. If they do carry grain, it is generally expensive and might not always work for wine, especially if you pick up something like "chocolate" malted barley! However, the lighter toastings of barley, assuming they are very fresh, will work very well and will color your wine nicely at the same time.

Just be sure to buy *good* quality whole grains for your wine and you won't go wrong.

There are even some cereals you can use, like Wheat Chex and Shredded Wheat, to help make wine. I'll show you how to use these cereals and toast to help things along.

I advocate using whole grains, cracked or rolled whole grains, and the like because of the flavor and body these foods have, though we don't want the starch they release. Using whole wheat flour WILL NOT WORK! Sometimes you can get away with a coarse meal, but not flour. Save it for bread.

So, get thee to the whole foods store, get some supplies, and let's get back to basics!

✸CRACKED WHEAT WINE✸

This one takes some advance preparation, but it's offset by the cheapness of the wine! Use this as a social wine.

2 lbs. cracked wheat (about four cups)
1 gallon water
1 lb. golden raisins (optional, but nice)
3 lbs. sugar or 3½ lbs. light honey
4 tsps. acid blend or juice and zest of 3 large lemons
juice and zest of 2–3 oranges (optional)
½ tsp. tannin
1 tsp. yeast nutrient

1 Campden tablet, crushed (optional)
1 tsp. pectic enzyme (if you use the oranges)
1 packet champagne or sherry yeast

The day before: Preheat your oven to 375–400°F. Spread the wheat out in a clean cookie pan or pans, and bake it for about 10 minutes, stirring it and turning it over with a spatula every couple of minutes. You want it to smell toasty and to be a light brown (but darker than it was originally). Be careful, because it is easy to burn.

Take the wheat out of the oven, stir it all again, and let it cool down.

After it is cool, put it in a clean glass or steel bowl with the chopped or ground raisins and enough of the water to cover.

The next day: Put it all, including the citrus zest if you are using it, in a *fine* nylon straining bag, and place it into a sanitized primary fermenter. Pour in the soaking water. Heat the rest of the water and the sugar or honey to boiling, skim if necessary, and pour over the nylon straining bag. Add the orange juice if you are using it. Add the acid blend, yeast nutrient, and tannin. Cover.

After it cools down, add the Campden tablet, if you choose to use one. Cover and fit with an air lock. Twelve hours after the Campden tablet, add the pectic enzyme. If you don't use the tablet, merely wait until the must cools down to add the pectic enzyme.

Twenty-four hours later, take the PA and add the yeast. If you want to, you can give the yeast a nudge by starting it in boiled, cooled orange juice.

Stir daily. After a couple of weeks, when the PA is down to 3 to 4 percent, take out the bag and let it drain. Do not squeeze. Discard the grain. Let the wine settle, then rack it into a secondary fermenter. Bung and fit with an air lock.

Rack once or twice in the next six months or so, depending on how much deposit it throws. It might take more time to clear. When it does, rack it out and bottle it. If you want a sweeter

NOTE: You can make this a very strong wine by adding another half pound of sugar to it. Wait until the PA reading is down to 6 percent or so, and boil the sugar with a pint of water and cool. Add the syrup to the wine, then continue the fermentation.

wine, stabilize and sweeten it, then bottle. This keeps well, and is very useful for blending.

☙BARE BARLEY WINE❧

Barley water is traditionally drunk by English women to keep their complexions lovely. Barley wine is traditionally drunk by English men who want to get a buzz on. This would be a very strong beer if you made it with malt instead of sugar and added hops. However, we are making barley wine. The lemon seems to be traditional, and I like the wine better with it.

DO NOT USE PEARLED BARLEY! Use whole barley or cracked whole barley if you can get it.

1 lb. whole or cracked barley
3 lbs. sugar or 3½ lbs. light honey
½ lb. golden raisins (optional, but nice)
zest and juice of 2 large fresh lemons or 4 tsps. acid blend
zest and juice of 2–3 oranges (optional)
½ tsp. tannin
1 tsp. yeast nutrient
1 Campden tablet, crushed (optional)
½ tsp. pectic enzyme (if you use the oranges)
1 packet champagne or sherry yeast

You can toast the barley as in the recipe for Cracked Wheat Wine on page 168, if you like. If not, rinse it well, chop the raisins, put them in a clean glass or steel bowl with enough of the water to cover, and soak them overnight.

The next day put it all, including the citrus zests if you are using them, in a *fine* nylon straining bag, and place it into a sanitized primary fermenter. Pour in the soaking water. Heat the rest of the water and the sugar or honey to boiling, skim if neces-

NOTE: As mentioned above, you can buy or make barley that is toasted to different degrees to make this wine. The darker the barley, the darker the wine. However, be very cautious in your experiments to avoid any burnt taste. What works in beer is not as easily masked in wine, since we aren't using heavily flavored malts and hops.

sary, and pour it over the nylon straining bag. Add the orange juice if you are using it. Add the acid blend, yeast nutrient, and tannin. Cover and fit with an air lock.

After it cools down, add the Campden tablet, if you choose to use one. Twelve hours after the Campden tablet, add the pectic enzyme if you are using the orange juice. If you don't use the tablet, merely wait until the must cools down to add the pectic enzyme.

Twenty-four hours later, take the PA and add the yeast. If you want to, you can give the yeast a nudge by starting it in boiled, cooled orange juice.

Stir daily. After a couple of weeks, when the PA is down to 3 to 4 percent, take out the bag and let it drain. Do not squeeze. Discard the grain. Let the wine settle, then rack it into a secondary fermenter. Bung and fit with an air lock.

Rack once or twice in the next six months or so, depending on how much deposit it throws. It might take more time to clear.

NOTE: As with the wheat wine, you can increase the alcohol content by adding more sugar halfway through. Follow the directions on page 169.

☙NOT SAKE RICE WINE❧

This is not sake, which is made differently. People will want to call it sake, but resist them. You have to be a Japanese peasant or a skilled sake brewer or a multimillion dollar sake-making corporation to make it properly. Honest.

2 lbs. long grain brown rice
3 lbs. sugar or 3½ lbs. light honey
4 tsps. acid blend or zest and juice of 3 large lemons
1 lb. golden raisins
1 tsp. pectic enzyme
1 tsp. yeast nutrient
½ tsp. tannin
1 Campden tablet, crushed (optional)
1 packet champagne or sherry yeast

Rinse the rice well, chop the raisins, and put everything in a clean glass or steel bowl with enough of the water to cover it. Soak everything overnight.

The next day put it all in a *fine* nylon straining bag and place it into a sanitized primary fermenter. Pour in the soaking water. Heat the rest of the water and the sugar or honey to boiling, skim if necessary, and pour over the nylon straining bag. Add the acid blend, yeast nutrient, and tannin. Cover and fit with an air lock.

After it cools down, add the Campden tablet, if you choose to use one. Twenty-four hours later, take the PA and add the yeast. If you want to, you can give the yeast a nudge by starting it in boiled, cooled orange juice.

Stir daily. After a couple of weeks, when the PA is down to 3 to 4 percent, take out the bag and let it drain. Do not squeeze. Discard the grain. Let the wine settle, then rack it into a secondary fermenter. Bung and fit with an air lock.

Rack once or twice in the next six months or so, depending on how much deposit it throws. It might take more time to clear. This wine keeps well.

ᡂWE CALL IT MAIZE WINEᡂ

This wine is for my Native American friends. There was once a corn oil commercial on television in which a "beautiful Indian maiden" would solemnly intone, "We call it maize," when speaking of corn. We used to howl with laughter at the poor woman. No Native American we knew called it maize.

My British friends were merely puzzled, because to them the word *corn* refers to wheat, and yes, they do call corn maize. Having an international assortment of friends is always entertaining.

I once followed a recipe for cornmeal wine. It was terrible. I now suspect, since it was a European book, that the recipe really meant for the winemaker to use the coarse Italian polenta style cornmeal, rather than the finely ground stuff I tried to use.

You can buy cracked corn at feed stores, stores that sell bird feed, and some co-ops. Otherwise, I wouldn't try this wine unless you want to try using the coarsest polenta meal.

2 lbs. cracked corn
3 lbs. sugar or 3½ lbs. light honey
4 tsps. acid blend or zest and juice of 2 large lemons
zest and juice of 2–3 oranges (optional)
1 lb. golden raisins
1 tsp. yeast nutrient
½ tsp. tannin
1 Campden tablet, crushed (optional)
½ tsp. pectic enzyme (if you use the citrus)
1 packet champagne or sherry yeast

Rinse the corn well, checking for any pebbles, etc. Chop the raisins, and put everything in a clean glass or steel bowl with enough of the water to cover. Soak overnight.

THE NEXT DAY: Put it all in a *fine* nylon straining bag and put into a sanitized primary fermenter. Pour in the soaking water. Heat the rest of the water and the sugar or honey to boiling, skim if necessary, and pour over the nylon straining bag. Add the orange juice if you are using it. Add the acid blend, yeast nutrient, and tannin. Cover and fit with an air lock.

After it cools down, add the Campden tablet, if you choose to use one. Twelve hours after the Campden tablet, add the pectic enzyme if you are using the orange juice. If you don't use the tablet, merely wait until the must cools down to add the pectic enzyme.

Twenty-four hours later, take the PA and add the yeast. If you want to, you can give the yeast a nudge by starting it in boiled, cooled orange juice.

Stir daily. After a couple of weeks, when the PA is down to 3 to 4 percent, take out the bag and let it drain. Do not squeeze. Discard the grain. Let the wine settle, then rack it into a secondary fermenter. Bung and fit with an air lock.

Rack once or twice in the next six months or so. This wine is best dry.

These are just basic recipes. I haven't made amaranth wine, or quinoa, oat, or rye wine, but I don't see why you couldn't, following one of the recipes above. They are all pretty much alike. I've seen recipes using rolled wheat and rye, but I've never made them, either.

I suspect oat wine would have a bit TOO much body, as would flax or chia wine. There are some beer recipes that use a bit of oatmeal to thicken them up, though.

NOTE: You can use half a cup of Wheat Chex or Shredded Wheat or a piece or two of toast per gallon to give a wine a little color. Make the toast the usual way (don't use butter!) or put the cereal in a fine mesh nylon straining bag the first day or so of the primary ferment. It will give the wine a nice color and a little body. The darker the toast, the darker the wine. This technique is especially nice for coloring a sherry-type wine. Don't leave the cereal or toast in for more than a day or two. Eggs and hash browns are right out!

People used to use toast to float the bread yeast they used in home-made wines. Of course the toast sank as it got wet, but it also provided nourishment for the yeast. I don't recommend this use for the toast—I merely mentioned it for its historical interest.

PART THREE

Advanced Winemaking, Or The Big Time

CHAPTER NINE

Advanced Techniques and Equipment

This section deals with more complicated wines, but nothing you can't handle, I assure you! You now know the basic steps of home winemaking and the basic flavors you can achieve. You know what an apple wine should taste like, as well as raspberry, carrot, herb, and flower wines.

Now we will start to play around. Think about those basic wines you have made. Invite a few friends over, open some bottles, sip, taste, and think.

What would happen if you combined that apple that was a bit sweet with the carrot that was a bit dry? Mix up a glass and try it. What do you think? Is it better? Is there more balance? Is it simply insipid? Less apple, more carrot? More apple, less carrot?

When you bottled your wines, I hope you followed my advice and bottled several different wines at the same time, creating some Mystery Wines with the leftovers. Try a few of those.

What have you got? A few mistakes, for sure, but maybe some surprising successes. Go back through your notes.

Say one bottle is one-third cherry and two-thirds raspberry. The cherry may have seemed harsh when you bottled it, but then smoothed out delightfully later. Say the raspberry had good full flavor but was thin. Together in this one bottle, what are they like now? Is it a happy marriage? Is it OK, but not something you'd try again except for the luck of the draw at bottling time?

If you like it, try to think why, and keep good notes.

Blending is an art. In the big wineries, blending helps balance the final product into a wine with a predictable taste and body. Say the grapes from one vineyard tend to be thin and acid with a high alcohol content, while those from another vineyard are lush and fruity, with low alcohol. Do they bottle the results as two products, one thin and acid, and the other lush and fruity? No, they blend them to achieve a nice middle ground at 12 percent alcohol. They can make much more money that way. They even blend various vintages, which evens out the whims of Mother Nature from year to year. Certain types of grapes must be used to some extent for the different varieties of wine, but they can mix good grapes with indifferent grapes of another variety, and still call the result a Cabernet, as long as they stay within certain guidelines.

In the smaller wineries, blending serves a similar purpose, but with some different twists. If one part of the vineyard turns out grapes with less sugar and flavor and another part turns out loud, full-bodied ones, blending might save the day. Or the vineyard might decide to sell the insipid grapes and bottle only the wine from the better grapes and hope they mellow out.

More typically, they will blend GOOD kinds of wine together, allowing for the restrictions of vintage, of course, to produce an even better wine.

You, as the proprietor of your little winery, can do any of the above and more! You can also enrich the basic wines you make with a little more fruit, or a little more sugar. You can add spices, herbs, flowers, a touch of citrus.

There is also another way. How about starting off with two kinds of fruits in the first place? All through the middle section I showed you a few options, adding some spices, using raisins, grape concentrate, or honey to make the wine fuller and richer. In this section, you can really go to town!

But first, there are a few things we ought to discover and reemphasize.

ACID

So far I've been giving you a set amount of acid to add to the various wines, and I will continue to do so. However, acid content varies considerably even within one kind of fruit, and you are much better off TESTING the acid content of the must with an acid test kit, and then ADJUSTING the acid level by either adding or subtracting acid.

Almost any wine supply place has acid test kits. They are readily available by mail, as well. They usually cost less than ten dollars. Follow the directions that come with the kit.

It is generally agreed that fruit wines should be at no more than about 0.60 percent, red grape wines 0.65 percent, white grape wines 0.75 percent, sherry 0.50 percent, port 0.50 percent, and champagne 0.75 percent.

There are some fruits with which it is easy to go over the mark: all currants, lemons, limes, rhubarb, and quinces. Pie cherries, gooseberries, wild plums, and raspberries are up there, too, but not as high.

To avoid having too much acid in a wine, you can limit the amount of high-acid fruit you use; use more water; use food-grade calcium carbonate (or *chalk*) to the must. You can use a high-acid fruit with a low-acid fruit, as well, in order to balance the acid.

Remember that it is always easier to *add* ingredients than to try to remove them once they've been added.

Personally, since I am lazy and hate extra steps, I simply limit how much of the high-acid fruits I use. This is easy, since I don't have access to huge amounts of currants or quinces where I live, though rhubarb wine is a lovely thing. Luckily, I prefer my rhubarb wine on the light side. I also like lemon and lime as flavorings, not as the major fruit in a wine.

Food-grade chalk is available at most wine supply stores or mail order supply houses. Adding chalk is not difficult—it is merely an extra step. You figure out how much acid there is in the must, and figure out how much chalk you must add. There is a limit to how much you can get away with, of course.

With *food-grade* chalk, the general idea is that using ¼ ounce per gallon (about 4 teaspoons) will subtract about 0.25 percent acid per gallon. It is best to use it before fermentation, when you must add the chalk to the must in a sanitized primary fermentation bin. Don't use more than an ounce of chalk per gallon. It takes about 24 hours to work, and you must stir every three to four hours. It will produce a lot of foam. Rack off the must into a clean container, leaving the sediment behind, and proceed with fermentation.

Most of the time, your test kit will tell you to add acid when making fruit and vegetable wines. Testing gives you more knowledge and control over your wines.

YEASTS

Once again, try using the various yeasts on the market, and find out which ones best suit the wines you make. You can't go really wrong, but you can certainly improve your product. Study books on grape wines, and learn the characteristics of the different yeasts to better match the various kinds to your fruit and vegetable wines. I especially encourage you to use mead yeasts, and port and sherry yeasts for those particular wines.

Keeping a variety of yeasts on hand isn't always practical, though the dry granular yeasts are easy to store and not very expensive. Getting a sudden windfall of red wine grapes and only having champagne yeast on hand is not a disaster, but having a more suitable red wine yeast would be better.

Some people like to culture their own yeasts, though it is not advised. It's like San Francisco sourdough bread. You can buy the starter, take it back to wherever you live, and make a batch of bread with it. It will come out with that wonderful San Francisco tang. The second batch will be weaker, and by the third batch, the local sourdough yeasts will have taken over the culture and the San Francisco yeasts will have died out.

Some wineries in California are experimenting with local wild yeasts to see what they get. I suppose you could, too, but be prepared for disappointments. Nonetheless, some mead makers and cider makers are enthusiastic about wild yeasts.

SANITATION AND CLEANLINESS

Don't get sloppy just because you think you know what you are doing. Remain in a Zenlike state of humbleness, appreciating Mother Nature and her urge to nurture yeast and fruit, while remembering that she also loves molds and vinegar entities just as much. Clean everything, and sanitize everything. Then, if you do slip up or take a chance in a moment of madness, it might not turn out too badly.

It is a good idea to get rid of the plastics you are using every once in a while and buy new ones. Look at your primary fermenters. Some grungy scratches here and there? What about your siphoning and racking tubes? Can you still see through them? What's that weird stuff along the side of that tube? How long has it been there?

You don't have to throw your old containers away. Recycle or reuse. They can still be useful as bins and planters in the garden, or for storing things like toys, extra clothes that are out of season, and hobby items like your prize-winning rubber band collection. If you turn a primary bin upside down and pad and cover it, you can even make a footstool or a small occasional table. No one will know what's under there!

Racking tubes are great to have in the trunk of a car to help out another motorist or winemaker who has been stranded. You can use them for siphoning rainwater out of a barrel. Tacked up horizontally at short intervals in the garage they make good holders for shovels, rakes, and the like. Use your imagination.

MORE EQUIPMENT AND SOME REFINEMENTS

If you want to make more than five gallons of wine at a time, all you really have to do is get a bigger primary fermenter and some more carboys.

If you are getting seriously serious and have the room, bigger vats are available in the small winery market. There are instruments and other items that are impractical on the scale of most home winemaking but which make sense in a larger operation, such as a club.

Some people stay with fruit wines, others branch out into grape wines. There's a whole world out there waiting to be explored. I don't have the room or the expertise to cover everything about it in this book, of course, but you can grow your own wine grapes, you know, even in northern and southern climes. Even a few vines can produce a nice quantity of wine. Consult your agricultural extension service.

Other books delve more seriously into the chemistry behind making wine. I've just given a general overview. The science of winemaking is fascinating. Check out the library at your local agricultural college for further information.

CHILLPROOFING

Commercial winemakers, as well as some serious amateurs, put their wines through a simple process called chillproofing. After the wine is racked, but before it is bottled, the wine is stored at a temperature just above freezing for a period of about two weeks. This allows part of the tartaric acid to precipitate out, and it helps to smooth high-acid wines. It also aids in stabilizing the wine.

If you live in a cold climate, chillproofing can be done in a cold part of the garage or basement at certain times of the year. Otherwise, you can use an old refrigerator.

It's a nice refinement, but not totally necessary. You will still make perfectly good wine without chillproofing.

FINING AND FILTERING

Two other things you should consider doing are fining and filtering your wine. Most of the commercial wineries do so, although some of the fancier labels don't.

Fining isn't strictly necessary. Peasants and home winemakers have gotten along without it for thousands of years. If you rack your wine well, bottle it properly, and drink it within a few years, your wine will be perfectly OK for home use.

However, many people feel that fining and filtering are a big help, even on the small home winemaking scale. They are certainly necessary if you are going to be entering wine competitions.

Fining involves adding a substance to the wine after the fermentation is finished. The substance soaks up sediment and impurities and sinks to the bottom of the wine with them. This helps stabilize the wine and clears out dead yeasts that can sometimes give your wine an off taste over time. The old books had many esoteric methods of fining, which sometimes took all the taste, as well as any sediment, out of the wine. Whenever you see a mention of egg whites or isinglass, or even ox blood, that's what they were talking about.

Isinglass, gelatin, silica soda, and bentonite are all substances used for fining. There are several commercial brands available, and they all come with instructions. The brands change, and might be available in all areas, so I won't go too much into the merits of each kind. Sparkolloid and PolyClar are two of the fairly common ones. They both should be removed by filtering, although it isn't strictly necessary with Sparkolloid, just better aesthetically.

Gelatine and bentonite do not have to be removed.

Some finings require tannin in order to react, but tannin is easily added.

Filtering on a small scale with gravity methods isn't very easy, and it can hurt your wine through oxidation if you take too long to do it. The old books describe some of these gravity methods. I don't think they are a good idea. The benefits aren't great enough to merit the trouble and risk.

For larger amounts of wine, there are many devices available on the market that involve hand pumps or carbon dioxide pressure tanks combined with filter pads that can remove amazingly small particles. If you have carefully racked, then fined, your wine, it won't take very long to go through the filtering procedure—including setting up and taking down. It will give you the "star bright" wine of wine competition dreams. The devices, like Vinamat and Polyrad, cost less than one hundred dollars.

Investigate the brands carefully and make sure you know what is in the pads, how much they cost, how easy they are to replace, etc., before you decide to buy.

Talk it over with your wine supply merchant and any winemakers you know. Everyone has a different opinion about filtering.

Up to a few years ago, some filter pads for some systems contained asbestos. This may or may not be a concern to you. I drink commercial wines, which at one point all used pads with asbestos and still may. I haven't keeled over yet, but what about later?

CASKS AND BARRELS

Ah, the images that come to mind when one says the word winery! Dark, mysterious barrels of aged wood bound by sturdy hoops lined up in some subterranean cavern lit by guttering bees-wax candles, perhaps graced by the silent presence of a hooded monk . . . secret passages to the throne room . . . men in lace jabots leaping from cask to cask with flashing swords . . . lurking anarchists conferring secretly, plotting to overthrow who knows what . . . lovers meeting at midnight for that precious stolen kiss . . . etc.

Yeah. But.

Barrels are large and expensive. They can go bad in a day once the wine is out of them. Any mold or vinegar is there to stay! They have to be treated very carefully, and you have to keep a serious eye on the wine, because both the alcohol and the water content evaporate. Buying used barrels is a tricky business, unless you know and trust the person you are buying them from.

You can buy small wooden barrels, but the evaporation problems gets worse the smaller they are. Nope, just not worth it, I would say.

If you merely want the oak taste you get from oak barrels, you can use oak chips, sticks, or a liquid extract in your red wines.

Or buy half an old whiskey cask at the plant nursery, turn it upside down in your cellar, put a candle in the middle and some little log seats around it and use it for atmosphere and a tasting table. Much less risk and work.

If you are really serious, then you'll just have to do it. Truth be told, using wine barrels is becoming more popular as more people get serious about small-scale winemaking. As the popularity of barrels grows, materials will get cheaper and methods will become more standardized.

GRAPE OR FRUIT CRUSHERS

If you plan to make a lot of grape or apple wine from scratch, year after year, you need a crusher. A grape crusher is different from an apple crusher. Buy the best one you can afford, and ask the advice of a clerk at your wine supply place, or someone else who knows. There are some cheap crushers on the market that do not work well. Always buy from a wine supply source rather than a garden catalog.

You can club together with friends to purchase one of these. Sometimes you can rent one from a local wine supply place, as well. A good crusher is a blessing if you are making more than ten gallons of grape or apple must at a time. Besides, its presence will save you from giving into the temptation to put the grapes in a big tub and stomp on them while singing charming European folk songs. Remember what happened to Lucy and Ethel?

FRUIT PRESS

There are also grape presses and apple presses. They press the juice from the fruit you just crushed! The cautions apply here as above.

Advanced Wines

Combination wines comprise single fruit or vegetable wines that are enhanced with spice, herbs, flowers, or citrus; duos (two fruits mixed in fairly equal proportion); tutti-fruttis (many fruits mixed together with one or two flavors dominating); and "generic" reds and whites, in which no single flavor dominates.

These are some of the types of wines we are going to explore next.

SPICES

I haven't really talked about spices until now because some people get a bit overenthused about them, and it's easy to spoil a wine by adding too much spice.

Spices offer a good means of enhancing a basic fruit wine. Usually these wines work better as an aperitif for casual sipping or on social occasions. It's truly impressive what you can come up with—there won't be anything in the wine stores like it, that's for sure.

From Roman times all the way up to Victorian times, many wines were heavily spiced if the host could afford it. Sometimes this was meant to show off the wealth of the host, since spices were exotic and expensive. Sometimes it was to cover up the fact that the wine was either inferior to start with or beginning to turn into vinegar.

People also thought of spices as medicines. Spices were usually added just before serving, although there are many old mead and fruit wine recipes that call for the addition of spices during fermentation. In one I found, I was amazed that the recipe writer remembered to include the apples for which the recipe was named. It seemed almost like an afterthought.

Spices give wine a feeling of warmth as well as flavor. In some of the stately homes and castles in northern Europe, anything that gave the feeling of warmth, even in the heat of summer, was welcome, I'm sure. Those thick stone walls hold in the cold for months.

Today we take spices for granted, and that's a pity. There is much history and flavor in them.

SPICE WINES

Mostly, I use spices to flavor a bland fruit or vegetable wine such as pear or apple. However, some people like to use spices to make single-flavor wines. To do so, follow the herb wine recipe given on page 163, but use only an ounce of the whole spice. Ginger is an exception; you need to use 4 to 8 ounces of the freshly grated root. Do not use powdered spices. They go stale easily and are hard to clear. Use fresh whole spices only.

To use spice as an added ingredient, bruise the whole spice with the flat of a sturdy knife blade and add it to the contents of the nylon straining bag. If you will not be using a nylon straining bag, heat the spice with the sugar and water, then strain the spice out before adding the yeast.

PEPPERCORNS

Peppercorns are wonderful. I learned how to use them in wine from a book by Mettja C. Roate published in 1963.

Ten bruised peppercorns do not so much add flavor as lend a warmth. I frequently leave them in the straining bag when making beet or carrot wine. I've read that pepper was used by moonshiners to warm up their product and make people think it was higher in alcohol than it actually was. If this is true, it probably also helped to mask the off flavors from bad distilling and no aging.

CASSIA

Cassia buds are another winner in my estimation. Cassia tastes like cinnamon. In the United States most cinnamon you encounter will be made from cassia buds. These buds add a hint of spice to blueberry, blackberry, and apple wine. I've also used them (ten to twenty or so at a time) in carrot and potato wine.

CINNAMON

Cinnamon bark can be used if you are sure it is fresh. Otherwise it tastes just like wood. It has a sharper, sweeter flavor than cassia. Warning: I have seen some cinnamon bark for sale in craft stores that is impregnated with artificial cinnamon flavor. Don't use this! Buy only from a reputable spice merchant or co-op.

GINGER

Fresh stem ginger is another one I use a lot. You can add as little as a half ounce grated to perk up a wine, or as much as 8 ounces to really really add a kick to apple, peach, carrot, or meads. Ginger is warm, and, well, gingery. In cooking we use it as both a sweet spice and a pungent one. You can do the same in winemaking.

CLOVES

Cloves are easy to overuse. Use a few to help things along once in a while, or with other spices such as cinnamon and ginger.

The same goes for allspice, nutmeg, and other "sweet" spices.

STAR ANISE

Star anise has a very strong flavor, rather like licorice. Be careful how you use it, but DO use it. Lightly crush one or two of the "stars." They can add a lot of character to a potato or grain wine.

VANILLA

I have seen recipes for vanilla wine, but I've never made it. I should think that if you used apple as a base, 4 ounces of vanilla extract or a couple of actual vanilla beans cut up and added to the contents of the nylon straining bag would do the trick. Once or twice I have added a drop or two of vanilla to my wines, and I liked it. This might be something to try with a wine that needs a little help. Pour a glass and add a drop of vanilla and decide if you like it or not.

Do NOT use artificial vanilla flavoring.

OTHER SPICES

Coriander and cardamom and juniper berries are useful in small amounts. It depends on your taste. Juniper is the dominant flavor in gin, for instance. Gin wine is a favorite old-fashioned "country" wine.

WHOLE SPICE MIXTURES

Try using mixtures of spices in their whole forms, like the spices used for apple pie—cinnamon, nutmeg, and clove—or the mixture used in pumpkin pie—cinnamon, ginger, and allspice. I've always wanted to do pumpkin wine with pumpkin pie spices.

Use the basic pea pod recipe with peeled cucumbers, add fresh dill, a little garlic, and pickling spices, and you might have dill pickle wine. I don't know. Maybe it's time I found out!

There are also some nice combinations, tried and true, in French cooking, like quatre epice, which is mostly white peppercorns with a touch of nutmeg, cloves, and ginger.

Vermouth is an aperitif wine that is made with various herbs. One recipe I found included the following: 5 parts wormwood (not advised by me! This stuff isn't good for you!), 1 part balm, 1 part gentian, ¼ part yarrow, angelica root, chamomile, tonka bean, and a pinch each of cloves, nutmeg, cinnamon, and thyme. There is no reason why you can't start out with a glass of plain white wine of some kind, add spices, let it sit a while, and think about trying it in a whole gallon.

With experimentation and careful tasting, you can come up with some very interesting wines. Remember that subtlety is usually more successful than bravado.

I don't recommend mustard, bay leaves, sesame (nice flavor, too much oil), horseradish, turmeric, or fenugreek, but again, some people might like them.

Go easy with spices. Use them as accents. Don't overwhelm a perfectly good wine with a heavy hand. I used to know a person who was basically a good cook, but who gradually seemed to lose her sense of taste. People began to shy away from her dinner parties, which, up to that point, had been very popular. I remember one pheasant dish in which she proudly told us she had used a whole jar of juniper berries.

She shouldn't have gone to the expense of adding the pheasant. We couldn't taste it for the juniper. It was like eating a juniper-flavored sponge.

There are spice oils on the market, like cinnamon oil, clove oils, etc. I've never used these in wines, but I see no reason you couldn't, if you were careful about not adding too much. Use only the ones specifically marked for consumption, NOT for perfumes.

⌘SPICED APPLE WINE⌘

A basic recipe to work from. Nice for sipping on cold autumn evenings. Good in cider punch, as well.

8 lbs. apples, crushed and pressed, or a 24 oz. can of frozen juice
1 lb. chopped golden raisins
3¾ qts. water
2¼ lbs. sugar or 2½ lbs. mild honey
1 crushed Campden tablet (used in the pressed juice)
10 peppercorns, bruised
20 cassia buds or bark cinnamon, bruised
5 cloves, bruised, or 2–4 ozs. grated fresh ginger
½ tsp. acid blend
½ tsp. pectic enzyme
1 tsp. yeast nutrient
¼ tsp. tannin
1 packet Montrachet or champagne wine yeast

Put the water mixed with the sugar or honey on the stove to boil. Put the spices and chopped raisins in a small muslin bag and add them to the water. Heat to boiling and let it simmer for 10 to 15 minutes. Pour the hot sugar water over the pressed or frozen juice, along with the spices and raisins. If you prefer you can chill and reserve half the water beforehand, to add later to bring the temperature down quickly. Add the acid, tannin, and yeast nutrient, but wait till the temperature comes down to add the Campden tablet. Cover and fit with an air lock. Twelve hours after the Campden tablet, add the pectic enzyme. If you don't use the tablet, merely wait until the must cools down to add the pectic enzyme.

Check the PA and write it down. Remember, you can always sweeten later. This wine is going to be on the heavy, sweet side.

Twenty-four hours later, add your yeast made up with a little sugar water. You want the fermentation to start right away.

After two weeks, remove the bag (don't squeeze). Discard the contents. After the sediment has settled down again, rack the wine into a glass secondary fermenter. Bung and fit with an air lock.

Rack it again at least once during fermentation.

In four to six months, check the PA. Taste it, too. Write down your impression. Bottle and label it. Let it rest for at least a year, then open and enjoy. This wine keeps well.

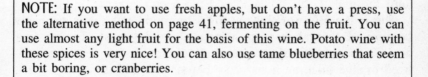

NOTE: If you want to use fresh apples, but don't have a press, use the alternative method on page 41, fermenting on the fruit. You can use almost any light fruit for the basis of this wine. Potato wine with these spices is very nice! You can also use tame blueberries that seem a bit boring, or cranberries.

☙FATHER SOLSTICE RAISIN SHERRY☙

This seems to be a traditional British idea. It's rich and needs to stay in the bottle for at least two years, but if you like sherry, it's well worth it. You can make it as a regular strength wine, or fortify it with some brandy or rum at the end so it is up to real sherry strength. You can use more raisins if you can afford them. See the dried fruit section on page 133 for details.

Chopping the raisins is a pain. The two best methods I have

found is to soak the raisins overnight and process them in small batches in a Cuisinart, or to put the raisins through a meat grinder. I make this several gallons at a time.

> *3 lbs. dark raisins*
> *1 gallon water*
> *1 lb. sugar or 1½ lbs. dark honey*
> *30 cassia buds, bruised, or 2–3 pieces bark cinnamon*
> *2–4 ozs. grated fresh ginger*
> *¼ piece nutmeg*
> *zest and juice of 2 lemons*
> *zest and juice of 3 oranges*
> *10 whole allspice, bruised*
> *1 tsp. yeast nutrient*
> *no tannin*
> *1 Campden tablet, crushed (optional)*
> *½ tsp. pectic enzyme*
> *1 packet Flor sherry yeast*

Put the chopped fruit, peels, and spices in a nylon straining bag. Simmer in the water with the sugar or honey. Put everything into a primary fermenter. Add the acid and nutrient. After the mixture cools, add the Campden tablet, if you choose to use one. Cover and fit with an air lock. Twelve hours after the Campden tablet, add the pectic enzyme. If you don't use the tablet, merely wait until the must cools down to add the pectic enzyme.

Check the PA. It might seem a bit high, but that's probably because of the raisin pulp suspended in the must. Twenty-four hours later, add the sherry yeast. You should start it in the sterilized orange juice an hour or so before you add it.

About two weeks later (maybe more; I tend to start this in the winter when the house is cool), check the PA and rack into a secondary fermenter. Bung and fit with an air lock. Sometimes it makes a lot of sediment, so be sure to have some cooled boiled water ready to make up the difference.

Rack this sherry two more times in the next six months or so. You can bottle this dry, or sweeten it. You can also add some brandy or rum to fortify it. Refer to the Pearson Square in the Port section on page 214.

Age improves this wine considerably. Ideally, it should be

served at Christmas, Solstice, or New Year's, amid much holly and ivy.

⌦BLUEBERRY SPICE⌫

I shamelessly tried to copy Nashoba Valley's blueberry wine. I'm still working on it, but it's pretty good like this.

2–3 lbs. fresh or frozen tame blueberries
1 can wild blueberries
3½ or so qts. water
2¼ lbs. sugar or 2½ lbs. mild honey
20–30 bruised cassia buds
1 oz. grated ginger
half a nutmeg, broken
1 tsp. acid blend
1 tsp. yeast nutrient
¼ tsp. tannin
1 Campden tablet, crushed (optional)
½ tsp. pectic enzyme
1 packet Montrachet yeast

Pick over the berries carefully. Watch for mold. Discard anything that looks odd. Wash the berries in cool water, and drain.

Wash your hands. Put the canned and fresh berries in a nylon straining bag and into the primary fermenter, then squish them with your hands or a sanitized potato masher. Add the liquid from the can of wild blueberries.

Put the spices in a smaller bag or a twist of clean cheesecloth that has been tied up, and add to the water. Boil the spices with the sugar or honey water, skimming off any scum.

Now pour the hot sugar water and spices over the crushed berries. This sets the color. If you prefer, you can chill and reserve half the water beforehand to use now to bring the temperature down quickly. Add the acid, tannin, and yeast nutrient, but wait till the temperature comes down to add the Campden tablet, if you choose to use one. Cover and fit with an air lock. Twelve hours after the Campden tablet, add the pectic enzyme. If you don't use the tablet, merely wait until the must cools down to add the pectic enzyme.

Check the PA and write it down.

Twenty-four hours later, add your yeast. Stir daily. After two weeks, remove the bag (don't squeeze), and after the sediment has settled down again, rack the wine into your secondary fermenter. Bung and fit with an air lock.

Rack it at least once during fermentation. You don't want any off flavors. Be sure to keep the wine in a dark jug, or to put something over it to keep the light from stealing the color.

In four to six months, check the PA. Taste it, too. When you bottle it, you might want to sweeten it. Use stabilizer, and add 2 to 6 ounces of sugar boiled in water. Keep it for a year before drinking, if you can.

> NOTE: Obviously, you can add spices to almost any wine you care to make. Vegetable and grain wines, along with apple and pear wines, work the best with spices. Remember my caveat above, though: Don't spice everything, just to fling spices around. Everything will taste the same. Let the true flavors of the fruits and vegetables come through.

FURTHER SUGGESTIONS FOR FLOWERS AND HERBS

After you've made plain herb and flower wines a few times, use them to enhance a single-fruit wine. Use apple, pear, carrot, citrus, potato, beet, or barley as a base for herb and flower wines. Just make the wines the way you normally would, using part of the water to decoct the flavor from the herb and part of it to dissolve the sugar or honey.

You can use herb teas to flavor wines, too. I've added Red Zinger to a mixed-fruit wine to help round off the flavor several times, and to meads that seemed a bit pale. You can use an ounce of so of Red Zinger tea in part of the water in a basic apple juice wine for a pleasant hibiscus flavor and pink color. Or you can use rose hip tea in a similar manner. If you have some rosebushes, you could get really creative and try this wine named after one of my nieces, whose name is Rosy:

☙ROSY APPLE MELOMEL☙

This is a bit of a risk. I've only done it once, though I plan to do it again.

The success of this wine depends on how potent your rose petals are. You are after color and flavor. Remember to pick the roses on a warm day after the dew has dried. Don Juan is a good tea rose for this recipe. The old-fashioned roses are best. If your red roses aren't very fragrant, you can use what you have for color, adding fragrant but paler roses for taste.

12. oz. can frozen apple juice or pressed juice of 8 lbs. fresh apples

petals from as many unsprayed red or dark pink roses as you can obtain, ideally 2 cups or more, the more fragrant the better

2 lbs. sugar or 2½ lbs. very light honey

1 gallon water

3 tsps. acid blend

¼ tsp. tannin

1 tsp. yeast nutrient

1 Campden tablet, crushed (optional)

½ tsp. pectic enzyme

1 packet champagne yeast

Put the rinsed petals into two cups of the water, heat to a simmer, turn off the heat, cover, and let sit for an hour or so. Heat the rest of the water with the sugar to dissolve. Strain and press the liquid off the petals into the primary fermenter. Add the rest of the water and sugar after it has cooled. You don't want it to be hot, because if it is it will drive off some of the fragrance of the roses. Proceed the way you normally would for apple wine (see page 85), checking the PA, etc.

NOTE: There are so many possibilities here. Apple with chamomile, apple with dandelion, apple with elderflowers, lavender, etc. Pear and barley wines would also be good enhanced with flower fragrances.

I wonder how raspberry and roses would come out? Cherry and roses?

At bottling time, remember this is better slightly sweet, not dry. If the fragrance is good but the color is pale, you can cheat and add a tiny bit of red food coloring to the wine. If the fragrance is too faint, you can hope it recovers. Or, I suppose, you could add some food-grade rose water. DON'T use perfume or anything else that hasn't been cleared for food consumption.

SINGLE ENHANCED WINES

☙STRAWBERRY LEMONADE WINE❧

Strawberry lemonade is an old-fashioned drink from which insipid canned pink lemonade seems to have evolved. I found an old recipe in a canning book from before World War II and decided to try it as wine. I had some strawberries that were kind of blah and needed help. So I enhanced them.

Use the Strawberry Wine recipe on page 121 for your base, and use a 6 ounce can of lemonade INSTEAD of the acid blend. Add the zest of two or three whole, fresh lemons to the strawberries in the straining bag. Don't use the lemon juice. Adding it here will create too much acidity. Proceed as normal. The resulting wine will have a bit higher alcohol content because of the sugar in the lemonade. Use it as a social wine or as the basis for a cooler in the summer.

Other ideas that are on my list to try are watermelon base enhanced with lime, apple with orange, blueberry with orange, blackberry with lemon, cantaloupe and spice, papaya or mango and lime.

ECONOMY ROSÉ WINES

Another idea when things are a little tight in the finance department but you still want to build your cellar is making wines with the inexpensive fruit juices like apple and white grape, or orange, adding a small amount of the more expensive or hard-to-get fresh fruits.

In a way, this is borrowing an idea from the bottled and frozen fruit juice companies. If you look closely at the ingredients they use, you see that they have a base of white grape juice or apple juice, with other juices added in to perk them up.

Cruise the aisles and check out the combinations. The better combos are at the whole food or co-op stores.

Use the Rosy Apple Melomel recipe on page 195 as a base, with sugar or honey and fruit instead of the rose petals. Use a 12–24 ounce can of frozen white grape or apple juice and add a pound or so of pie cherries, raspberries, or blueberries to the basic recipe, checking the PA carefully so you don't overdo it on the sugar.

Orange juice works well, too, but you will often get a more apricot color than rosé, though it depends on the fruit you use. Orange juice with absolutely dead ripe apricots or peaches added is VERY nice. In northern climes, trying to get really ripe apricots and peaches is difficult and expensive, so when you do happen upon a few, be ready!

DARING DUOS

We'd better consider flavors before we go much further.

By now you realize that some fruit and vegetable flavors are more assertive than others. The following isn't meant to be a complete list, and your opinions may differ from mine.

STRONG	MEDIUM	MILD
raspberry	strawberry	apple
blueberry	cherry (sweet)	apricot
cherry (pie)	melon	grape (white)
grape (red)	beet	peach
elderberry	citrus	pear
citrus (sometimes)	gooseberry	pineapple
black currant	rhubarb	some tropical
	red currant	banana
	dried fruits	vegetable
	parsnip	grains

Duos are wines that have two flavors that are of about equal strength, give or take a little, like:

apricot-pineapple

carrot-apricot

apricot-peach

strawberry-rhubarb

watermelon-blueberry

blackberry-raspberry

beet-blueberry

cherry-strawberry

cherry-raspberry

orange-pineapple

raisin-banana

parsnip-raisin

blueberry-raspberry

Sometimes one fruit might be a little more assertive than the other, but you make up for this by using more of the blander fruit.

The only trick to making these wines is to watch the acidity. Either measure it with a kit or use half the acid recommended for one fruit (of the medium acid fruits) and half from the other. I like to make these a bit richer in fruit than the single-fruit wines. It seems to work better that way.

Duos are also a good use for a batch of fruit that isn't quite good enough to make into a top-notch single-fruit wine. So, one berry is not as flavorful as you would like? Add another kind of fruit that *is* up to par. However, you should NEVER use inferior, spoiled, or unripe fruit. It's never worth it.

These are usually good table wines that are easier to match with various menus than single-fruit wines are.

Here are a few of my favorites.

☙ LATE JUNE SWOON ❧
(STRAWBERRY AND SWEET CHERRY)

Here in the upper Midwest, the high point for local strawberries is late June, when sweet cherries from other parts of the country are coming in. I had some of each leftover from batches of jam, and was delighted with this combination.

3 lbs. sweet cherries, any kind
2 lbs. sweet local strawberries
1 gallon water

2½ lbs. sugar or 3 lbs. light honey
1 tsp. acid blend or juice and zest of 1 lemon
¼ tsp. tannin
1 tsp. yeast nutrient
1 Campden tablet, crushed (optional)
½ tsp. pectic enzyme
1 packet champagne yeast

It isn't necessary to stone the cherries. Stem and wash them well in cool water. Cherries are sprayed with pesticides, and they get dust and dirt on them. Stem and wash the strawberries for the same reasons.

Boil the sugar or honey in the water and skim if necessary. Put the fruit into a nylon straining bag. Wash your hands carefully, and squish the fruit from outside the bag. You'll be able to feel the cherry pits as lumps. Don't pound them with anything; just let them be. They won't hurt anything.

Pour the hot syrup over the fruit and cover. When cooled, add the yeast nutrient, acid, and tannin, and the Campden tablet, if you choose to use one. Cover and fit with an air lock. Twelve hours after the Campden tablet, add the pectic enzyme. If you don't use the tablet, merely wait until the must cools down to add the pectic enzyme.

Twenty-four hours later, check the PA and add the yeast. Cover and stir daily for a week or so until the PA comes down to 3 to 5 percent. Rack the wine into a secondary fermenter. Bung and fit with an air lock. Rack it twice in about six months, till fermented out dry. This wine is fine dry, but you might like it sweeter.

Use stabilizer and sweeten the wine with 2 to 4 ounces of sugar in a syrup. Bottle. Keep it for six months, at least.

☜WATERMELON BLUES WINE☞
(LET'S BE CAREFUL OUT THERE)

You never know when a winemaking opportunity will knock. I threw a party in the summer, and spent hours carving a watermelon into a peacock and seeding the fruit. Then I added some nice frosty blueberries to the watermelon cubes, for contrast and flavor. Everyone admired it. Said it was the nicest peacock watermelon they had seen all week.

No one ate it. After the party I stared at all the leftover watermelon and berries. People had mistaken the berries for seeds, it seemed.

Well, heck. On impulse, I threw all the fruit (minus the peel) into a nylon straining bag, added the usual suspects, and made wine. Six months later, I was bottling, and my goodness! A star was born!

I now make this every year. It's a little unusual, but it can still be used as a table wine. If you are too busy during the summer, get a couple of melons when they are at their cheapest, and freeze the pulp for future use. You don't have to remove the seeds.

Since the blueberries are more assertive than the melon, you don't need many.

1 lb. fresh blueberries
3 lbs. watermelon centers
2 lbs. sugar or 2½ lbs. light honey
3¾ qts. water
2 tsps. acid blend
½ tsp. tannin
1 tsp. yeast nutrient
1 crushed Campden tablet (recommended)
½ tsp. pectic enzyme
1 packet champagne yeast

Wash the berries. Cube the watermelon. If you want to, you can get rid of the seeds by putting the melon through a strainer or feed mill, but it isn't necessary. Put it all in a nylon straining bag, and with very clean hands, squish the fruit.

Boil the sugar or honey in the water and skim if necessary. Pour hot syrup over the fruit and cover. When cooled, add the yeast nutrient, acid, tannin, and include a Campden tablet. Cover and fit with an air lock. Twelve hours later, add the pectic enzyme.

Twenty-four hours later, check the PA and add the yeast.

Cover the must and stir daily for a week or so till the PA comes down to 3 to 5 percent. Rack the wine into a secondary fermenter. Bung and fit with an air lock. Rack it twice in about six months, till fermented out dry.

If you like, use stabilizer and sweeten it with 2 to 4 ounces of sugar in a syrup. Bottle. Keep it for six months, at least.

☙LIQUID SUNSHINE❧
(CARROT AND APRICOT)

This wine has to be good for you!

3 lbs. carrots
2 lbs. dry apricots or 3 lbs. fresh apricots
1 lb. golden raisins (optional but nice, especially if using
*   fresh apricots)*
zest and juice of 3 oranges
2½ lbs. sugar or 3 lbs. light honey
1 gallon water
2 tsps. acid blend or zest and juice of 2 large lemons
¼ tsp. tannin
1 tsp. yeast nutrient
1 Campden tablet, crushed (optional)
½ tsp. pectic enzyme
1 packet champagne yeast

Wash the apricots. There's no need to peel them. If you're using dry fruit, cut it into pieces and soak overnight in some of the water. If you're using fresh fruit, pit it and put into a nylon straining bag with the citrus zests and the soaked raisins, if you are adding them. Put the bag in the primary fermenter.

SIMMER the sliced carrots just as you would for normal carrot wine. Remove the carrots and add the sugar or honey and dissolve, skimming if necessary. Pour hot syrup over the apricots and raisins in the fermenter and cover. When cooled, add acid, yeast nutrient, and tannin, including a Campden tablet, if you choose to use one. Cover and fit with an air lock. Twelve hours after the Campden tablet, add the pectic enzyme. If you don't use the tablet, merely wait until the must cools down to add the pectic enzyme.

Twenty-four hours later, check the PA and add the yeast.

Cover and stir the wine daily for a week or so till the PA comes down to 3 to 5 percent. Rack it into a secondary fermenter. Bung and fit with an air lock. Rack it twice in about six months, till fermented out dry.

So you see, there's no real trick to this. Just use your head and the recipes in part two to come up with your own interesting combinations. As always, you can make these wines in bigger batches if you like.

TUTTI-FRUTTI

In these wines, one or two fruits or general categories of fruits still dominate. You might mistake some of these for grape wines, but probably not. I tend to make them in five-gallon batches because I like them and it is usually less expensive to buy the fruit in larger amounts. I also feel that bigger batches of these wines let the fruit flavors meld together more, though it is easy to make them in one-gallon batches. All you do is divide the ingredients by five, except for the yeast.

⚘REINCONATION CITRUS MELOMEL⚘
(FOR KAREN SCHAFFER)

I'd been making wine for about seven years when I came up with this one. It wasn't my first experiment, of course (see Mulberry Revenge, page 113).

This was first made from supplies left over from a punch that's a favorite of some friends of mine; at the end of a big party we found that some of the backup fruit juices had thawed. On a bet, I recklessly used a ten-pound jar of local honey and made up the recipe as I went along, attempting to duplicate the punch in wine form. The idea was to serve the wine at the next annual party.

We did. It was a big hit. I didn't quite duplicate the punch, but no one minded. We can always make punch.

ReinConation Citrus Melomel is light, crisp, almost effervescent. A delicious summer wine, it's fine to serve with appetizers as well as with a meal. Serve chilled.

4–8 ozs. fresh ginger, sliced and simmered in two cups of water
12 bruised peppercorns
zest of 2–4 good oranges
10 lbs. rich but light-colored honey
sufficient water to make up the five gallons
1 12 oz. can lemonade
3 12 oz. cans limeade
1 12 oz. can orange juice
NO ACID!!
2½ tsps. pectic enzyme
5 tsps. yeast nutrient
1 tsp. tannin
5 Campden tablets, crushed (optional)
1 packet champagne yeast

Simmer the ginger for at least two hours, adding the pepper-corns and the zest toward the end. Boil the honey with a couple of gallons of the water (you might want to do this in two batches). Skim, if necessary. (Local honeys tend to have a few bee parts here and there.) Reserve the orange juice to make up the starter for the yeast.

This is a one-stage fermentation, so start with a glass carboy.

Strain the now-thawed juices into the carboy. Strain the ginger-pepper-orange liquid into the carboy, and then the somewhat cooled honey water. DON'T pour this in hot—you could crack the carboy!

Add some cool water. Leave a little more room than usual, in case you get a lot of froth. You can top it up later.

Add everything but the pectic enzyme and the yeast. Cover with plastic and a rubber band. Wait till the temperature drops to below 90°F, and add the Campden tablets, if you choose to use them. Twelve hours after the Campden tablets, add the pectic enzyme. If you don't use the tablets, merely wait until the must cools down to add the pectic enzyme.

Twenty-four hours later, check the PA (probably seems a bit high, but don't worry), add your champagne yeast starter, add a bung and an air lock, and let 'er rip.

Check during the first few days and weeks to make sure nothing is getting out of hand, then top up the wine with enough cool boiled water to fill the carboy to within a few inches of the top. Rack the wine carefully at least twice.

Remember, honey takes longer to ferment out. The second time you rack, taste for spices. You might want to add more ginger water. When it ferments out dry, bottle it, and wait six months, then taste it. I served this almost exactly a year from when it was first made, but it benefited considerably from another couple of years in the bottle. Who knows what the future will bring with this melomel?

☜TUTTI-FRUTTI I☞

This was my first serious tutti-frutti, made after a wild morning in the farmers' market. The berries dominate. It makes five gallons at a pretty reasonable price and doesn't taste like spumoni at all.

4 lbs. strawberries
2 lbs. raspberries
1 lb. blueberries
2 lbs. peaches
2 16 oz. cans sour pie cherries
1 12 oz. can frozen red grape juice
1 12 oz. can "tropical" (pineapple, banana, passion fruit) drink
   OR orange juice
6 lbs. sugar
2 lbs. light honey
sufficient water to make up five gallons
10 tsps. acid blend
1½ tsp. tannin
2½ tsps. pectic enzyme
6 tsps. yeast nutrient
5 Campden tablets, crushed (optional)
1 packet champagne yeast

Prepare all the fruit and put it in one big or two smaller nylon straining bags. Thaw the juices. Place them in the bottom of a sanitized primary fermenter.

Boil about 1 to 2 gallons of the water with the sugar and honey, depending on how big a kettle you have. Skim if necessary.

Pour the hot sugar water over the fruit and juices. Add the rest of the water needed to make up the five gallons and a little over (because of the fruit bulk). Add the yeast nutrient, acid, and tannin, including the Campden tablets, if you choose to use them. Cover and fit with an air lock. If you use the Campden tablets, wait at least 12 hours before adding the pectic enzyme. In another 12–24 hours, check the PA and add the yeast.

Stir daily. In a week or two, lift out the fruit bags, and let them drain without squeezing. Discard the fruit. Check out the volume of wine and the PA. If you need to add more water, do. If you have a little too much, don't worry. Life is too short as it is.

When the PA goes down to 2 to 3 percent, rack the wine off into a glass carboy, and fit it with an air lock.

Rack it twice more during the next six months or so. Wait till the wine clears and it ferments out.

This wine is good dry, but you can sweeten it by stabilizing and adding 8 to 10 ounces of sugar in a syrup solution.

Bottle it in large and regular sized bottles. Wait six months before trying.

⌘FREEZER ROSÉ⌘

Another version of the above, this one is a lighter rosé. It gets its name from the time I cleared all the previous year's leftover fruit out of the freezer and made it into wine. It's good summer wine.

4 lbs. strawberries
1 lb. raspberries
2 lbs. fresh grapes
2 lbs. dark plums
4 lbs. peaches
2 12 oz. cans frozen red grape juice
water sufficient to make up five gallons
6 lbs. sugar AND 2 lbs. honey
10 tsps. acid blend
1½ tsp. tannin
5 tsps. yeast nutrient
5 Campden tablets, crushed (optional)
2½ tsps. pectic enzyme
1 packet champagne or Montrachet yeast

Prepare all the fruit and put it in one bag or two smaller nylon straining bags. Thaw the juices and place everything in the bottom of a sanitized primary fermenter.

Boil about 1–2 gallons of the water with the sugar and honey, depending on how big a kettle you have. Skim if necessary.

Pour the hot sugar water over the fruit and juices. Add the rest of the water needed to make up the five gallons and a little over (because of the fruit bulk). When cool, add the yeast nutrient, tannin, acid, and chemicals, including the Campden tablets, if you choose to use them. Cover and fit with an air lock. If you use the Campden tablets, wait at least 12 hours before adding the pectic enzyme. In another 12–24 hours, check the PA and add the yeast.

Stir daily. In a week or two, lift out the fruit bags, let them drain without squeezing, and discard the fruit. Check out the volume of wine and the PA. If you need to add more water, do. If you have a little too much, don't worry. Be happy.

When the PA goes down to 2 to 3 percent, rack the wine off into a glass carboy, and fit it with an air lock.

Rack it twice more during the next six months or so. Wait till the wine clears and it ferments out.

This wine is good dry, but you can sweeten it by stabilizing it and adding 8 to 10 ounces of sugar in a syrup solution.

Bottle it in large and regular sized bottles. Wait six months before trying.

GENERIC WINES

These are wines that either come close to tasting like grape wines or to not tasting of any particular fruit. I am giving the recipes in one-gallon batches because you will have your own ideas about them and might want to experiment with several versions at once. It's nice to have a basic white and a basic red around.

☙GENERIC RED❧

2 lbs. fresh or frozen blueberries
2 lbs. fresh or frozen blackberries or mulberries
½ pint red wine concentrate or 1 lb. dark raisins
water sufficient to make up the gallon
2 lbs. sugar or 2 lbs. light honey
1 tsp. acid blend
¼ tsp. tannin
1 tsp. yeast nutrient
1 Campden tablet, crushed (optional)
½ tsp. pectic enzyme
1 packet Montrachet or Burgundy yeast

Prepare all the fruit, including the raisins if you use them, put in nylon straining bag, and place the bag in the bottom of a sanitized primary fermenter. Mash the fruit with clean hands or a sanitized potato masher. Pour in the fruit concentrate. Boil the water with the sugar or honey, skimming if necessary. Sugar gives a more ''generic'' taste than honey does.

Pour the hot sugar water over the blueberries and blackberries or mulberries and grape concentrate. Add the rest of the water needed to make up the quantity. Add the yeast nutrient, acid, and tannin, including the Campden tablet, if you choose to use one. If you use the Campden tablet, wait at least 12 hours before adding the pectic enzyme. In another 12–24 hours, check the PA and add the yeast.

Stir daily. In a week or two, lift out the fruit bags and let them drain without squeezing. Discard the fruit. When the PA goes down to 2 to 3 percent, rack off the wine into a glass carboy, and fit with an air lock.

Rack it twice more during the next six months or so. Wait till the wine clears and it ferments out dry. You can sweeten this a little, if you like, but don't add more than two ounces of sugar. Bottle and sample it in six months.

⛧ANOTHER GENERIC RED⛧

1 lb. fresh elderberries or ¼ lb. dried elderberries
2 lbs. dark plums or blackberries
2 lbs. beets
sufficient water to make up the gallon
2 lbs. sugar or 2 lbs. light honey
2 tsps. acid blend
no tannin
1 tsp. yeast nutrient
1 Campden tablet (optional)
½ tsp. pectic enzyme
1 packet Montrachet or Burgundy yeast

Prepare all the fruit, put in nylon straining bags, and place the bags in the bottom of a sanitized primary fermenter. Mash the fruit with clean hands or a sanitized potato masher. Simmer the cleaned, sliced beets in 2 quarts of the water JUST until tender. Discard or eat the beets.

Boil the water with the sugar or honey, skimming if necessary. Sugar gives a more "generic" taste than honey does.

Pour the hot sugar water and beet water over the elderberries and plums or blackberries. Add the rest of the water needed to make up the quantity. Add the yeast nutrient, acid, and tannin, including the Campden tablet, if you choose to use one. Cover and fit with an air lock. If you use the Campden tablet, wait at least 12 hours before adding the pectic enzyme. In another 12 to 24 hours, check the PA and add the yeast.

Stir daily. In a week or two, lift out the fruit bags and let them drain without squeezing. Discard the fruit. When the PA goes down to 2 to 3 percent, rack off the wine into a glass carboy and fit with an air lock.

Rack it twice more during the next six months or so. Wait till the wine clears and it ferments out dry. You can sweeten this a little, if you like, but don't add more than 2 ounces of sugar. Bottle and sample it in six months.

⫷GENERIC WHITE⫸

½ lb. golden raisins
2 lbs. fresh or frozen peaches or apricots
1 12 oz. can frozen apple juice
1 6 oz. can frozen orange juice
2 lbs. sugar or 2 lbs. light honey
sufficient water to make up the gallon
2 tsps. acid blend or juice of 2 large lemons
½ tsp. tannin
1 tsp. yeast nutrient
1 Campden tablet, crushed (optional)
½ tsp. pectic enzyme
1 packet champagne yeast

Soak and chop the raisins. Clean, pit, and chop the fruit. Put the fruit in a nylon straining bag and place it in the bottom of a sanitized primary fermenter. Thaw the juices. Mash the fruit with clean hands or a sanitized potato masher.

Boil the water with the sugar or honey. Skim if necessary. Sugar gives a more "generic" taste than honey does.

Pour the hot sugar water over the fruit and thawed juices. Add the rest of the water needed to make up the gallon. Add the yeast nutrient, tannin, and acid. After the must has cooled, add the Campden tablet, if you choose to use one. Cover and fit with an air lock. If you use the Campden tablet, wait at least 12 hours before adding the pectic enzyme. In another 12 to 24 hours, check the PA and add the yeast.

Stir daily. In a week or two, lift out the fruit bag and let it drain without squeezing. Discard the fruit. When the PA goes down to 2 to 3 percent, rack off the wine into a glass carboy and fit it with an air lock.

Rack the wine twice more during the next six months or so. Wait till the wine clears and it ferments out dry. You can sweeten this a little, if you like. Add 2 to 4 ounces of sugar in a syrup. Bottle it and sample in six months.

✿A WHITER SHADE OF PALE GENERIC WHITE✿

3 large grapefruit, preferably organic
1 lb. golden raisins or ½ pint white grape concentrate
1 12 oz. can frozen apple juice
2 lbs. sugar or 2 lbs. light honey
water sufficient to make up a gallon
1 tsp. acid blend or juice of 1 lemon
1 tsp. yeast nutrient
1 Campden tablet, crushed (optional)
½ tsp. pectic enzyme
1 packet champagne yeast

Prepare the zest of one of the grapefruit. Then peel the fruit and remove as much of the white pith from the sections as possible. Put the fruit into a nylon straining bag. Add the soaked and chopped raisins if you are using them. Mash the fruit with a sanitized potato masher or your very clean hands. Thaw the juice.

Boil about three quarts of the water and sugar or honey and pour the hot sugar water over the fruit and apple juice or concentrate if you use it. Add the rest of the water needed to make up the gallon. Add the yeast nutrient and acid or lemon juice. Wait until the must cools down to add the Campden tablet, if you choose to use one. Cover and fit with an air lock. If you use the Campden tablet, wait at least 12 hours before adding the pectic enzyme. In another 12 to 24 hours, check the PA and add the yeast.

Stir daily. In a week or two, lift out the fruit bag and let it drain without squeezing before discarding the fruit. When the PA goes down to 2 to 3 percent, rack off the wine into a glass carboy and fit it with an air lock.

Rack the wine twice more during the next six months or so. Wait till the wine clears and it ferments out dry. You can sweeten this a little if you like: add stabilizer and 2 to 4 ounces of sugar in a syrup. Bottle and sample in six months.

⟨⟨GENERIC ROSÉ⟩⟩

To me, most grape rosés are kind of bland. They seem like watered-down reds or whites without much integrity, although of course there are exceptions.

Fruit rosé wines are much more interesting and produce some glorious rosés. When you think about it, most of the "reds" in this book are actually dark rosés. There is nothing bland about any of them. I feel they offer an exciting new dimention to wines in general.

Try using Freezer Rosé as a generic rosé, or try this recipe a.k.a. in our household as Pink Plonk. Feel free to adjust the fruit composition to suit your tastes. By all means, become a rosé enthusiast.

½ lb. fresh or frozen strawberries or raspberries
½ lb. fresh or frozen blueberries
1 12 oz. can frozen cran-raspberry drink
water sufficient to make up a gallon
1½ lbs. sugar or 2 lbs. light honey
1 tsp. acid blend
¼ tsp. tannin
1 tsp. yeast nutrient
1 Campden tablet, crushed
½ tsp. pectic enzyme
1 packet champagne yeast

Prepare the fruit and put it into a nylon straining bag. Mash the fruit with a sanitized potato masher or your very clean hands. Thaw the juice.

Boil about three quarts of the water and sugar or honey and pour the hot sugar water over the fruit and cran-raspberry juice. Add the rest of the water needed to make up the gallon. Add the yeast nutrient, tannin, and acid or lemon juice. Wait until the must cools down to add the Campden tablet, if you choose to use one. Cover and fit with an air lock. If you use the Campden tablet, wait at least 12 hours before adding the pectic enzyme. In another 12 to 24 hours, check the PA and add the yeast.

Stir daily. In a week or two, lift out the fruit bag and let it drain without squeezing before discarding the fruit. When the PA goes down to 2 to 3 percent, rack off the wine into a glass carboy, and fit it with an air lock.

Rack the wine twice more during the next six months or so. Wait till the wine clears and it ferments out dry. You can sweeten this a little if you like, adding stabilizer and 2 to 4 ounces of sugar in a syrup. Bottle and sample in six months.

CHAPTER ELEVEN

Fortified and Sparkling Wines

PORT

Port is a Portuguese red wine that has been fortified with Portuguese brandy up to about 20 percent alcohol and is properly called Porto. It has a long history and many imitators.

The original grape wine was harsh, dry, and it didn't travel well. Brandy was added to stabilize it so it could be sweeter and longer-lived for shipping—a wonderful example of making a silk purse out of a sow's ear.

Fine port is expensive but worth it if you have the money. Good port-type wines are made outside Portugal (such as those from California and Australia), but the best stuff comes from Portugal.

There are many different styles of port, from the young ruby port (no relation to Ruby Tuesday) to tawny port, to the vintage ports. Some people keep their port cellared for decades before drinking it. It gets left to relatives in wills. Choose your ancestors carefully!

It is said that some cheaper ports and port-type wines have been "adulterated" with other fruits, such as elderberries, to fake the richness of true Porto.

You and I can't make port. But we can make port-like wines that are pretty good!

Now that you know the characteristics of the dark fruit wines, you can use your imagination to mentally taste some combinations. Combinations of dark fruits do the best job of mimicking the rich complexity that is port. I like to use fresh or frozen fruit for the most part, though some dried fruits, such as elderberries and raisins, are good to add.

The addition of brandy or spirits also contributes to the flavor and body of the wine. Good brandy is better than cheap brandy for this purpose (big surprise, huh?), and really good brandy is wasted (whew). You can also use high-alcohol grain alcohol (120 to 140 proof) if you can get it in your area. You don't need as much, and it doesn't dilute the taste of the wine the way brandy does. Also, the addition of the alcohol kills off any leftover yeast, stabilizing the wine and allowing you to sweeten it if you choose.

Another means of fortification is to use flavored brandies. Commercial fruit brandies are frequently too sweet for my taste, and they are also low in alcohol, so I usually make my own, using high-alcohol grain spirits. Check out the Extra Helpings chapter on page 234 for some simple recipes. It's very easy to make your own fruit brandies using brandy, vodka, etc. as a base.

When making wine that you plan to fortify, try to use a wine yeast that allows a maximum amount of alcohol, if you can, and use the maximum amount of sugar you think you can get away with (up to 14, or even 15, percent). Port or sherry yeasts are best. The best method I have come up with for making these wines is to have a long, slow fermentation, ferment the wine out dry, and then fortify it.

You can tease the yeast into making more alcohol by adding controlled amounts of thick sugar syrup (two parts sugar to one part water) in very small doses during the secondary fermentation. This is called syrup feeding. (It is not necessary to call out "Sooeee, sooee, sooee, here yeast yeast yeast," but you can if you are feeling particularly full of beans.)

As soon as the wine ferments out, add enough sugar syrup to bring the alcohol up a tiny bit, and let it ferment out again. Do this several times, then rack the wine and clear. This is where the Specific Gravity reading becomes really important, rather than merely the Potential Alcohol! You want to start out at 1.000 SG, and raise it only to 1.0900 or less, then ferment back to 1.000 again. Don't try to put more than another pound of sugar into a gallon this way.

I find it hard to remember to monitor everything, so I usually take the expensive way out and get the highest alcohol content I can in the basic fermentation and fortify with alcohol.

PEARSON SQUARE

The Pearson Square is a useful tool depending on how good you are with math. Here is how it looks:

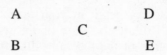

It's very simple algebra.

A is the percent of alcohol in the spirit you are going to use to fortify your wine. (80 proof would be 40 percent alcohol, 120 proof is 60 percent. The "proof" is always twice the actual alcohol content.)

B is the alcohol content of the wine at hand (which you know from having kept track, right?).

C is the degree of fortification you want in the finished product.

D equals C minus B, and gives you the proportion of spirit to use.

E equals A minus C, or the proportion of the basic wine you need.

Or: A = C + E. B = C – D. C = B + D. D = C – B. E = A – C.

So, say A is 40 percent, and B is 12 percent, and C is 20 percent. Then D is 8 and E is 20, which indicates that some hefty fortifying is needed. That's eight parts spirit to twenty parts wine in the finished product—an improbable 40 percent result, which will give a strong alcohol content and a weak taste at an expensive price.

So what happens if we start with wine with a higher percent, and alcohol with a higher percent? A is 60 percent, B is 15 percent, and C is still 20 percent. C minus B is 5 (D), and A minus C is 40 (E), which gives us five parts alcohol to forty parts wine, a 12 percent result, which is a lot better and a lot more drinkable.

☙BLUEBERRY PORTAGE❧

5 lbs. blueberries
¼ lb. dried elderberries
2–4 ozs. banana flakes or ½ lb. dark raisins (optional)
sufficient water to make up a gallon
1¾ lbs. sugar or 2 lbs. honey, adding another ½ lb. later
½ tsp. acid blend
no tannin (the elderberries have plenty)
1 tsp. yeast nutrient
1 Campden tablet, crushed (recommended)
½ tsp. pectic enzyme
1 packet sherry, port, or Montrachet yeast
brandy, grain alcohol, or fruit brandy to fortify the result to the percentage you desire later

Pick over the berries carefully. Watch for mold. Discard anything that looks odd. Wash the berries in cool water, and drain. Soak the dried elderberries for a half hour in a cup of hot water. Drain the elderberries and reserve the water.

Wash your hands. Put the berries in a nylon straining bag and into the primary fermenter, then squash with your hands (you might want to use sanitized rubber gloves) or a sanitized potato masher. Be sure you press the berries well. Add the dried elderberries and (optional) banana flakes or raisins (these give even more body and flavor).

Boil the water and sugar or honey. Skim if necessary. Pour the hot sugar water over the crushed berries. You can chill and reserve half the water beforehand, adding it now to bring the temperature down quickly. Add the elderberry water, acid, and yeast nutrient, but wait until the temperature comes down to add the Campden tablet, if you choose to use one. Cover and fit with an air lock. Wait 12 hours to add the pectic enzyme.

Check the PA and write it down. You can adjust the PA up a bit at this point.

Twenty-four hours later, add the yeast. Stir it daily. Keep it a little warmer than usual, but not over 75°F. After about two weeks, remove the bag (don't squeeze). Discard the fruit. After the sediment has settled down again, check the PA. It will probably need to go another week. When it gets to 3 to 4 percent PA, rack the wine into your glass fermenter. Bung and fit with an air lock.

Add the extra half pound of sugar, dissolved in water, to the must gradually, watching the SG as described on page 214. Make a note of it. If the beginning PA was higher than 14 percent, don't add the sugar. The yeast may not take it. (The engines will na take it, Cap'n . . .)

Rack the wine at least twice during fermentation. You don't want any off flavors. Be sure to keep it in a dark jug, or put something over it to keep the light from stealing the color.

In six to eight months, or even more, check the PA, and judge the clarity. Taste it, too. There should be plenty of tannin from the elderberries—maybe what seems to be too much. Do you think it will gain in smoothness and flavor over the next couple of years? Here you have to decide if you want to go to the expense of adding the grain alcohol, the brandy, or the fruit brandy.

To be accurate, use the Pearson Square to figure out how much alcohol, of what proof, you will need to bring it up to 19 or 20 percent. If that gives you a headache, figure about two to three cups of 80 proof brandy to the gallon. You might want to add some sugar syrup, too, so add four to six ounces dissolved in water. The alcohol will kill off the yeast, so you don't have to worry about the additional sugar.

Fruit brandies (unless you made them with high alcohol and low sugar) will make more volume, and you probably won't need to add sugar. Taste them to make sure. I would use a blackberry brandy to deepen the flavor, or a raspberry to brighten it up a bit. You could also use elderberry or blueberry brandy, of course. To make very sure you are killing off the yeast, you can add a stabilizer or a Campden tablet.

Rack off the wine and add the alcohol. Then bottle, label, and store the wine. Try it in a year, then in two, or even three, years. Consider using some half bottles, so you can taste it more often as it progresses.

You could also just bottle the wine as it is, without fortifying it, and enjoy it, of course! In that case, stabilize and sweeten with four to six ounces of sugar in syrup. Keep for at least a year before trying.

☙PORTLY BLACKBERRY❧

5 lbs. blackberries, loganberries, Marionberries (dead ripe)!
¼ lb. dried elderberries
2–4 ozs. banana flakes or ½ lb. dark raisins (optional)
1¾ lbs. sugar or 2 lbs. honey, adding another ½ lb. later
sufficient water to make up a gallon
½ tsp. acid blend
no tannin (the elderberries have plenty)
1 tsp. yeast nutrient
1 Campden tablet, crushed (recommended)
½ tsp. pectic enzyme
1 packet sherry, port, or Montrachet yeast
brandy, grain alcohol, or fruit brandy

Pick over the berries carefully. Watch for mold. Discard any-
thing that looks odd. Wash the berries in cool water and drain.
Soak the dried elderberries for a half hour in a cup of hot water.
Drain the elderberries and reserve the water.

Wash your hands. Put the berries in a nylon straining bag and
into the primary fermenter, then squash with your hands (you
might want to use sanitized rubber gloves) or a sanitized potato
masher. Be sure you press the berries well. Add the dried elderberries and (optional) banana flakes or raisins (these give even more
body and flavor).

Boil the water and sugar or honey. Skim if necessary. Pour the
hot sugar water over the crushed berries. You can chill and reserve
half the water beforehand, adding it now to bring the temperature
down quickly. Add the elderberry water, acid, and yeast nutrient,
but wait until the temperature comes down to add the Campden
tablet, if you choose to use one. Cover and fit with an air lock.
Wait 12 hours to add the pectic enzyme.

Check the PA and write it down. You can adjust the PA up a
bit at this point.

Twenty-four hours later, add the yeast. Stir it daily. Keep it a
little warmer than usual, but not over 75°F. After about two weeks,
remove the bag (don't squeeze). Discard the fruit. After the sediment has settled down again, check the PA. It will probably need
to go another week. When it gets to 3 to 4 percent PA, rack the
wine into your glass fermenter. Bung and fit with an air lock.

Add an extra half pound of sugar, dissolved in water, to the must, gradually, watching the SG as described on page 214. Make a note of it. If the beginning PA was higher than 14 percent, don't add the sugar. The yeast may not take it.

Rack the wine at least twice during fermentation. You don't want any off flavors. Be sure to keep it in a dark jug, or put something over it to keep the light from stealing the color.

In six to eight months, or even more, check the PA, and judge the clarity. Taste it, too. There should be plenty of tannin from the elderberries—maybe what seems to be too much. Do you think it will gain in smoothness and flavor over the next couple of years? Here you have to decide if you want to go to the expense of adding the grain alcohol, the brandy, or the fruit brandy.

To be accurate, use the Pearson Square to figure out how much alcohol, of what proof, you will need to bring it up to 19 or 20 percent. If that gives you a headache, figure about two to three cups of 80 proof brandy to the gallon. You might want to add some sugar syrup, too, so add four to six ounces dissolved in waster. The alcohol will kill off the yeast, so you don't have to worry about the additional sugar.

Fruit brandies (unless you made them with high alcohol and low sugar) will make more volume, and you probably won't need to add sugar. Taste them to make sure.

I would use a blackberry brandy to deepen the flavor, or a raspberry to brighten it up a bit. If you can get or make apple or pear liqueur, it's good, too.

Rack off the wine and add the alcohol. Then bottle, label, and store the wine. Try it in a year, then in two, or even three, years. Consider using some half bottles, so you can taste it more often as it progresses.

You could also just bottle the wine as it is, and enjoy it, of course! In that case, stabilize it and sweeten with four to six ounces of sugar in syrup. Keep for at least a year before trying.

⌐ANCIENT MIDNIGHT⌐

You have to like black currants for this one. If you don't, substitute another dark fruit brandy.

2 lbs. blueberries
1 lb. fresh elderberries or ¼ lb. dried elderberries
2 lbs. blackberries or mulberries

2–4 ozs. banana flakes or ½ lb. dark raisins (optional)
1¾ lbs. sugar or 2 lbs. honey, adding another ½ lb. later
sufficient water to make up a gallon
½ tsp. acid blend
no tannin (the elderberries have plenty)
1 tsp. yeast nutrient
1 Campden tablet, crushed (recommended)
½ tsp. pectic enzyme
1 packet sherry or Montrachet yeast (or port, if you can get it)

Black currant brandy (cassis) or 8 ozs. Ribena (black currant syrup) AND brandy or grain alcohol. (Black currant syrup can be found in grocery stores specializing in Greek, Italian, or eastern European foods. I have found Ribena, an English syrup, in Oriental grocery stores. Don't ask me why it was there.)

Pick over the berries carefully. Watch for mold. Discard anything that looks odd. Wash the berries in cool water and drain. Soak the dried elderberries for a half hour in a cup of hot water. Drain the elderberries and reserve the water.

Wash your hands. Put the berries in a nylon straining bag and into the primary fermenter, then squash with your hands (you might want to use sanitized rubber gloves) or a sanitized potato masher. Be sure you press the berries well. Add the dried elderberries and (optional) banana flakes or raisins (these give even more body and flavor).

Boil the water and sugar or honey. Skim if necessary. Pour the hot sugar water over the crushed berries. You can chill and reserve half the water beforehand, adding it now to bring the temperature down quickly. Add the elderberry water, acid, and yeast nutrient, but wait until the temperature comes down to add the Campden tablet, if you choose to use one. Cover and fit with an air lock. Wait 12 hours to add the pectic enzyme.

Check the PA and write it down. You can adjust the PA up a bit at this point.

Twenty-four hours later, add the yeast. Stir it daily. Keep it a little warmer than usual, but not over 75°F. After about two weeks, remove the bag (don't squeeze). Discard the fruit. After the sediment has settled down again, check the PA. It will probably need to go another week. When it gets to 3 to 4 percent PA, rack the wine into your glass fermenter. Bung and fit with an air lock.

Add an extra half pound of sugar dissolved in water, to the must, gradually, watching the SG as described on page 214. If the beginning PA was higher than 14 percent, don't add it. The yeast may not take it.

Rack the wine at least twice during fermentation. You don't want any off flavors. Be sure to keep it in a dark jug, or put something over it to keep the light from stealing the color.

In six to eight months, or even more, check the PA, and judge the clarity. Taste it, too. There should be plenty of tannin from the elderberries—maybe what seems to be too much. Do you think it will gain in smoothness and flavor over the next couple of years? Here you have to decide if you want to go to the expense of adding the grain alcohol, the brandy, or the fruit brandy.

Rack off the wine and add the black currant brandy (cassis) or Ribena (black currant syrup) plus brandy or grain alcohol. Then bottle, label, and store the wine. Try it in a year, then in two, or even three, years. Consider using some half bottles, so you can taste it more often as it progresses.

You could also just bottle the wine as it is, and enjoy it, of course! In that case, stabilize it and sweeten with four to six ounces of sugar in syrup. Keep for at least a year before trying.

☞ RED PORT ☜

Intense; not for everyone!

3¾ qts. water
2¼ lbs. sugar or 2½ lbs. mild honey
3–4 lbs. fresh or frozen raspberries
1 lb. fresh or frozen blackberries or blueberries
1 lb. white raisins or 1 pint white grape concentrate
½ tsp. acid blend
1 tsp. yeast nutrient
¼ tsp. tannin
1 Campden tablet, crushed (optional)
½ tsp. pectic enzyme
1 packet champagne or sherry wine yeast
raspberry or red currant or lingonberry brandy

If using the raisins, soak them overnight.
Put the water mixed with the sugar or honey on the stove to

boil. Pick over the berries carefully, discarding any that are not up to par. Rinse lightly. Put the berries into a nylon straining bag with the raisins, if you are using them, and tie the top tightly.

Put the bag of fruit into the bottom of your primary fermenter and crush the fruit within the bag. You can use a potato masher if you prefer, but hands are the best.

Now pour the hot sugar water over the crushed fruit. This sets the color. If you prefer, you can chill and reserve half the water beforehand, adding it now to bring the temperature down quickly. Add the acid, tannin, and yeast nutrient, but wait till the temperature comes down to add the Campden tablet, if you choose to use one. Cover and fit with an air lock. Twelve hours after the Campden tablet, add the pectic enzyme. If you don't use the tablet, merely wait until the must cools down to add the pectic enzyme.

Check the PA and write it down.

Twenty-four hours later, add the yeast, made up with a little sugar water.

After two weeks, remove the bag (don't squeeze). Discard the fruit. After the sediment has settled down again, check the PA. If it is still above 3 to 4 percent, let the wine ferment for another week, then rack into your glass fermenter and add the white grape concentrate if you are using it. Bung and fit with an air lock.

Rack the wine at least twice during fermentation. Be sure to keep it in a dark jug, or put something over it to keep the light from stealing the color.

In six to eight months, check the PA and clarity. If the wine has fermented out, rack it and fortify it with whatever brandy you have decided to use, using the Pearson Square.

You can use any red liqueur with this, but you'll have to add more unless you make your own using higher proof alcohol. Raspberry (framboise) will make it more intensely raspberry, while strawberry might be nice, or cranberry, or lingonberry. You can also use apple or pear.

One thing I've always wanted to try is rose liqueur!

Rack off the wine and add the alcohol. Then bottle, label, and store the wine. Try it in a year, then in two, or even three, years. Consider using some half bottles, so you can taste it more often as it progresses.

You could also just bottle the wine as it is, and enjoy it, of course! In that case, stabilize and sweeten with four to six ounces of sugar in syrup. Keep for at least a year before trying.

☞WHITE PORT☜

Some people consider white port to be an abomination, but they'd consider our fruit ports in the same light, so what the heck?

water to make up the gallon, as needed
2¼ lbs. sugar or 2½ lbs. mild honey
8 lbs. crushed or chopped apples or 24 oz. can frozen apple juice
3 lbs. fresh or 1 lb. dried apricots or peaches
2 tsps. acid blend
1 tsp. yeast nutrient
¼ tsp. tannin
1 Campden tablet, crushed (optional)
½ tsp. pectic enzyme
1 packet sherry wine yeast
Brandy, Calvados (apple brandy), or fruit liqueur

Put the water mixed with the sugar or honey on the stove to boil. If you are using crushed or chopped fresh fruit, do it as quickly as possible. Tart apples mixed with sweeter apples are better than all sweet dessert apples. Peels are OK, though it's best to get rid of the seeds if you can. Pit the apricots or peaches and chop. If using dried fruit, chop. Put the crushed or chopped fruit into a nylon straining bag and put it in the bottom of your primary fermenter.

Now pour the hot sugar water over the fruit or the frozen apple juice. If you prefer, you can chill and reserve half the water beforehand, adding it now to bring the temperature down quickly. Add the acid, tannin, and yeast nutrient, but wait till the temperature comes down to add the Campden tablet, if you choose to use one. Cover and fit with an air lock. Twelve hours after the Campden tablet, add the pectic enzyme. If you don't use the tablet, merely wait until the must cools down to add the pectic enzyme.

Check the PA and write it down.

Twenty-four hours later, add the yeast. After one or two weeks, remove the bag (don't squeeze). Discard the fruit. After the sediment has settled down again, check the PA. If it is still above 3 to 4 percent, let it ferment another week or so, then rack it into your glass fermenter and fit with an air lock.

Gradually add an extra half pound of sugar, dissolved in water, to the must, watching the SG as described on page 214.

Rack the wine at least twice during secondary fermentation.

In six to eight months, check the PA and clarity. If the wine has fermented out, rack it again and add whatever brandy you have decided to use.

A white or yellow liqueur will be nice here: you can use apple, pear, peach, or apricot. Don't use applejack unless you are sure you like it. Most domestic brands I have tried have not been very good. Calvados, the French apple brandy (no sweetener) is better, but hideously expensive.

Rack off the wine and add the alcohol. Then bottle, label, and store the wine. Try it in a year, then in two, or even three, years. Consider using some half bottles, so you can taste it more often as it progresses.

You could also just bottle the wine as it is, and enjoy it, of course! In that case, stabilize it and sweeten it with four to six ounces of sugar in syrup. Keep for at least a year before trying.

These are the basic methods. You could make any wine in this book into a sort of port, just by fortifying it and sweetening it. I recommend using only your best wines for this purpose. Combos or tutti-fruttis produce the best flavors.

SHERRY

Back in part two, in the section on dried fruits, I pretty well covered sherry-type wines. There are also a few in part three under spiced wines.

Sherry-type wines are fortified pretty much the same way port-type wines are; however, many people prefer dry sherries to sweet, or "cream," types. So for sherries, you simply don't add very much sugar in the final fortification—use brandy or vodka instead of fruit brandies.

Remember also that you don't have to fortify these wines if you don't want to. They'll keep a reasonable time and taste very nice on their own.

In general, raisins and other dried fruit very effectively provide that "oxidized" flavor and the characteristic brown color so familiar in sherry. But in this section I will offer some examples of some more classic home winemaking recipes. When you rack these wines, let them splash a bit. They need the oxygen.

☜GOLDEN PARSNIP SHERRY☞

If you use store-bought parsnips, remove the wax coating that is sometimes applied to them—otherwise, you'll have a waxy mess. You'll have to scrape and peel them.

2 lbs. dark raisins
6 lbs. parsnips
10 or 20 bruised peppercorns (optional)
zest and juice of 3 oranges
juice and zest of 2 large lemons or 3 tsps. acid blend
1 gallon water
2 lbs. sugar or 2½ lbs. honey
1 tsp. yeast nutrient
1 Campden tablet, crushed (optional)
½ tsp. pectic enzyme
1 packet sherry yeast

Soak the raisins overnight. Drain, reserve juice, and chop.

Scrub the parsnips well; cut off the tops and the root ends. Cut or shred them finely. SIMMER, do not boil, with the peppercorns (if you are using them) until tender.

Remove the zest from the citrus fruit (no white pith), and squeeze the juice. Place zest and raisins in a small nylon straining bag and place in your primary fermenter.

Strain the parsnips (and peppercorns) from the water. Remove about a quart of the water to add back later if you don't have enough. It's hard to say how much you will have lost in steam while cooking. Add the sugar or the honey, and simmer until the sugar is dissolved. If using honey, simmer 10–15 minutes while stirring, and skim any scum.

Pour the hot water into a sanitized primary fermenter over the zest. Add the fruit juices. You can reserve a bit of the orange juice and extra parsnip water to start the yeast later, if you like. Check to see if you have a gallon of must. If not, make it up with the reserved water. Add yeast nutrient, tannin, and acid blend if you didn't use lemons. Cover, and attach an air lock. Let the must cool, then add the Campden tablet, if you choose to use one. Twelve hours after the Campden tablet, add the pectic enzyme. If you don't use the tablet, merely wait until the must cools down to add the pectic enzyme.

Twenty-four hours later, check the PA and add the yeast.

Stir daily. In two weeks or so, lift out the bag of raisins and let it drain back into the container before removing it. Do not squeeze. Let the wine settle, and rack into a secondary fermenter. Bung and fit with an air lock. Rack it as necessary in the next six months or so. Check the PA.

If you want to try to tease the alcohol up, use an extra half pound of sugar in a syrup solution as described on page 214. Sherries are usually lower than port in alcohol content, though. When it ferments out, fortify using plain brandy or grain alcohol. Bottle. Keep it for two years at least.

NOTE: As a variation, substitute carrots or potatoes for the parsnips in the amounts suggested in chapter 7.

☙PRUNED APPLE SHERRY❧

4 lbs. dark prunes, pitted
zest and juice of 3 oranges
2 tsps. acid blend or zest and juice of 2 large lemons
1 12 oz. can frozen apple juice
2 lbs. sugar or 2½ lbs. dark honey
¼ tsp. tannin
1 tsp. yeast nutrient
1 Campden tablet, crushed (optional)
½ tsp. pectic enzyme
1 packet sherry yeast

Soak the pitted prunes overnight in some of the water. Drain, chop, and place them in a nylon straining bag with the zest of the oranges and lemons, if you are using them. Put the bag in the bottom of a sanitized primary fermenter. Thaw the apple juice.

Boil the rest of the water and sugar or honey, and skim, if

necessary. Pour over the prunes, prune soaking water, and frozen juice.

You can reserve a bit of the orange juice to start the yeast later, if you like. Add the yeast nutrient, tannin, and acid blend if you didn't use lemons. Cover, and attach an air lock. Let the must cool, then add the Campden tablet, if you choose to use one. Twelve hours after the Campden tablet, add the pectic enzyme. If you don't use the tablet, merely wait until the must cools down to add the pectic enzyme.

Twenty-four hours later, check the PA and add the yeast.

Stir daily. In two weeks or so, lift out the bag of prunes and let it drain back into the container before removing it. Do not squeeze. Let the wine settle, and rack into a secondary fermenter. Bung and fit with an air lock. Rack as necessary in the next six months or so. Check the PA. When it ferments out, fortify it with plain brandy or grain alcohol. Bottle. Keep for two years at least.

☙CITRUS SHERRY❧

10 heavy juice oranges
1 lb. pitted dates
10 bruised peppercorns (optional)
3¾ gallons water
2 lbs. sugar or 2¼ lbs. dark honey
no acid
1 tsp. yeast nutrient
½ tsp. tannin
1 Campden tablet, crushed (optional)
½ tsp. pectic enzyme
1 packet sherry yeast

Pare the zest from four or five of the oranges. Then peel the fruits and section them, getting rid of as much white pith as you can. Put the segments and the zest in a nylon straining bag, and put it in the bottom of a primary fermenter with the pitted dates. Add the peppercorns, if you use them. Mash with very clean hands or a sanitized potato masher.

Boil the water and sugar or honey, and skim if necessary.

Pour the hot sugar water over the crushed fruit. If you prefer, you can chill and reserve half the water beforehand, adding it now to bring the temperature down quickly. Add the tannin and yeast nutrient, but wait until the temperature comes down to add the Campden tablet, if you choose to use one. Cover and fit with an air lock. Twelve hours after the Campden tablet, add the pectic enzyme. If you don't use the tablet, merely wait until the must cools down to add the pectic enzyme. Be sure to use the pectic enzyme!

Check the PA and write it down.

Twenty-four hours later, add the yeast. Stir down daily. After about one week, remove the bag (don't squeeze). Discard the fruit, and after the sediment has settled down again, check the PA. If it is above 3 to 4 percent, let the must ferment for another week or so and rack into your glass fermenter. Fit it with an air lock.

Rack once or twice during fermentation.

In four to six months, check the PA and clarity. If fermented out, fortify with plain brandy or grain alcohol if desired and bottle. This might be more to your liking if sweetened with 4-6 oz sugar, as well. Keep it for at least two years.

☙SPICED BANANA SHERRY❧

1 lb. dark raisins
3 lbs. very ripe, black (but not rotten) organic bananas
3–4 sticks cinnamon or 20 bruised cassia buds
several bruised allspice
4 ozs. grated ginger
1 gallon water
2 lbs. sugar or 2½ lbs. dark honey
2 tsps. acid blend or juice of 2 large lemons
1 tsp. yeast nutrient
¼ tsp. tannin
1 Campden tablet, crushed (optional)
½ tsp. pectic enzyme
1 packet sherry wine yeast

Soak the raisins overnight in some of the water. Drain, chop, put them in a nylon straining bag, and place in the bottom of a sanitized primary fermenter.

Wash and slice the bananas, peels and all (which is why I suggest using organic bananas). Put them in another nylon straining bag and simmer for half an hour in half the water. Lift the bag out of the water and let it drain, then pour the banana water into a primary fermenter. Boil the sugar or honey in the rest of the water, and skim if necessary.

Now pour the hot sugar water over the must and the raisins and spices bag. Add the acid, tannin, and yeast nutrient, but wait until the temperature comes down to add the Campden tablet, if you choose to use one. Cover and fit with an air lock. Twelve hours after the Campden table, add the pectic enzyme. If you don't use the tablet, merely wait until the must cools down to add the pectic enzyme.

Check the PA and write it down. It might seem a bit high because of the pulp escaping the nylon bag. It will probably look a little alarming.

Twenty-four hours later, add the yeast.

Stir daily. Check the PA. After a week, lift out the bag and drain; do not squeeze before removing. You might have to make up the gallon with a little extra boiled water to make up for the sediment. Rack the wine into a secondary fermenter. Bung and fit with an air lock.

Rack it at least twice during fermentation.

In six months, check for clarity and check the PA to see if it has fermented out. Sweeten and fortify with plain brandy or grain alcohol if desired. Keep for two years before sampling.

Feel free to experiment with combinations. Aim for a rich, complex taste. Don't forget that it's easy to add color to sherry-like wines by adding toast or grains as discussed back in chapter 8.

APERITIF WINES

Europe has developed many aperitif wines. These are wines that are meant to wake the appetite. Byrrh, Dubonnet, Campari, and vermouth all come to mind.

Some of them are fortified, and some aren't. Some of them are very sweet, some are dry, some include a lot of herbs and taste almost medicinal. Herb and seed wines may actually qualify as aperitifs.

It is my sneaking suspicion that most aperitif wines started out as wines that didn't make good table wines, so people decided to make "lemonade" out of their "lemons." I could be wrong.

Almost any wine can be served as an aperitif; Champagne and

sherry are both accepted as aperitifs. You can also serve one of your fruitier wines like blackberry over ice with a twist of lemon or lime or orange.

You can also buy vermouth flavoring and experiment with adding it to one of your white wines.

SPARKLING WINES

It's hard not to love a sparkling wine. There is just something about bubbles that fascinates, makes wine taste better, and lends a feeling of celebration to any festive occasion.

Real Champagne comes from the Champagne region of France. Everything else is sparkling wine. It might be made by the Champagne method, but it is still "merely" sparkling wine.

There are six basic ways to get the sparkle into wine:

- accident
- *methode Champenois*
- closed tank fermentation, a.k.a. *cuvée close*
- Andovin method
- carbon dioxide forced into the wine
- cheat

Accidents do happen. Sometimes you think you've fermented out the wine, and lo, after bottling and aging it, you open the wine and you get a pleasant gush. The wine is *petillant,* or fizzy. You could refrigerate the rest of that batch before you open it, hoping that none of the corks blow and that none of the bottles break. The best thing to do is to stabilize the wine and rebottle it. I've had a few surprises, but I've been lucky, losing only a few corks and some wine. However, I don't recommend you do things by accident; it's too dangerous and messy.

The traditional method, *methode Champenois,* takes time and skill. The grapes are grown in a region with chalky soil, then they are harvested and made into wine. Later in the winter the wines are blended to each house's specification, and the wine is bottled in extra-strong bottles with a heavy cork that is tied down. Then the wine is allowed to ferment and build up carbon dioxide. It is put upside down in a rack called a *pupitres,* which looks like a huge sandwich signboard with holes cut out at various angles.

A skilled worker gradually moves the bottle up the rack, shaking down the sediment till the bottles are upside-down and the sediment is lodged in the neck.

Then the cork is loosened, and the sediment is allowed to spurt out. Afterward the bottle is topped up with wine, and the *dosage,* a bit of sugar in syrup, is added. The bottles are corked again and allowed to ferment out.

Nowadays, most wineries using the Champagne method have modified things a bit by using a bottle cap instead of a cork the first time around and freezing the neck of the bottle so that when the sediment is propelled out, it goes out in a solid plug of ice; that way, not as much wine is lost.

The Andovin method is much simpler, but it requires a large empty freezer. It modifies the sediment procedure considerably by pouring the wine off the sediment into bottles containing frozen dosage. It is still a somewhat dangerous, tricky method.

These methods produce fine, long-lasting bubbles and don't traumatize the wine.

I have tried the Champagne method and concluded that my nerves and coordination are not up to the excitement of this particular winemaking tradition. The shower stall ever afterward seemed to have a faint winy smell to it, as well.

As an older gentleman who makes 200 bottles of rhubarb sparkling wine every year explained to me, "God hates a coward."

I had not thought of it as a religious issue before.

As you can see, there are dedicated amateur winemakers who love sparkling wines and seem to have no trouble with *methode Champenois.* If you want to try it, I suggest that you read a good book on the subject (see bibliography), get to know someone who uses this method, and get them to show you.

I only recently heard of the Andovin method, and one day I'll try it, when the freezer isn't full of fruit waiting to be made into wine. It is described in the Andersons' *Winemaking* book (see bibliography).

Cuvée close is just not doable by amateurs. You need equipment only a commercial winery or a very rich person could afford to own.

Forcing in carbon dioxide—which is how most cheap sparkling

wines (and soda pops) are made—works fine and is easily
achieved at home by using a soda syphon. Cool the bottle of wine
for several hours in the refrigerator, then open it and pour it into
the soda syphon. Cool that for a few more hours, and there you
are, sparkling wine! The bubbles are large and don't last as long
as those produced by the traditional method, but it works.

Then there is that method known in the scientific world as
cheating.

Cheating has a long and noble history in the world of professional and home winemaking. It works pretty darned well if you
don't mind the possibility of a little sediment now and then and
some extra work.

If you have ever made beer or hard cider, you are probably on
to me now.

To *cheat,* you make a nice dry wine of about 10 percent alcohol
and the all-important *dosage,* before bottling it in champagne bottles as you would beer, using either bottle caps or plastic champagne stoppers and wires.

First, you need to make the wine. Use any of the light-colored
wines from part two, or even the frozen juice wines from part
one. You want a wine that you already know you like, that will
ferment out dry, and that will taste fine when young. Some that I
have tried are apple, peach, potato, apricot, citrus, mead, strawberry, raspberry, and Pink Plonk. Uncomplicated single-fruit wines
such as apple seem to work out best.

Other wines that have traditionally been used to make sparkling
wines are gooseberry, rhubarb, elderflower, dandelion, white grape,
plum, and pineapple.

There is absolutely no reason why you can't make sparkling
red wines. Remember that most of our fruit reds are actually
dark rosés.

However, there is a reason why you can't make sparkling sherry
or port: once you've fortified them, the alcohol will kill off any
dosage you add.

When making sparkling wine, champagne yeast is nice but not
essential. Champagne yeast ferments out fast and leaves a firm
deposit, which is why it has become champagne yeast. However,
there is no reason why you can't use another yeast.

The way to proceed is to keep the PA at 10 percent or so, so
you *know* it will ferment out and leave room for the dosage. Don't

get cute and try for more alcohol or sweetness. Don't use sodium metabisulphite after you've added the yeast in the initial fermentation. The acidity should be 0.60–0.75.

Put the wine into a glass secondary fermenter and let it go for six months at least, racking twice. Ferment it out dry, dry, dry and clear, clear, clear. Rack the wine into a sanitized primary fermenter.

Then add NO MORE than HALF A CUP (NOT HALF A POUND!!!!) of sugar to five gallons, or 1½ tablespoons per gallon. Stir it in well. If you like, you can make it into a syrup first, to make sure it gets distributed evenly. There should still be enough live yeast in the wine to take care of the sugar. Traditionally more yeast is used, but I rarely have a problem working with young wines, and I don't think adding the yeast is a safe thing to do in this method.

Rack the wine into sanitized champagne bottles that have been rinsed out with boiling water after you have sanitized them. You don't want to kill off the leftover yeast in the wine.

You can get champagne bottles from the wine supply store, some caterers and restaurants, or friends who have just had a wedding or large New Year's party. Clean the bottles and soak them carefully, just as you would any wine bottle. Champagne bottles tend to get more mold in them because no one ever rinses them out after festivities. Sigh.

NEVER USE NORMAL WINE BOTTLES!!!!! They weren't meant for this job. Don't use beer bottles, either. There is too much potential for mistakes, which, with the percent of sugar we are using when making the wine, could be disastrous.

For capping you will need a bottle capper that will accommodate champagne bottles, and champagne bottles that will accommodate crown caps. Most of them will. You can buy a capper at most wine and beer supply stores. They're known as bench cappers, because you use them on a workbench. They cost more than the simpler handheld capper, though usually well under fifty dollars.

To use the plastic champagne corks, you just have to whack in the cork gently with a padded mallet, and wire it down with a soft-wire assembly, which you can usually get at your wine supply store along with the plastic corks.

I would prefer that you use the champagne corks, because I

know if you've made a mistake, the cork will go before the bot-tle does.

If by some wonderful chance you have access to cork champagne corks and have the device you need to insert them, please do so.

Twist on the wire hoods carefully so that you fasten them snugly, but don't break the wire. Rinse the bottles off and let them dry, then label them and lay them in a moderately warm, quiet place for a while. You don't have to lay them on their sides like regularly corked bottles if you don't want to, but it doesn't hurt.

If you are nervous, you can put the bottles near a floor drain with a heavy cardboard box over them for a couple of weeks. After years of experience in making beer, wine, and soda pop, I'm pretty sure everything will be OK.

After a month or two, you can try a bottle, just to see how it is doing, but you are better off waiting three to six months.

Before opening, refrigerate the bottle, standing it upright in the refrigerator for two to three hours, or ice it for an hour or so in an ice bucket. If you used a cap, open the wine over the sink, with glasses handy.

If you used the plastic corks, carefully remove the wire. As the Flying Karamazov Brothers say during one of their acts when open-ing a champagne bottle, the prophylactic is off! Get a pair of pliers or one of those rubber disks for opening jars, and ease the cork out over the sink. ALWAYS make sure the cork is not pointing at any-one, including yourself, and not at anything breakable, either.

And there you are. Sparkling wine. Cheers!

If you enjoyed this section, then I encourage you to study fur-ther. Get some books on the subject of sparkling wines and learn all you can, including the proper methods, from other people.

NOTE: For making hard cider, perry, or soda pop, use glass beer or glass soda bottles that will take a crown cap, and sanitize them just like wine bottles. Rack in the fermented-out cider, perry, or soda pop, and cap the bottles with sterilized crown caps. Turn each bottle on its side to check for leaks. Store upright for at least two weeks for soda, two months for cider and perry. Chill before opening or you'll be sorry!

All of this is described more carefully in the last chapter under soda pop, but it's pretty simple.

Extra Helpings

COMPETITIONS AND JUDGING

Y̶ou might be interested in competitions and judging. It's a good way to test your palate and your winemaking skills. Even if you don't compete yourself, it's always fascinating to see what wins. Alas, unless you are a judge, you probably won't get to taste the winners or losers.

Amateur wines are frequently judged on the Davis system, named after the Davis campus of the University of California, which has done many good things for winemaking in general and home winemaking specifically.

Even if you never intend to enter a competition, it is useful to know how wines are generally judged. The Davis system is based on a 20-point scale. Canada and Europe use a different scale, but the idea is the same.

- Appearance or clarity = 1 or 2 points
  A bit of sediment on the bottom is allowed, but the wine itself should be absolutely bright and clear. "Star-bright" is the usual phrase.

- Aroma and bouquet = 5 points
  This gets tricky, depending on if it is a young wine or an older one. You should be able to smell the ingredients, and the general overall smell should be pleasant, as well. Any chemical or off smells costs points.

- Astringency = 1 point
  This refers to tannin, not acidity. You don't want the wine to have a puckery effect in the mouth nor do you want it to be insipid. Red wines have more astringency, white ones, less. A young red could have a lot.

- Body = 2 points
  How does the wine feel in the mouth, aside from the sugar and tannin? Can you tell there is something there besides water? Red wines call for more body, while most whites are expected to be on the thin side.

- Color = 1 point
  Red wines should be red, never brown. White wines can vary from really white to gold. Rosé should be a nice color, not tan or muddy. How spinach wine is judged I have no idea. There are no plaid wines.

- Flavor and balance = 5 points
  Does this taste like wine? Or does it taste like yeast, aluminum siding, mice, rubber, caramel corn, or old athletic shoes? Even if you don't like red wines, can you tell this tastes good (for a red)?

- Sugar = 1 point
  This depends on the type of wine the label declares it to be. If it is a sweet port, it should be sweet. If it is a dry table wine, it should be dry.

- Total acid = 2 points
  Again, this depends on the type of wine. White wines are usually higher in acid than reds. Don't confuse acid with tannin.

- General impression = 2 points
  Well, would you buy it? Would you trade for it? Would
  you take it as a gift with a smile of joy or a polite, tight
  grin—and pour it down the sink later?

A standard kind of bottle is usually expected. Make it clean
(even polished) and fill the bottle up to about ¼ inch from the
cork. Sometimes a label is provided, sometimes not. Label the
wine clearly.

You might want to get together with some of your winemaking
and non-winemaking friends and hold a blind wine judging. Have
an impartial person cover the labels of the bottles with paper and
mark them by assigned numbers from a master list.

Bring out the wines in rounds of three or four bottles of like
kinds and have people put down their impressions by the number
on the bottle. Later, unmask the bottles and provide a master list.

Some friends did this with commercial wines. In the Cabernet
section, it was discovered that the two most popular were a $50
bottle and a $3 bottle. Needless to say, there was a run on Bulgar-
ian reds the next day at the wine store.

COMMERCIAL WINEMAKING

If you get a chance to visit a commercial winery, do so. It's
a fascinating experience. Smaller wineries are usually more
interesting.

Compared to the small lots you and I work with, the sheer bulk
of the operation is exhilarating.

Many wineries use mechanical harvesting, but the better (and
smaller) wineries still use people, which is kinder to the grapes and
the vines. One would prefer that it were also kind to the people.

Trucks bring the grapes in from the fields. They are then tum-
bled into huge vats that are covered with grills to keep out stray
branches (and rabbits and dogs, I suppose).

Stalks are sometimes removed before crushing, but not always.
Many red wines are fermented in open containers, and are stirred
or pumped regularly to make sure that the "cap," or floating mass
of grapes and skins, doesn't cause problems with the wine below
by cutting off all of the oxygen or rotting.

When enough tannin and color have been extracted into the

wine, the wine is pressed. There are many different ways of doing this, but in the old-fashioned way, grapes are loaded onto huge mats, the mats are stacked, and the juice is pressed out by means of winching a huge screw, like a printing press (hmm, is this where Gutenberg got the idea?). The wine pours out the sides and is then pumped back into a sealed vat.

The pomace, or what is left of the skins and stems, is used as compost or silage.

And you know what happens to the wine!

There is also a lot of science behind grape winemaking these days, which improves methods more universally than mere guessing used to. Much of the time spent in the laboratory is devoted to simply finding out *why* old Jose's or Drucilla's techniques worked.

Winemaking is still a very human process and will remain so, no matter how much wine is produced. In California alone there are now so many small, specialized wineries compared to twenty years ago that wine stores are treasure-houses of discovery. You never know what you will find. Heck, even the Smothers Brothers make wine! And now so do you and I.

HOMEMADE LIQUEURS OR CORDIALS

Commercial liqueurs are made two ways—by distillation of a fruit wine or by infusing the fruit, seeds, or herbs into already distilled alcohol.

Private citizens are not allowed to make distilled alcohol in this country. You can buy it, though! Then you can use it to make liqueurs and cordials.

There are two basic ways of doing this. You can buy the liqueur extracts ready-made and add them to your own alcohol and sugar, or you can use real fruit and soak it in the alcohol and sugar.

I've done both. For the most part, I prefer using real fruit, but the extracts are fun.

USING EXTRACTS

The most commonly available extracts are the Noirot brand, available in most wine supply places. Directions come with the extract, but basically, you use 2 cups of sugar made into syrup with one cup of water, or 2½ cups of mild honey with less than one cup of water, a bottle of the extract, and 16 ounces of 80 proof vodka. This gives you about a quart of a 40 proof (20 percent alcohol) product.

If you use high-proof alcohol, you get a higher alcohol content. Forty proof is perfectly fine for sipping.

USING REAL FRUIT

Using real fruit is almost as easy. I keep the sugar at a minimum at first, but it is necessary to use some because it helps draw out the flavor, as does the alcohol. *Never* squeeze the fruit at the end of the process. You'll just make the drink harder to clear.

If you are making liqueurs to fortify your wines, use the highest-proof alcohol you can get.

These keep for a long time, but they do deteriorate after several years. Keep liqueurs cool and in a dark place.

⚭RASPBERRY LIQUEUR⚭

1–2 lbs. of the best raspberries you can pick or buy
1 cup white sugar
1 bottle vodka or high-proof alcohol
1 sterilized quart canning jar or other glass jar with an air-tight lid

Boil the canning jar or wash it well, rinse it in warm water, and pour boiling water into it. When the jar has cooled, pour out the water and put in the raspberries. Pour in the sugar and as much vodka as the rest of the jar will hold, leaving an inch or two clearance. Fit the jar with a sterilized canning lid and ring, or some other tight-fitting lid, depending on the jar.

Sometimes I put a barrier of plastic wrap between the jar and lid if I am not using a canning jar lid.

Put the jar in a dark place, but somewhere where you will see it every other day or so, perhaps near the coffee or tea. Shake the jar every day, or at least a few times a week for a month.

The sugar will dissolve gradually, and the color of the liquid will become a lovely red, while the raspberries will turn pale and uninteresting.

After the raspberries are almost white, let the jar settle, and

NOTE: You can use this recipe for any berry or cherries. Every year I make pie cherry liqueur. Pit the sour cherries, add them to the vodka, and tie the pits in a bit of cheesecloth and add them as well. Some people crack a few of the pits for that almond flavor.

Also note that, especially with strawberries, you might get some globs of pectin floating around in the finished product. They are harmless but look disgusting. Filter them out when they form. I've never tried it, but it might be interesting to see if mashing the strawberries and adding half a teaspoon of pectic enzyme for twelve hours before adding the sugar and alcohol would help.

carefully pour out the liquid. Some books say the fruit is now wonderful on ice cream, but I find it repulsive and throw it away.

Taste the liqueur. If you want it sweeter, boil another ½ to 1 cup of sugar with half the amount of water, cool it, and add in increments, tasting as you go. You will find that this procedure makes you quite cheerful.

I now filter the liqueur through a paper coffee filter, probably losing some alcohol content as I go, but that's life. You can also use several thicknesses of clean cheesecloth.

Store the liqueur in another jar or pretty bottle that has been cleaned and rinsed out with boiling water. Make sure the lid is tight. Keep in the dark to maintain the color.

NOTE: Liqueurs are superb for after-dinner sipping instead of a dessert. They are also wonderful to put *in* or *on* desserts. As long as you have a good vanilla ice cream in the freezer and this liqueur or others in the cupboard, you have an elegant easy dessert. Put out your selection of liqueurs and let the guests choose their favorite. Toasted almonds are a nice touch, too.

Another easy dessert is to make one layer of a dense chocolate cake, sprinkle liqueur over it (raspberry, orange, or cherry) and top it with fruit to match or contrast, or drizzle chocolate icing over the cake. Pound cake is great this way, too.

☙ORANGE LIQUEUR❧

This takes some forethought. During the winter, eat lots of aromatic oranges and tangerines, preferably organic. Peel them in large pieces, enjoy the fruit, and save the peelings. With a grapefruit spoon, carefully scrape away as much of the inner white pith of the peel as you can, then lay the peels out to dry. When you get about a pint jar's worth, you are ready to begin making this useful liqueur.

1 pint dried orange and tangerine peels
1 cup sugar
1 bottle vodka
1 quart jar

Boil the canning jar or wash it well, rinse it in warm water, and pour boiling water into it. When the jar has cooled, pour out the water and put in the orange peels. Pour in the sugar and as much vodka as the rest of the jar will hold, leaving an inch or two clearance. Fit the jar with a sterilized canning lid and ring, or some other tight-fitting lid, depending on the jar.

Sometimes I put a barrier of plastic wrap between the jar and the lid if I am not using a canning jar lid.

Put the jar in a dark place, but somewhere where you will see it every other day or so. Shake the jar every day, or at least a few times a week for a month.

The sugar will dissolve gradually, and the color of the liquid will become a pale orange. It will take several months to leach the flavor out of the peels. Taste it once in a while to see how it's doing. There is likely to be a very firm layer of pectin on the bottom of the jar. Ignore it.

Let the jar settle, and carefully pour out the liquid.

Taste the liqueur. If you want it sweeter, boil another ½ to 1 cup of sugar with half the amount of water, cool it, and add in increments, tasting as you go.

Filter the liqueur through a paper coffee filter or use several thicknesses of clean cheesecloth.

Store the liqueur in another jar or pretty bottle that has been cleaned and rinsed out with boiling water. Make sure the lid is tight. Keep in the dark to maintain the color.

This liqueur is infinitely useful. I make this with Everclear and use it for orange flavoring in cookies and cakes.

❧NUT LIQUEUR❧

A bit expensive, but very nice! You *must* use fresh nuts. Be picky when you buy them. I suggest going to a co-op.

2 lbs. fresh, unsalted, unblanched almonds, chopped OR the same amount of filberts or hazelnuts (though be sure they are fresh!)
1 cup sugar
1 bottle vodka or brandy
1 half-gallon jar or 2 quart jars

Rinse the jar out with boiling water.

Put the chopped nuts in the jar, and add the sugar and the vodka or brandy. Shake daily for a month or more until fragrant, then strain off the nuts, and add sugar syrup if desired. The color will be brown or tan. Filter or stand to clear. Nuts have oil in them, and so this will, too—it won't keep as long as fruit will, but it is quite nice to have around. Don't invite any squirrels over.

❧SEED LIQUEUR❧

You can use anise or caraway for this. It might not be to everyone's taste. If you aren't sure, make a small batch at first.

4 tablespoons anise or caraway seeds, bruised or half ground
1 cup sugar
1 bottle vodka or brandy
1 quart jar

Put the seeds into a clean jar that has been rinsed out with boiling water. Add the sugar and the vodka or brandy. Shake daily for a month or more until fragrant, then strain off the seeds, and add sugar syrup if desired. The color will be tan. Filter or stand to clear.

⤜APPLE LIQUEUR⤝

You want tart, flavorful apples for this. Grocery store apples won't do.

2–3 lbs. tart/sweet flavorful apples
1 cup sugar
1 bottle vodka or brandy
1 half-gallon jar

Wash and core the apples, but don't remove the peel. Chop them finely. Rinse out the jar with boiling water. Add the sugar and the brandy and fit the jar with a lid. Shake every day for one to two months. Sometimes the peel will give it a rosy tint.

Strain out the fruit, filter, and add sugar syrup to taste. This also might develop a pectin haze, so be sure to filter.

NOTE: This recipe also works for pears. The pears should be firm but ripe.

Either fruit takes a little spicing very well. Add some cinnamon stick and/or ginger to the fruit when soaking. Be sure not to use ground spices, as they will make the liqueur cloudy.

⤜APRICOT OR PEACH LIQUEUR⤝

1–2 lbs. dead-ripe apricots or peaches
1 cup sugar
1 bottle brandy or vodka
1 half-gallon jar or 2 quart jars

Wash and pit the apricots. Rinse the jar out with boiling water, add the apricots or peaches, sugar, and alcohol. Cover and shake once a day or so for one to two months. Strain and filter, then sweeten to taste with sugar syrup. These fruits are also nice lightly spiced with whole spices. Some people like to add a couple of the cracked pits to the fruit during soaking.

☙COFFEE VANILLA LIQUEUR❧

This isn't exactly cheap to make, but it's very nice.

2 ozs. good instant coffee
2 cups sugar
4 ozs. really good vanilla (do not use imitation vanilla)
1–2 Madagascar or Tahitian vanilla beans (optional)
1 bottle brandy or vodka

Rinse the jar out with boiling water. Drain.

Heat the water, coffee, and the sugar to simmer. Remove from the heat and cool. If you are using the vanilla beans, chop them fine, losing none of the black inner seeds, and put them in the jar. Add the 4 ounces of vanilla. Pour in the coffee/sugar/water and stir. After two to three months, strain out the vanilla beans. Bottle. You might want to add more sugar.

A tablespoon or two of this in chocolate cookies, cake batter, or icing is a wonderful addition. It doesn't overwhelm the chocolate but instead gives it more depth.

You can pour some rum or brandy over the vanilla beans after you have removed them; you will get more flavor out of them if you let them stand for another few months.

☙EASY WHISKEY LIQUEUR❧

Don't use the best whiskey for this. A blended whiskey is just fine.

1 bottle whiskey
2 cups orange blossom honey
zest of 2 oranges or tangerines
4 tablespoons coriander seeds, bruised

Rinse out the jar with boiling water. Drain.

Mix everything together in the jar, put the lid on, and shake once a day for a month. Taste, and decide if you want more honey or more orange flavor. Strain or filter, and bottle the liqueur.

☙HERBAL OR FLOWER LIQUEUR❧

This could be tricky. It really depends on what you like and how you like it. Many commercial liqueurs have herbs and spices in them. I think blends work better than single herbs, spices, or flowers (except for roses).

I tried making lemon balm liqueur once, and it tasted like my favorite bath shampoo. I made mint liqueur once, and it tasted like sweet Listerine. If you can get the tiny, low-growing Corsican mint, you've got the proper kind for crème de menthe.

The general idea is the same in the previous recipes. Flowers should be only those you are certain are not poisonous. Herbs can be fresh or fresh dried. Spices should be used with a judicious hand. Citrus is always a nice note.

For flowers, use 1–2 cups fresh petals; for fresh herbs, about 1 cup; for spices, 2–3 tablespoons. You can make small batches and see which ones you like and which ones you don't, and then blend to see what combinations you like.

Don't hesitate to try other fruits. You really can't go too far wrong. The stronger the flavor of the fruit, the less of it you need to use. The softer the flavor, the more you need. Experiment and have fun.

FOR CHILDREN OF ALL AGES

For those of you who don't like or can't tolerate alcohol, homemade soda pop is fun and easy. There is a little alcohol in it, but only a tiny bit. Many commercial soda pops have a little bit in them, too.

Extracts are easily available at a grocery store or at the wine and beer supply store. I prefer the kinds from the wine supply store. You can get cola, root beer, sarsaparilla, ginger ale, cherry, raspberry, and probably a few others.

There is also no reason you can't use regular flavoring as extracts. The colors won't be as attractive, and you might have to double the amount of extract you use, but hey, coconut soda pop? Pineapple? It might be worth a try.

The kind from the wine supply store comes in 4 ounce bottles, and supposedly you can get four gallons of soda from each one, but it is my experience that only a very young child will care for the weak taste if you make them at that dilution!

If you know how to make and bottle beer or cider, you are halfway there. You can follow the various directions the extracts give, or you can follow mine, which makes less soda but has pretty good flavor.

First, I recommend that you use champagne yeast for this. In a pinch you can use a beer yeast, but champagne comes out the best. You don't want to use the whole packet of yeast, only a little of it, so you could start some wine while you make the soda, or you could make more than one kind of soda!

If you wrap it up tight and keep it in the fridge, the leftover yeast keeps for about a month.

Use only the returnable kind of beer or soda bottles, washed clean, and soaked overnight in a tub of water with 2 ounces chlorine bleach per five gallons of water to sanitize. Use new crown caps, boiled for five minutes and left in the water until you use them. Sanitize a primary fermenter.

ᗢSODA POPᗣ

4 ozs. Homebrew brand extract, any flavor OR 4–6 ozs. other
  extracts (be sure to shake the bottle before using)
2½ gallons water
4½ cups sugar
¼–½ tsp. champagne yeast
24–28 12 oz. beer or soda bottles and crown caps

Dissolve the yeast in one cup of the water at body temperature, and let it sit for five minutes.

Mix the sugar and most of the extract with enough of the rest of the water to dissolve the sugar in the primary fermenter at warm body temperature (not over 100°).

They say to use warm tap water, but I've heard it isn't good for you to use warm or hot tap water for anything other than washing, so I would advocate using cold tap water, adding boiling water until you get the right temperature. Use your floating thermometer or apply the scientific guess-and-by-golly test of dipping your wrist in the water to see how hot is it . . . carefully. Dipping in your big toe is not acceptable.

Stir until you don't hear any of the sugar scraping along the sides and bottom and you are sure the sugar is dissolved. A clean metal spoon is fine for this purpose.

Now add the yeast and the rest of the warm water. Taste it and see how you like it. Add the last ounce or so of the extract. Sometimes the strength differs from package to package, so this is a way of making sure it isn't too strong. You can always add a little more water and sugar, too.

Fill the drained, rinsed bottles with your racking tube, leaving an inch or two in the neck. Seal with a crown capper. Make sure the seals are good.

Rinse off the outsides of the bottles, and put them in a covered cardboard box (a beer case is good). Keep them in a cool (but not cold), dark place for a couple of weeks. If you are nervous, place the box near a drain in case you mismeasured the sugar.

Before you serve, chill the bottles for at least an hour, and open them carefully over the sink. There will be a little sediment on the bottom, so once you start pouring, just keep going until you get to the sediment and stop. The sediment won't hurt you, but it isn't pretty. Serve your sparkling beverage with pride.

I tend to make a sugar syrup instead of going the dry sugar route, because I think the carbonation is more even.

If using honey, use a tiny bit more than you would sugar. Boil it into a syrup, especially if you are serving this to very young children, who should not eat uncooked honey.

Champagne bottles and a bench capper make this whole process go a lot faster.

There's no law saying you can't blend extracts!

I make my own ginger beer extract by simmering four to eight ounces of fresh sliced ginger for an hour or two. However, it's trickier to do because you can't always predict how much flavor any one stem of ginger will have. Still, sometimes it's fun to live a little dangerously, and Jamaican ginger beer spoiled me. If you try this, add the zest and juice of two to three lemons or 2 to 3 teaspoons citric acid to the brew.

NEVER add more sugar than is recommended in the instructions!!!

Soda pop made this way will keep for up to a year if it is kept cool, or about three months in warm weather.

DREGS

There is a lot to be learned about home winemaking—more than I could ever put into this book, and there's still more to learn. I hope this book gets you off to a good start. Let me know how things go.

I'd like to thank all the other writers of winemaking and home-brewing books for all the work they have done over the years. I hope that I will have helped future winemakers and writers in my own peculiar way.

Most especially, I'd like to thank Charlie Papazian, whom I have never met, for his superb books, which gave me the courage to make my own beer, and which expanded my knowledge and horizons. No, I didn't worry, and yes, I had a home brew! Thank you, sir!

I will now give you all a gentle shove and launch you out into the home winemaking world. Keep growing, keep fermenting, keep bubbling, read everything you can get your hands on about winemaking, and teach someone else how to make wine. Knowledge is a wonderful thing.

Like my grandmother said: Do the best you can and don't worry.

Cheers, prost, salud, l'chaim, and here's how!

WINEMAKING GUIDELINES AND CHEAT SHEETS

The quick references are for your convenience AFTER YOU'VE READ THE TEXT!! Don't think that these are a substitute for knowing what you're doing. It's always a good idea to go back and reread once in a while.

QUICK REFERENCE: SANITIZING EQUIPMENT AND BOTTLES

- Use a proprietary sanitizer according to the manufacturer's directions.
- OR use a solution of 12 mashed Campden tablets (sodium metabisulphite) dissolved in a quart of water
- OR use a solution of 4 ozs. sodium metabisulphite crystals in 1 quart of water
- OR use 1½ teaspoons of household bleach in 5 gallons of water.

Remember:

- Heat destroys the above sanitizers.
- ALWAYS rinse anything soaked in bleach solution with hot water to remove the chlorine.
- It is OK to leave Campden tablets or sodium metabisulphite

solutions unrinsed in equipment or bottles if you pour out the solution before using the equipment or bottles—*unless you are sensitive to the chemical.*

- NEVER mix sanitizers.

QUICK REFERENCE: WINEMAKING

- Gather your equipment.
- Sanitize your equipment.
- Prepare the ingredients and put them in the primary fermenter.
- Add the water and sugar or honey.
- Cover and fit with an air lock.
- Cool the must to tepid.
- Add chemicals. If you are using sodium metabisulphite (Campden tablet), wait 12 hours before adding the pectic enzyme, and another 24 hours before adding the yeast.
- Check the PA.
- Add the year, cover, and add an air lock.
- Stir daily.
- Check the PA in 5 to 7 days (remove fruit at some point).
- Rack into a sanitized secondary container and add an air lock.
- Rack once or twice in the following 2 to 8 months until fermentation is finished and wine is clear.
- Stabilize and sweeten if you like.
- Bottle or store in bunged jug or cask.

QUICK REFERENCE: RACKING

- Clean and sanitize all equipment.
- Check PA.
- Rack.
- Check all other air locks for good luck.
- Re-sanitize all equipment.
- Make notes about dates, conditions, ingredients, etc.

QUICK REFERENCE: BOTTLING

- Choose wines to bottle, checking PA and clarity.
- Clear area of any dust, cats, dogs, birds, children.
- Clean and sanitize all equipment and bottles.
- Stabilize and sweeten any wines that you want to.
- Lay down paper or plastic on surfaces.
- Drain bottles and line them up.
- Rack wine into bottles.
- Cork.
- Rinse outsides of bottles.
- Dry and label.
- Sanitize and clean all equipment.
- Store wine and equipment.

APPENDIX B

TROUBLESHOOTING: WHEN GOOD WINES GO BAD

Bad things can happen to wines. Most of the time, they don't, but you'd better know the worst that can happen, I suppose.

Acetification: This means vinegar! Acetification can happen for several reasons, but mostly it happens because you didn't keep the vessel topped up and the air lock full. People used to blame this on the "vinegar" fly, which was probably a fruit fly. If you notice a faint vinegar smell, you might be able to head it off at the pass by adding a Campden tablet per gallon and checking it again in a day or so. Usually, however, the wine is doomed. Dump it or let it go and use it for salad vinegar. Don't use it for canning unless you know for sure that it is 5 percent acid.

Insipid wine: Insipidity is usually due to a lack of tannin. Add a small amount (⅛ to ¼ teaspoon per gallon) and see if that helps.

Too much sweetness: Easy to do at first. Too much sweetness comes from not measuring how much sugar you are adding, and not testing for PA in the first place. Use your hydrometer and keep track of what you add. You reduce sweetness by blending a too-sweet wine with one that is dry, of a similar or complementary ingredient. Be sure that the wine has stopped fermenting—you could have a stuck ferment (see below).

251

Funny smell: A funny smell can be caused by inferior ingredients or by some kind of contamination of equipment, such as not rinsing the soap away completely. Sometimes you can get rid of a smell by fining or filtering (see page 182), sometimes not. If it smells really nasty send it down the drain.

Ropey wine: Ropey wine looks as if egg whites got mixed into it. It is caused by a harmless lactic bacteria. Sometimes you can get rid of it by beating the wine, adding a couple of crushed Campden tablets, and filtering. Personally, I've never seen the stuff.

Flowers of wine: Flowers of wine are little flecks of a yeast that will ruin the wine. Again, I've only heard of this, never seen it. Various sources suggest sulphiting and filtering.

Too much or too little acid: Sometimes you can tell if a wine has too much or too little acid by the taste, other times you need to buy a test kit at the wine supply store to find out. Follow the manufacturer's instructions to test the wine. For too much acid, you can dilute the wine. For too little acid, you just add some.

Wine won't clear: Give it more time. Some wines take a long time to settle out, sometimes much longer than the actual fermentation. Rack a little more often. If the wine still refuses to clear, you can try adding pectic enzyme and keeping the wine warm for a few days (not above 85°). If this doesn't work, and the wine smells good, you can try fining it with a fining agent (such as bentonite) and filtering it. This is a very rare occurrence; I would be very suspicious of the wine and get rid of it.

Stuck ferment: A ferment gets stuck when the wine stops fermenting but still has a lot of sugar in it. Check the temperature of the area—it might be too cold for the yeast. If this is not the case, try adding some more yeast nutrient and stirring the wine very gently. Occasionally a nitrogen deficiency is the cause. One to two tablets of diammonium phosphate will help; so will a quarter teaspoon of Marmite. If nothing helps, you should discard the wine and start over again.

APPENDIX C
GLOSSARY

Acetic acid: The acid that makes vinegar taste sour. You don't want any of it in your wine!

Acid blend: Generic name for a combination of acids used in winemaking—usually citric, tartaric, and malic acids. (No '60s jokes, please.)

Acidity: The amount of acid that is present in a wine or a fruit.

Aerobic fermentation: Fermentation in the presence of air, usually called the primary fermentation. It has nothing to do with Jane Fonda.

Age: After the fermentations are done, the wine is put aside in bulk or in bottles to age. During this time, chemical changes occur that, up to a point, improve the wine.

Air lock: A.k.a. fermentation lock, a device that lets gases out of the fermenter but does not allow air or anything else back in.

Amelioration: Adding water, sugar, and chemicals to the must in order to make a better wine. Commercially, this is very strictly regulated.

Anaerobic fermentation: Secondary fermentation, or fermentation without the presence of air (or very little).

Aperitif: A wine made for perking up the appetite or for enjoying at times other than meals.

Aroma: The fragrance that arises from the fruit or herbs used in a wine.

Astringency: The slight "dry tongue" feeling that tannin gives a wine, creating a dry sensation on the tongue and palate.

Balling: A scale to show how much sugar is present in must. Interchangeable with Brix.

Bentonite: An inorganic fining or clarifying agent made from diatomaceous earth.

Blending: Putting two or more wines together to achieve a more balanced wine.

Body: Thickness of the liquid wine in the mouth.

Bouquet: The scent of the wine when you open the bottle. Bouquet of roses and vanilla is OK; bouquet of cat box is not.

Brix: See Balling.

Calcium carbonate: Food-grade chalk used to counter over-acid wines. Two teaspoons per gallon will reduce the acidity by 0.1 percent–0.15 percent. Use no more than six teaspoons per gallon.

Campden tablets: Metabisulphite in half-gram tablet form, invented by the Campden foundation in England.

Capsules: Plastic or metal coverings to put over the upper part of the bottle after it has been corked.

Carbon dioxide (CO_2): The gas produced as a by-product of fermentation. You want it to go away.

Carboy: A glass jug, anywhere from one to fourteen gallons, but most commonly five gallons, used as a secondary fermenter.

Cellar: Wherever you decide to put your finished wine (besides your stomach), but traditionally a cool underground chamber, usually under a house.

Chateau bottled: Bottled at the house or place where the wine was made. Most of your wine will be chateau bottled. Chapeau bottled would be bottled in a hat, very different.

Citric acid: The acid most commonly present in citrus fruits, used to acidify and help preserve wines.

Clarify: The process of letting the wine "settle," or clear itself of minute bits of dead yeast, etc.

Concentrate: Grape or fruit juice that has had much of the water removed so it doesn't take up so much space.

Country wines: A term used by some people to mean wines that are not made of grape juice. It is one of the more polite terms.

Cuvée: A blend of old and new wines for champagne production. Pronounced <cu-vay>.

Decant: Remove the wine from the sediment in the bottle into a clean container for presentation at table.

Dessert wine: A sweet wine served for or with dessert.

Diammonium phosphate: A source of nitrogen for stuck ferments.

Disgorging: The process of removing the sediment from a bottle of champagne before it is charged with the dosage. With small children and cats this word has a very different meaning.

Dry: A wine that has fermented out, meaning the sugar has been completely used up to make alcohol.

Fermentation: The process by which yeast changes the must or juice into wine. Sugar, oxygen, and yeast create alcohol, carbon dioxide, and energy in the form of heat. Wine is fermented, beer is brewed.

Fermentation lock: See Air lock.

Fermenter: Vessel in which fermentation takes place, preferably one in which you meant it to happen.

Filtration: Filtering a finished wine to remove finings and/or impurities. A process that helps stabilize the wine as well as clarify it further.

Fining: The addition of fine particles of organic or inorganic matter to help clarify the wine. The finings attract impurities and sink to the bottom of the fermenter. The wine is then racked off the finings.

Fortification: Adding alcohol to a wine to make it stronger in alcohol and to stop the possibility of more fermentation. Sherries, Madeira, and ports are fortified wines.

Glycerin: A substance used to give body and some sweetness to a wine.

Hydrometer: A simple device that is made of glass and floats in a must or wine to measure the density, or specific gravity, or potential alcohol in a wine.

Lees: The small dead bodies of the noble yeasts that have worked so hard to produce your wine. They form a sediment on the bottom of the fermenting vessel (and under a microscope can be shown to have smiles on their faces).

Malic acid: Another acid present in fruits that is used to acidify wine.

Mature: When your wine settles down and gets a job? Nah, when the wine has aged properly and is ready to drink.

Metabisulphite: Sodium or potassium metabisulphite, used to sanitize equipment and must, and to stabilize wine. See Campden tablet.

Must: The juices, sugars, and water that become wine when the yeast has finished its work.

Oak chips, sticks, or extract: Used to give red wines an oaky taste, as if they had been aged in a romantic white oak barrel instead of glass. Easy to overuse.

Oxidation: The chemical reaction between air and wine that renders the wine brown and disappointing, unless the wine is sherry, at which point all bets are off. Generally to be avoided.

Pectic enzyme: An enzyme that destroys pectin, the substance in some fruits that causes them to gel. Pectin is good in jelly, bad in wine.

Petillant: A polite way of saying fizzy wine, pronounced <pay-tee-yawn>.

pH: An acidity/alkalinity scale that will tell you, if you use your acid test kit, how acid (or not) your must is.

Potassium sorbate: See Stabilize.

Proof: How much alcohol is present in a wine. Proof is roughly twice the percent alcohol. For example, if something is 30 proof, it has 15 percent alcohol in it.

Racking: Siphoning the wine off the lees, or sediment. No torture is actually used.

Saccharometer: See Hydrometer.

Siphon: Using gravity and a tube to persuade a liquid to migrate from one vessel to another. The process of racking uses siphoning to take the wine off the lees.

Social wines: Wines that are too unusual to drink with food, so you palm them off on your friends when they come to your parties or after they help you pull the VW engine out of the car. Potato/ mint is much easier to drink when you are not trying to make it go with enchiladas.

Sour: You don't want your wine to be sour. Sour is for lemons and vinegar.

Sparkling wines: Wines with little bubbles in them, more than when the wine is merely petillant. Champagne is a sparkling wine (some would say the ONLY sparkling wine, but some people will say anything to get a laugh).

Specific gravity: The measurement of the density of a liquid, particularly when sugar is added. Sugar is heavier than water, and alcohol isn't. Nice how it works out.

Stabilize: Using a chemical such as potassium sorbate or extra alcohol to make a wine stable and to prevent further fermentation.

Still wine: A wine that has no bubbles. A Zen wine.

Stuck fermentation: A fermentation that has halted before all the sugar is transformed into alcohol and needs to be coaxed back into action so you can get on with your winemaking.

Table wine: Wine successfully served with food, open to many opinions.

Tannin: An astringent. It usually refers to grape tannin, although it is also present in oak (ask anyone who has ever eaten acorn mush). Winemakers add it to fruit musts that lack tannin, to give the wine some bite and to help clear the wine. Traditionally more present in red wines than in white.

Tartaric acid: Another helpful acid present in most fruits, especially grapes, and part of most acid blends.

Titration: A method used in some tests for acid in the fruit or wine.

Varietal: A term used to describe the variety of grapes a wine has been made out of. In California, the wine must contain at least 51 percent Cabernet grapes to be called a Cabernet.

Vintage: The year a wine was made. Nonvintage wines are made of a blend of different years. That's all it means. Thus when someone says they own a vintage '56 Chevy, they mean none of its parts were made in other years. If more than 51 percent Studebaker parts were used, you couldn't call it a Chevy anymore. See Varietal.

Wine enthusiast: A person who will cheerfully converse with almost anyone about wine and/or winemaking with the simple goals of furthering knowledge and having a good time.

Wine snob: A person whose opinions and tastes are invariably superior to anyone else's.

Wombat: A medium-sized marsupial from Australia. Just wanted to see if anyone ever actually reads the glossary besides librarians and editors.

Yeast: Our hero. This "sugar fungus" eats the sugar, makes alcohol and carbon dioxide, and turns our must into wine, then conveniently expires. Isn't Mother Nature wonderful?

Yeast nutrient: Extra vitamins and food to feed the yeast in our fruit, vegetable, and grain wines.

APPENDIX D
BIBLIOGRAPHY

Some of these books are really old. You can still find them in used bookstores or in libraries. Some are journals, the best of which are *American Journal of Enology and Viticulture* out of Davis, California, *California and Western States Grape Grower* out of Fresno, California, and *Wine Spectator* out of New York. Many out-of-print journals are still available in large library collections. Ask your local library. Some of these books are concerned with commercial winemaking, but that doesn't mean you can't learn from them.

Books marked with an asterisk are highly recommended. Books marked (OP) are out of print.

Ace, Donald, and James H. Eakin. *Winemaking as a Hobby.* The Pennsylvania State University College of Agriculture, 1977. (OP)

Amerine, M. A., and C. S. Ough. *Methods for Analysis of Musts and Wine.* New York: John Wiley and Sons, 1980.

Amerine, M. A., & V. L. Singleton. *Wine: An Introduction.* Berkeley and Los Angeles: University of California Press, 1977.

*Anderson, Stanley F., and Dorothy Anderson. *Winemaking: Recipes, Equipment, and Techniques for Making Wine at Home.* New York: Harcourt Brace and Co., 1989.

*Berry, C. J. J. *First Steps in Winemaking.* Ann Arbor, Mich.: G.W. Kent for Amateur Winemaker, 1991.

———. *130 New Winemaking Recipes.* England: Amateur Winemaker Publications, 1985.

————. *Winemaking With Canned & Dried Fruits.* Andover, England: Amateur Winemaker, 1972. (OP)

Bravery, H. E. *Successful Winemaking at Home.* New York: Arco Books, 1984.

Cooke, George M., et al. *Making Table Wine at Home.* Oakland, Calif.: Publications Division of Agricultural and Natural Resources, University of California, 1988.

De Chambeau, André. *Creative Winemaking.* Rochester, N.Y.: WWWWW/Information Services, 1977. (OP)

Dart, C. J., and D. A. Smith. *Woodwork for Winemakers.* England: Amateur Winemaker, 1972. (OP)

Deal, Josephine. *Making Cider.* Ann Arbor, Mich.: G.W. Kent, 1985.

Delman, Philip. *Ten Types of Table Wines.* London: Mills & Boon, 1971. (OP)

Duncan, Peter. *Progressive Winemaking.* Ann Arbor, Mich.: G.W. Kent for The Amateur Winemaker, 1991.

Gayre and Nigg. *Brewing Mead: Wassail.* Boulder, Colo.: Brewers Publications, 1986.

Hopkins, Albert A. *Home Made Beverages.* New York: The Scientific American Publishing Company, 1919. (OP)

Irwin, Judith. *A Step by Step Guide to Making Home Made Wine.* Stamford, Conn.: Longmeadow Press, 1993.

Jackson, Ron S. *Wine Science: Principles and Applications.* San Diego: Academic Press, 1994.

Jagendorf, M. A. *Folk Wines, Cordials & Brandies.* New York: The Vanguard Press, 1963.

Johnson, Hugh, and James Halliday. *The Vintner's Art: How Great Wines Are Made.* New York: S&S Trade, 1992.

Keers, John H. *How to Make Liqueurs at Home.* New York: Manor Books, 1974. (OP)

Lichine, Alexis. *Alexis Lichine's New Encyclopedia of Wines and Spirits.* New York: Alfred A. Knopf, 1985.

Lucas Cyril. *Making Sparkling Wines.* Toronto: Mills & Boon, 1971. (OP)

Lundy, Desmond. *No Sour Grapes: Introduction to Winemaking.* Victoria, BC: Fermenthaus, 1987.

Lyon, Richard. *Vine to Wine.* Napa, Calif.: Stonecrest Press, 1985.

*Massaccesi, Ramond. *Winemaker's Recipe Handbook.* place and publisher unknown, but every wine supply place carries it, 1976.

Mitchell, J. R. *Scientific Winemaking Made Easy*. England, The Amateur Winemaker. (OP)

Morse, Roger A. *Making Mead*. Ithaca, N.Y.: Wicwas Press, 1992.

Ough, Cornelius S. *Winemaking Basics*. New York: Haworth Press, 1992.

*Papazian, Charlie. *The New Complete Joy of Home Brewing*. New York: Avon Books, 1991.

Pinnegar, Francis. *How to Make Home Wines and Beers*. London: Hamlyn Books, 1971. (OP)

Proulx, Annie, and Lew Nichols. *Sweet and Hard Cider*. New York: Garden Way, 1980. (OP)

Roate, Mettja C. *How to Make Wine in Your Own Kitchen*. New York: McFadden Books, 1963. (OP)

Robinson, Jancis. *The Oxford Companion to Wine*. Oxford: Oxford University Press, 1994.

Seltman, Charles. *Wine in the Ancient World*. London: Routledge and Kegan, 1957. (OP)

Sperling, L. H. *Fruit Wine: a Home Winemaker's Guide to Making Wine from Fruits*. Rochester, N.Y.: American Wine Society, special issue # 17, 1993.

Tritton, S. M. *Amateur Wine Making*. London: Faber & Faber, 1971. (OP)

Turner, B. C. A. *Fruit Wines*. Toronto: Mills & Boon, 1973. (OP)

Turner, B. C. A., and C. J. J. Berry. *The Winemaker's Companion*. London: Mills & Boon, 1968. (OP)

Wagner, P. M. *Grapes into Wine*. New York: Alfred A. Knopf, 1976.

Ward, Philip. *The Home Winemaker's Handbook*. New York: Lyons & Burford, 1994.

Wright, Helen S. *Old Time Recipes for Homemade Wines*. Boston, Mass.: Dana Estes and Co., 1909. (OP)

MISCELLANEOUS INFORMATION

FORMULA FOR METRIC CONVERSION

ounces to grams	multiply ounces by 28.35
grams to ounces	multiply grams by 0.035
pounds to grams	multiply pounds by 453.5
pounds to kilograms	multiply pounds by 0.45
cups to liters	multiply cups by 0.24

METRIC EQUIVALENTS

1 cup	230 milliliters
2 cups	460 milliliters
4 cups (one quart)	0.95 liter
4 quarts	3.8 liters

VOLUMES

1 U.S. gallon=4 quarts=8 pints=16 cups
1 U.S. quart=2 pints=32 ounces
1 U.S. cup=8 ounces=16 tablespoons=48 teaspoons
3 teaspoons=1 tablespoon
4 tablespoons=¼ cup

LIQUOR BOTTLE CAPACITIES

OLD SIZE	U.S. FLUID OUNCES	LITERS
1 pint	16	500 ml
1 fifth (4.5 qt.)	25.6	750 ml
1 quart	32	1.1

WINE BOTTLE CAPACITIES

SIZE	U.S. FLUID OUNCES	LITERS
split	6.3	187 ml
half bottle	12.7	375 ml
standard	25.4	750 ml
liter	33.8	1
magnum	50.7	1½

TEMPERATURES

To convert Fahrenheit to centigrade, subtract 32 from Fahrenheit, multiply by 5, then divide by 9.

To convert centigrade to Fahrenheit, multiply centigrade by 9, divide by 5, then add 32.

APPENDIX F

WINE SUPPLY ADDRESSES

Check your local Yellow Pages listings under Winemaking. Also check under Beer Making Supplies, because someone who supplies beer brewers will frequently have some supplies for home winemaking.

Here are some reliable mail order houses:

WINE ART INC.
6080 Russ Baker Way, Unit 120
Richmond, BC V7B 1B4
Canada
1-800-881-6110 (Canada only)
1-604-278-2370
1-604-278-1761 (fax)

WINE ART INDIANAPOLIS
5890 N. Keystone Ave.
Indianapolis, IN 46220
1-317-546-9940
1-800-255-5090

SEMPLEX
Box 11476
Minneapolis, MN 55411
1-612-522-0500

AMERICA BREWS
9925 Lyndale Ave. S
Minneapolis, MN 55420
1-612-884-2039

CELLAR HOMEBREW
14411 Greenwood Ave. N.
Seattle, WA 98133
1-800-342-1871
E-mail: homebrew@aa.net
World Wide Web: http://www.aa.net/~homebrew/catalog.html

PORTAGE HILLS VINEYARDS
Suffield, Ohio
1-800-418-6493
World Wide Web: http://www.portagehill.com/portage/
  welcome.html

WINE EMPORIUM
950 Wilson Ave.
North York, Ontario M3K 1E7
Canada
416-636-2827
World Wide Web: http://www.can.net/wine/wine.html

APPENDIX G
ON-LINE

If you have a computer and a modem, there are a lot of wine-makers out there waiting to talk to you. Almost every commercial electronic mail outfit has hundreds of "discussion lists"—people who have a specific topic in mind who want to talk to other people about that topic. Home winemaking is one of them!

On the Internet, check under Usenet for rec.crafts.winemaking, and look around for discussion groups specializing in mead, cider, and perry, as well.

It's a very interesting world out there. You can talk to people in New Zealand, Germany, India, and every other place that has electricity and someone willing to post a message on the net.

The World Wide Web is growing by leaps and bounds, too. If you look back at Appendix F, you will notice that a few of the wine supply places I listed have either E-mail or a WWW address, as do many wineries.

The Portage Hills site is particularly interesting and has many links to other wine interest sites, such as the WWWW page at http://www.uidaho.edu/stevep/wine/winehome.html. WWWW stands for World Wide Web of Winemaking, and it can lead you to discussion lists and FAQs (lists of Frequently Asked Questions). There are also links for some universities that have a special interest in winemaking, such as UC Davis and Cornell University.

Subject Index

Recipe Names Index

Recipe Ingredients Index